I0816674

MONEY PROUD

MONEY PROUD

THE QUEER GUIDE TO GENERATE WEALTH, SLAY DEBT, AND BUILD GOOD HABITS TO SECURE YOUR FUTURE

NICK WOLNY

wm

WILLIAM MORROW

An Imprint of HarperCollins*Publishers*

HarperCollins books may be purchased for educational, business, or sales promotional use. For information, please email the Special Markets Department at SPsales@harpercollins.com.

hc.com

FIRST EDITION

Designed by Kyle O'Brien

Illustrations by Jason Snyder

Library of Congress Cataloging-in-Publication Data has been applied for.

ISBN 978-0-06-343660-2

25 26 27 28 29 LBC 5 4 3 2 1

CONTENTS

PART III: MONEY PROUD POWER MOVES

INTRODUCTION

It's time to come out to yourself about your money.

For a long time, I struggled with this. I still do in some ways. I came out as gay when I was 18. I came out as Beyhive at 26 after Beyoncé dropped that damn self-titled album and blew our minds. But I still wasn't ready to come out to myself about my relationship with money until much later in life.

It scares me to tell you this, because most personal finance gurus and authors of money books seem to have always been good with money. They learned about money while growing up, found well-paying jobs, saved diligently, and became financially independent early in life. Not me. Name any aspect of money and I've probably stepped in its dogshit over the years. Did my taxes wrong, then got audited. Quit a job with no safety net, then burned down my life savings (later rebranded this as a gap year). Did some *Mortal Kombat*–level damage to my checking account during a weekend of impulsive spending, then avoided looking at my bank balance for days, sometimes weeks.

Despite these mistakes, I was still living what felt like a great queer life. I would lose my voice singing along to Pride headliners' sets at the top of my lungs. I would get tipsy at the gay bars and kiss boys. But beneath all this YOLO energy was a constant feeling of unease about my money. What happens if I get in an accident? What would I do if I suddenly couldn't work anymore? Why does my account suddenly have fourteen dollars left? These thoughts often lurked, and I'd shrug them off, preferring to feel invincible.

This brings me to what I'm *really* scared to tell you, which is that personal finance has been a spiritual journey for me as an LGBTQ+ person. It's terrifying to say that, because (1) I'm not religious, and (2) organized religion is the origin point for most discrimination and outright terrorism against queer people throughout the world. "Spiritual" also gives woo energy, and despite my editors assuring me woo is in these days, it freaks me out as a personal finance writer and columnist to acknowledge this feeling (if I recommend a crystal at any point as a budgeting solution, please intervene). But spiritual is probably the correct word to describe how my relationship with money has evolved.

Please don't take this as toxic positivity, or contrived white cis throwaway advice, or an attempt to minimize the very real obstacles and intra-community inequalities we face as queer people. Also don't take it to mean that I'm suddenly living this monastic, monk-in-the-mountains life in order to save money (although the robe would be cute—could pull the hood down, add a brooch, and wear it as a cape). What I know in my heart is that small tweaks to both my money and mindset have made a difference in my self-esteem as a queer person. I'm out and proud and gayer than ever, and if I can do it, you can do it.

Even my career in personal finance was very unlikely. I grew up in the rural Midwest, in a single-parent home that brought in about $34,000 a year, the median American household income in the mid-nineties.[1] My parents, a carpenter and a health-care administrator, divorced when I was eight, and my mom took custody. When my dad would pick me up for the day, we'd sometimes stop off at job sites, and I'd help him bag up the extra sawdust so he could later portion it into brick-sized plastic bags—"Sawdust burritos," he called them—and throw them into the wood burner to save a few bucks on his heating bill.

Like many people, I wasn't taught much about financial literacy growing up, but I doubt I would have cared about it if I had, because every waking second of my adolescence fixated either on the agony of realizing my sexuality or the ecstasy of loitering in the men's underwear section at JCPenney. For teenage "I prefer wearing boxers, but prefer *looking* in the briefs aisle" Nick, money success meant getting a college scholarship so I could leave town, start fresh as a gay man, and figure out the financial stuff later.

Example: I joined band in sixth grade, because when you got to high school and signed up for marching band, you were given a gym class waiver, which meant I wouldn't have to be near naked men in a locker room and risk popping an erection that would reveal my deep, dark secret (marching band was my high school's unspoken gay mecca for this reason). I played the French horn because instruments were assigned by last name, and when they got to the *W*'s, only the French horn and tuba remained, and the tuba would have been heavier to carry home. But I ended up loving it. Music became my craft, my vehicle for expression and a confidence-builder at a time when I was too afraid to express my true self, so I decided to study it in college.

Unbeknownst to me at the time, two degrees in classical French horn do not make you the most employable person on the planet. So it was off to entry-level work life I went, juggling odd jobs throughout my twenties to make ends meet. Barista. Yoga teacher (great for bossy gays like me). Administrative assistant. Digital marketing generalist. I eventually found my groove as a marketing copywriter, perhaps because writing feels a lot like classical music to me. It's a craft you can practice, something that demands a balance of creativity and technique, and an art form with the power to change the world . . . or at least put food on the table by selling more supplements and skincare.

For six years, I did the entrepreneur thing full-time, helping small businesses market and sell themselves online. I did about $900,000 in total revenue over this time period, which sounds like hustle porn without context. After taxes and costs and software and subcontractors, however, I was left with a middle-class salary most years. Still, I knew how to fish well enough to afford to live in a city, have good time freedom, and enjoy my queer life.

Then the darkness came.

I was warming up on the squat rack at the gym when something in my lumbar spine shifted. With the slip and slide of a single vertebra, my life changed. The pain was immediate and intense. I'd tweaked my back before and shaken it off, but this time around the pain didn't fade. It persisted and worsened, for days, then weeks, then months.

"No. *Noooooo,*" I thought to myself. "Not this. Not me. *Not yet.*"

The thing that was never supposed to happen had happened. My back injury turned my life upside down. I could barely stand up straight, let alone rustle up income. For months, I needed at least eight ibuprofen a day and two fat edibles a night to function. (The way it all happened was so pedestrian, too: I hadn't crawled my way out of a burning building, or carried a grandma to safety, or tussled with a bunch of homophobes trying to ruin steak night at my local queer-owned establishment. I was warming up at the squat rack, my back tweaked, and, uh, that's it.)

Everything came to a screeching halt. My mood was trash, constantly. And it was right around this time that all my money malnourishment began to bubble up to the surface. I wished I had more financial resources. I wished even more that I had lived it up in my younger years and spent my blow money differently. I needed a day job, and better health insurance, so I crawled back into the trenches of the job hunt to look for a nine-to-five. Eventually, I landed one as an editor, covering personal finance. I expected the paycheck and benefits would bring me more stability. What I didn't expect was a new outlook on how to live my best queer life.

Personal finance is a longevity skill set. And sadly, as a gay man I didn't see value in longevity skill sets or money management because I didn't expect to be around long enough for them to matter. From the endless barrage of political vitriol, to the imagery and stories of AIDS in the late eighties and early nineties (the time period I was born into), much of queer life has a temporary, transient feeling. My new relationship with money has helped me cultivate qualities I once valued but had steadily lost over the years. Empathy. Moderation. Patience when the person ahead of me in line at the café asks questions about *every single item on the menu,* then orders a black coffee. So when I say personal finance is spiritual for me, I don't mean it in a gaslight-y, vision quest-y, "attract the abundance" kind of way. Applying the fundamentals of personal finance has helped me go from letting my emotions run the show to having more peace of mind. It's been therapeutic to explore and heal my relationship with money, a healing that has then spilled over into other areas of my life.

Personal finance also made me realize that, uh, I'd been the villain for quite some time. Whoops! A marketing copywriter's whole job is to persuade people to part ways with their coins, which is the complete opposite of most personal finance. And to be clear, we copywriters can be manipulative AF, because we know that people don't buy a product or a service; they buy a feeling or a result. Good copywriters use this to their advantage. They burrow five levels deep into your brain, leveraging the principles of psychology to sharpen pain and amplify desire, then sprinkle the perfect amount of storytelling on top to convince you to whip out your wallet.

This consumerism is deeply ingrained in modern culture, and it has a million more cool points than personal finance does. The advertisements we see throughout the day mold how we think and behave, which is why our exploration of personal finance will begin with looking at how media influences and reinforces your desires. Marketing makes money by highlighting the gap between who you currently are and who you aspire to become, then selling you something to plug the hole. If you've ever felt deflated about not being attractive enough, successful enough, smart enough, or interesting enough, consumerism is patting itself on the back for a job well done.

WHO WE ARE

"What does being LGBTQ+ have to do with my money?" A lot, actually.

First, simply being queer (or any other minority, for that matter) leads to "minority stress," defined by the American Psychological Association as "the resultant conflict with the social environment experienced by minority group members."[2] Chronic stress physically changes your brain, which can then increase the risk of developing a mental health disorder. Approximately 40 percent of LGBTQ+ adults experienced a mental health illness in 2024, compared to 18 percent for all adults, and LGBTQ+ teens are six times more likely to experience depression than non-LGBTQ+ teens, according to data from the Trevor Project.[3] We're also more casual with therapy speak these days ("Girl, I was so depressed after that client meeting!" "Same!" *clinks martini glasses*), which sometimes downplays how much our stressors affect us.

Mental health isn't simply the absence of a disorder. It's a blanket term that refers to your overall psychological and emotional well-being. The *Merriam-Webster* dictionary defines mental health as "feeling comfortable about oneself, positive feelings about others, and the ability to meet the demands of daily life."[4] Even when we aren't diagnosed with a mental health disorder, we often still feel this way, so we use avoidance and numbing behaviors to cope, and these behaviors often influence how we manage our money. We also yearn for belonging and safety, so when we feel socially isolated we go into survival mode, which ratchets the minority stress up.

Second, queer people have a long history of enduring economic discrimination. Mainstream entertainment frames queer people as bubbly SINK and DINK (single/double income, no kids) households, splashing around in a jacuzzi of disposable income without a care in the world. This is untrue. Even the LGBTQ+ wage gap, 90 cents on the dollar, is too generalized, because the wage gap varies dramatically by race and gender (for example, it's 96 cents for cis queer men, but 60 cents for trans women).[5]

As an overall group, though, one thing we have in common is we've been getting fired for decades because of our sexual orientation or gender identity. One reason gayborhoods developed is because out queer people couldn't secure work or housing, and these communities gave not-out queer people trapped in homophobic households a way to escape. For some, when they were outed, they were kicked to the curb by their families (which still happens today; an estimated 40 percent of homeless youth are LGBTQ+).[6] Nevertheless, queer people keep kicking ass. Look at this culture we developed and fashioned in times of economic oppression that everyone wants a piece of now. Our history of perseverance is something to be proud of and draw energy from.

Third, politics are downright diabolical these days because politicians have realized that anger is a motivator, and to leverage anger properly, you need a villain—preferably something your constituents don't interact with much or care to understand. Fifty years ago, a dumbass orange juice heiress branded her homophobic campaign as "Save the Children," and the messaging stuck. Fast forward to modern times, where more than $215 million was spent on anti-trans election ads in 2024 and hundreds of anti-LGBTQ+ bills are being introduced in state legislatures.[7] Many of these politicians admit behind closed doors that they have nothing against queer people, but anger sells, so here we are. As a result, mainstream acceptance of queer people dipped in 2024, the first time in nine years to do so.[8]

The scapegoating most affects queer youth, which is bad, because they're our fabulous future. Nearly one in three queer young people said hearing about anti-LGBTQ legislation made their mental health "poor" most of the time, and two in three said hearing about legislation that would ban talking about LGBTQ+ people at school made their mental health "a lot worse." We must seize the opportunity to empower and protect young queer people because they've shown us they're ready to further our revolution and take up space. In recent Gallup polls, overall LGBTQ+ identification has more than doubled, mainly due to Gen Z, the generation born between 1996 and 2010, coming into adulthood. In the 2023 Gallup poll, 22 percent of Gen Z identified as LGBTQ+; for millennials, it was just under 10 percent; Gen X, 4.5 percent; and boomers, 2.3 percent.[9] Similar to how left-handedness gradually rose in surveys as it became increasingly destigmatized (we used to burn left-handed people at the stake, y'all), our yearslong efforts to encourage queer acceptance are paying off.

An outcome of all these stressors is that we lag behind the overall population in many aspects of financial well-being, and your boy's got the receipts to back this up. According to surveys from the Center for LGBTQ Economic Advancement & Research, 57 percent of queer Americans report having an annual income of less than $50,000 (vs. 36 percent for non-LGBTQ+); 87 percent make less than $100,000 (vs. 66 percent non-LGBTQ+); a majority of queer people have less than $5,000 in savings; 20 percent have no savings at all; we're twice as likely to be unemployed; we're 45 percent more likely to have over $75,000 in student loans, and just over 20 percent of us are underbanked or "unbanked," meaning we have no checking or savings account and must transact entirely in cash.[10] [11]

So yes, being queer affects your money. And financial literacy can empower queer people to overcome these challenges and secure their future, no matter where they're currently at. But there's a problem: A lot of personal finance is *boring*.

"This target date fund is perfect for when you retire in the year 2065!" Um, what? Read the room, boo; rent is expensive, we need solutions now. Personal finance tends to focus only on managing money you already have, at a time when many people have no money left over at the end of the month to save or spend. That's why I've been brought in—to zhuzh things up. Much of our efforts together will focus on the steps that come *before* personal finance, like making more money and understanding the motivations that drive our habits, so we can live a less burdened life.

Personal finance also sometimes clashes with queer culture. Personal finance loves to go on and on about the virtues of frugality and delayed gratification (there's definitely a purity culture vibe at times), but queer culture rejects these virtues because they've historically been used against us. We deserve queer gratification now by being out, proud, visible, and expressive. Our goal here is to maintain that, but more sustainably. Queer culture challenges us to embrace creativity and rise to the occasion, efforts that build confidence and character, so it's critical we don't lose connection to our queer selves as we go on this personal finance journey together.

And can I rant for a moment? (*Steps back on soapbox*) I believe it is my *duty* to live a joyous queer life because many generations of queer people before me never got to. Our ancestors couldn't gather at Pride parades or local gayborhoods. They couldn't hold hands in public. (They couldn't legally be intimate *in their own homes,* either; gay sex was considered sodomy in thirteen states until 2003.) We're supposed to have hundreds of thousands of mentors right now, but don't, because the AIDS crisis devastated our community and was ignored by the federal government for years. Much of queer culture has been shaped by premature death and injustice. So when I say "live a joyous queer life," I don't mean that in a superficial way, in which you go to all the white parties and eat all the caviar and wear all the outfits. To me, joyous means having the courage to be honest with yourself, getting your shit together, and cultivating time freedom so you can do as you please. Our queer ancestors would not have wanted us to carry around the chronic stress that is worrying constantly about money—not even as a handbag. It's our duty as out-and-proud LGBTQ+ people to cultivate financially independent lives, not only for ourselves, but also to model this wellness for future generations.

We need an A-to-Z guide to personal finance tailored specifically toward the fourteen million out LGBTQ+ adults living in America, a number that will rise in coming years as younger generations report their queer identity more openly. My hope is that the book you hold in your hands delivers on this assignment. To lift a phrase from ballroom culture, reading is fundamental, and that doesn't just apply to building wit or poise. The statement can be taken literally to educate ourselves about money: How to make, save, and spend it in order to live more vibrant queer lives.

WHAT YOU WILL LEARN

Here is how we will fulfill on our duty in this book.

We will chart a roadmap for financial independence. You will walk away from this book with a clear action plan for your money that is aligned with your priorities as a queer person. Monthly income will go up, buyer's remorse will go down, and debt will leave the house party on its own (great, because it was rude and everyone kind of wanted it to leave anyway). You will unlock new levels of financial awareness that may shift or even transform the hopes and dreams you have for your lifetime.

We will redefine wealth. Wealth usually refers to money, but we will broaden its definition to include time, attention, health, relationships, and personal growth. We will stress-test how much money is "enough" for you, which will in turn help you more evenly prioritize other facets of wealth in your life. You will overhaul your attitude toward budgets and expenses, because you will know your money is going toward matters that are important to you. By keeping your queer identity front-and-center throughout this book, we ensure you set goals that are aligned, sustainable, and fun. This effort will be grounded in what we call the 7-word plan for building wealth: lower expenses, increase earnings, invest the difference.

We will cultivate a work life that doesn't make us want to numb out every weekend. Most of us will work for most of our adult lives, so this one's important. When work is lucrative and fulfilling, it feeds and energizes you. When work is draining and demoralizing, you drag ass during the week, detonate your bank account every weekend to numb out from it all, then start over again on Monday morning. The career advice in this book will help you make work your ally rather than your enemy, without it having to be your bestie—and certainly not your personality. If you want to someday stop working altogether, whether that be sooner or later, we also cover how to turn that fantasy into reality.

We will live joyous queer lives. Most importantly, we will reimagine your relationship with money management such that you can bask in queer joy now. At a time when both young people's queer self-acceptance and anti-LGBTQ legislative bills are breaking records, living a life of purpose and peace is one of the most activist things we can do. The money work we do in this book will lead to more time freedom, which you can then use to learn more about yourself and the world.

HOW TO READ THIS BOOK

Each chapter of this book covers one standalone money topic, and the chapters are intended to be read in order, since each chapter builds on the ones before it. Together, they give you a roadmap on how to manage one of the most influential resources of your lifetime. The different money tools you acquire along the way are what will help you move toward your financial independence finish line.

This book is organized into three parts.

Part I: Reading Is Fundamental. None of this money stuff works unless we are willing to take a good look at our thought patterns and behaviors first. Therefore, we must explore where these thought patterns come from and why, so that we can begin to spot them and course-correct them in the moment. Part I introduces a debt payoff plan for those who have it, explains how to set a simple budget that doesn't feel restrictive or tedious, and introduces a valuable metric, saving rate, that quiets the economic noise and can always act as your personal finance dashboard.

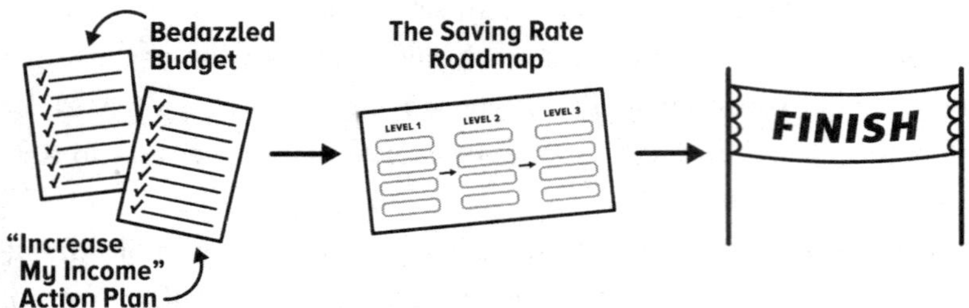

Part II: It's Giving Confident. With these fundamentals in place, we then go deep on the 7-word plan for building wealth: lower expenses, increase earnings, invest the difference. Each of the chapters in part II correlate with one aspect of the 7-word plan and will give you a tool you can start using right away to take action. For expenses, we have the Bedazzled Budget; for earnings, we have the "Increase My Income" action plan; and for saving and investing, we have the Saving Rate Roadmap, which looks a bit like a Scantron but won't be graded by a robot, so scribble outside the lines as much as you want. (In crayon.) By building fluency in each of these actions, you'll become smart, strong, and savvy, not only with how to make and save money, but also how to stay nimble when job markets take an unexpected turn. We also go through a hype-free primer on investing and how it helps your money make money. These instructions work for queer people of all stripes, ages, and income levels.

Part III: Money Proud Power Moves. Part III is a series of "Money Proud Power Moves," in which each chapter is a standalone rundown on one aspect of money you will likely encounter often in your lifetime. We'll make topics like taxes, entrepreneurship, retirement, and estate planning fun and accessible so that you actually absorb this information once and for all. As the saying goes, if a drag queen death drops in the forest, and no one's around to tip her a dollar, did she really make a sound? (Might be paraphrasing there.) We use fun as a learning technique throughout this book, and you just might laugh to yourself a time or two along the way.

Also—we do the homework during class. You're welcome. You're busy, we don't have much time together, and I want you to get maximum value and utility out of this book. Each chapter has exercises for you to apply what you learn to your own finances as we go. Do not be that person who reads self-help books, implements none of what they learned, and then sits on the sidelines and talks shit about the people who *are* implementing. You are here to evolve your relationship with money. I am here to help you achieve that goal. Let's give this work the attention it deserves—for the ancestors.

Revisit as often as needed. This book is designed to live on your bookshelf and be an ongoing reference guide.

° ° °

Queer people deserve to live confident, expressive, and self-sufficient lives. Money is a tool that can help cultivate these outcomes, particularly in a world where we often must look out for ourselves. Hope is not a financial plan. Neither are thoughts and prayers. It's time for action.

When you know your way around money, you can take meaningful actions that empower both yourself and the queer community at large. Aspire to become more comfortable with your money and yourself. The best is still ahead.

Hit the music, DJ—let's begin.

MONEY PROUD

PART I

READING IS FUNDAMENTAL

1

THOUGHT PATTERNS

Why Your Favorite Mindset-Money Collabs Are Overdue for a Remix

It's an exciting and tumultuous time to be a queer person in Dolly Parton's America.

LGBTQ+ people don't just exist. We *thrive*. We build houses. We style hair. We lead organizations and take care of families. We pay our fair share of property taxes and create the best house music. But we're also not above slipping you a free cocktail after takeoff because the plane was delayed on the tarmac. We're increasingly out and proud, and deserve lives of financial stability and social acceptance, just like everyone else.

As queer adults, we encounter a variety of responsibilities—and stressors. Jobs and bills. Parades and brunches. Politicians saying we are unequal and maybe shouldn't exist at all, often to distract from their own sex scandals (oop). Fifty-eight dollars in our checking account. Nineteen *RuPaul's Drag Race* franchises to keep up with. And then often, in the background, a mountain of debt, large and looming. It's giving "scary mountain," thunder and lightning, and castles and such, rather than a cute lil' "I'm sporty and like rock climbing" mountain.

Much of the chronic stress queer people experience relates back to money. Lame, right? Unless you're super rich and have bottomless resources to fall back on, or came into a fat inheritance, your thoughts and decisions about money are constant. You go to work, a value exchange in which you swap two currencies (time and energy) for one (cash), then go spend the money you just made to numb yourself from the job you just did. The pursuit of money likely dominates your calendar, and it certainly dominates the space between your ears. Money is many things all at once: your saving grace, your worst nemesis, the object of your professional desire, the subject of your resentment, the protagonist of a Cardi B bop, and a barometer for your self-worth. And don't forget the shame, darling! Money is riddled with shame triggers that keep you quiet and stuck.

I didn't learn much about money growing up. It took me a long time to get a grip on the basics, and my money shame gremlins had built up quite the hoarded home in my brain before I finally evicted them. Turns out that's really common: We rarely talk about money to one another, so we don't encounter different perspectives, and subsequently never challenge our own. This leads to thinking the same thoughts over and over, until they become patterns and beliefs. Whether it's how your parents viewed money growing up, drifting in and out of stable work in a tight job market, or overspending to feel seen and accepted, these money thought patterns lead to money habits, and habits often determine what is (or isn't) in your bank account as time goes on.

To be clear, I'm not saying our challenges with money are due to attitude alone. It is *tough* out here on these economic streets right now. Rising prices, housing shortages, and fifty years of wage stagnation have made just about everything more expensive. Most of society's economic progress has now been gobbled up by billionaires. Credit card debt is at both record-high balances and record-high interest rates. The cost of college tuition and fees at public four-year institutions has increased by 141 percent in the last twenty years.[1] Consumers lost $10 billion to scams in 2023.[2] One analysis from *The Washington Post* found that, between 2019 and 2024, home prices alone increased by 54 percent.[3] The average American household now saves less than half of what they did in the 1980s, and for queer people, the situation is typically worse: Multiple studies have found we're more likely to have lower earnings and higher debt burdens than our non-queer counterparts.

"*EAT THE RICH!*" we scream. Except, uh . . . where's the buffet for that, again? And how long is the wait? Many of these external factors are systemic, and with our federal government increasingly turning into a reality TV show (but still taking itself way too seriously, so the camp element is completely lost), this stuff isn't going to get resolved overnight. Meanwhile, your thought patterns and financial literacy are factors you *can* start changing now. Not when Congress has the right ratio of representatives, not when another planet moves into retrograde causing chaos for your Scorpio Rising, not next year, not next month—now.

For these healthy new money thoughts to stick, we must ensure they will have enough space in your mind to take root. This means taking inventory of the thoughts and beliefs that influence your day-to-day decisions and becoming more aware of where they come from, along with why you act on them. As you do this, you might discover that some of your existing thought patterns around money are actually weeds: ugly, homophobic weeds that take up space, strangle the good stuff in your mental garden, and hide in plain sight by cosplaying as fun, interactive flowers (looking at you, dandelions). Before we can plant new ideas around money—and maybe a few hydrangeas, too, while we're at it—we must first find these weeds and dig them up. This work builds mental resilience, and resilience is useful for queer people in both money and life as we navigate the current moment.

If you dread looking at your money, I've got you. We're going to lock arms and frolic forward by looking at other people's money first. This helps you practice the productive thinking that leads to healthy money management without having any of your own personal baggage attached to your decisions. Then, with your post-glow-up brain, you'll apply the same approaches to your own money, based on your unique circumstances.

We're gonna cover a lot in this book: debt, saving, income, investing, taxes, and more. You will walk away knowing not only how to transform your finances, but also how to cast a new vision for what's possible in your life, then go there. And it all starts with thought patterns. You've got this. You were the queer kid who made the volcano for the science fair in elementary school. If you can do that, you can do anything.

To make space for all the good stuff that is to come, let's identify the homophobic weeds that are sapping you of valuable thinking energy, then start applying your new perspectives to your money right away.

Homophobic Thought Patterns to Unlearn

1. Inherited beliefs
2. Money malaise, avoidance, and numbing
3. "Just to be safe"
4. Binary perspectives
5. "I'm a starving artist, this is just how it is"
6. Comparison culture
7. "More is better"

THOUGHT PATTERN NO. 1: INHERITED BELIEFS

You actually did inherit something: a whole bunch of janky beliefs! Not as much fun to shove in your purse and go shopping with, unfortunately.

Many of your thought patterns are not your own—you inherited them. Things like your family lore, socioeconomic class, and queer journey shaped how you now see yourself as a person. This happens with money, too. We see or experience a financial faux pas, make a conclusion about how money works in the world, then live our lives based on that belief, even when the belief is misguided or flat-out wrong.

We sometimes make decisions about money based on what our parents directly or indirectly signal to us. And because money is such a weird, taboo topic for people, these experiences don't get talked about much in social settings. Instead, they get quietly reinforced. Most of us receive zero financial literacy education in school (or we don't pay much attention, because compound interest is typically first taught in pre-algebra class during the most awful, angst-y years of junior high), so these inherited belief weeds often have years to take root.

The risk to letting inherited beliefs run your life is that you miss out on exploring who you really are. Inherited beliefs can be homophobic because much of society was imagined and engineered as though queer people don't exist. Overcoming them requires the uncomfortable-but-necessary task of questioning what's true and what isn't (in a hot scientist way, not a conspiracy theorist way) to discover our true identity. When we don't do this, inherited beliefs about money and the world determine our identity instead.

This was certainly me. Since I grew up in a lower-income household, my perception of money was that it was never available, and that if you had some, you needed to hold onto it for dear life. Ironically, even with this scarcity mentality, I still wasn't great about holding onto money, so it was like a double-whammy: I missed out on queer experiences and adventures in my twenties, but also didn't have much to show for my efforts at the end of that first decade of adulthood because I had poor financial literacy along the way.

We often relate to other queer people's journeys, even when their journeys are very different from our own. And this money mindset inertia is very real. To help you realize you're not alone, I put out a request to queer people around the country to share their money testimonies with us throughout this book. Several dozen donated their time and energy to do so, because that is how we roll (and why I love our community so much).

Here's what some of them had to say about inherited beliefs and identity:

Matthew, 46, Massachusetts: *I used debt as a stopgap for anything I felt I needed to keep up and fit in, from a Rolex to a law degree. A combination of expected and unexpected expenses caused my debt to creep up to $108,000. I'm just trying to fix my life. It feels like my life is slipping away from me. I didn't come out until I was 41, and then the pandemic happened. I feel like money and coming out are completely connected because I was trying to live this life that I thought society wanted me to live, and now I've realized that I don't need to do that.*

Kira, 27, Kentucky: *I identify as a woman now. I had an inkling that something was going on, but never really thought it was an option for me, having grown up in rural Ohio. As my identity evolved, it has informed how I want to spend my money: what is important to me financially, what kind of opportunities I want, and how I invest the resources I have. All my friends from high school have kids now. I don't foresee myself having kids anytime soon, but I banked sperm before my transition to potentially have some in the future.*

Musah, 23, Rhode Island: *A big deterrent for me [in going to college] was thinking that I wasn't smart enough. Impostor syndrome. I feel that in a lot of spaces because the culture I was raised in was pretty different. I was born in Ivory Coast to a Liberian mother, she was a refugee of the Liberian Civil War, and we moved here when I was eight months old. My impostor syndrome comes from a mixture of things, one of which is trying to make my family proud of me.*

Joshua, 39, California: *My upbringing had narratives. "Blessed are the meek." "Your riches are in heaven." Well into adulthood, I believed that I didn't deserve money. I didn't dream about owning or achieving grander* *things. I would also filter what I put on social media, especially Facebook, because that demographic mostly knew me from church. "Oh, I can't post this—too gay." When the Pulse shooting happened in Orlando, it deeply affected me. I remember seeing the victims' faces and thinking that could have been me on a night out with my friends. It empowered me to live unapologetically. There's a future to be built, and it's up to me.*

Tamika, 50, Texas: *My mother became a cash-and-carry person after seeing my dad get into debt repeatedly. I think she conflated debt with addiction because he was an alcoholic, so I did the same. I was just like, "That's bad." As a queer Black person, I have this relationship with money where it's about building as much as possible inside of the generation that's living, but not necessarily leaving anything behind. It's about current safety.*

Ryan, 41, New York: *My parents acted like the worst thing you could ever do is take out a student loan. You could borrow money for God-ordained reasons, like a house or a car or a business. Going to college was not one of those God-sanctioned reasons. The only way I could figure out how to go to college without taking on a student loan was to join the army. So I did. Later in life, I figured out that my parents were actually terrible with money because of their religion. They went bankrupt.*

K (pseudonym), 18, location redacted: *I am a full-time college student who still lives at home and works about thirty hours a week at a part-time job. I came out to my parents as bisexual two years ago. We haven't talked about it since. It's as if I never said anything about it. As for my gender identity, my parents are much more transphobic than they are homophobic. I'm not certain they wouldn't kick me out for being non-binary, so I currently plan on never revealing my gender identity to them. If I were to do so, it would be after I have secured a place on my own. I spend my money very scarcely because I am trying to save up to be able to move out. Ideally I'd like to have about $40,000 in savings before I move out to cover college and living expenses. I am over halfway there. I am hoping to be out* *in a year, but it just depends on if I can find a roommate and how many hours I can get at work. Between work and school, there is not much time for anything else.*

You will hear from more queer people throughout the chapters of this book. If your past has shaped your relationships with money, know you're not alone. Often, your inherited beliefs are not the real you.

THOUGHT PATTERN NO. 2: MONEY MALAISE, AVOIDANCE, AND NUMBING

Your brain can be quite the diva sometimes. Self-inflicted drama seeps into our bank accounts in three ways: avoidance, numbing, and money malaise.

Avoidance is intentionally not looking at your bank accounts: "Out of sight, out of mind." Great for ex-boyfriends, less great for your budget. In avoidance, you purposely avoid reality and shut out uncomfortable feelings so that things look great on the surface, but it's a *Hoarders*-level hot mess behind the scenes. Numbing is a type of avoidance; it's when we soothe unpleasant feelings or emotions to feel better, and is sometimes our response to flailing mental health.

There's also **money malaise**, which is when we feel helpless or resigned about our money situation and the future of society in general. Money malaise is slightly different from avoidance and numbing. It's a darker, more nuanced thought pattern. Here are some of the ways it shows up:

- **Long payoff timelines.** "I have $100,000+ in student loans. People will be living on Mars by the time I pay this shit off. Who cares if I buy this pair of earrings?"
- **Hating on the system.** "Oh, so I have to cough up almost 20 percent of my pay to taxes, but billionaires don't? I am so over this country—bartender, another vodka soda, please."

- **Climate nihilism.** "At this rate, there's not going to be a planet in fifty years, so why even think about retirement?"
- **Post–coming out Renaissance realness.** "I spent a lot of my life in the closet, not living it up. I'm done with that. It's time to do what I want, and whatever that costs doesn't matter."

Money malaise can also stem from resentment and regret. If you feel financially unmotivated because of events from the past, forgive yourself—for not studying the "right" thing in college to have a more lucrative career; for squandering your income or a windfall of cash in your earlier years; for not realizing how fast credit card debt grows; for making a dumb investment or getting swindled; for going bankrupt. Forgive yourself, remove the mind weeds, treat yourself to a martini or mocktail by the pool to reinforce the productive behavior of confronting your thought patterns, and then move on.

None of these money malaise behaviors are destructive in the moment. The problem is when your justified thoughts become a pattern and you follow through on them repeatedly, to the point in which they become habits. To break a habit, we must start with awareness and self-reflection.

Think of a time when you bought on impulse. Did you know you had the money, or did a cloud of "I wonder if this will come back to bite me in the ass later" linger over the thrill? Spending some fun money here and there is fine (and we budget for that later in this chapter to keep you motivated!), but if you're in a hole and want to get out of it, you have to stop digging yourself deeper at some point.

CONTENT WARNING: IN THE FOLLOWING TESTIMONY, A QUEER PERSON DESCRIBES THINKING ABOUT SELF-HARM.

Paul, 40, California: *I knew I didn't like girls when I was 14 but didn't come out until my last semester of college. There was this eight-year period where I figured I would either stay in the closet forever or kill myself. Those seemed like my only two options. When I came out,* *the mindset became "Don't save. F***ing spend it. You've earned it." So I did. Happy hours with top shelf drinks. Taking $75 cabs that should have been $2 trains. There was a period where I lived at home, but still spent all of the money I was "saving" on going out and conveniences. It's only been in the last few years that I've gotten to a better place with the financial stuff.*

Proactive planning helps you have more of what you want in life, as well as the sexy sheen of freshly boosted confidence. Avoid using your situation as an excuse to just keep spending.

THOUGHT PATTERN NO. 3: "JUST TO BE SAFE"

If your cash flow is tight, and you're not sure you'll have enough to make it to your next paycheck, you'll be more inclined to throw expenses on a credit card "just to be safe." This innocent four-word tagline is keeping you broke.

You buy the plane tickets, but aren't sure you'll have the cash, so you put it on the credit card "just to be safe." You slice your finger open cutting tortilla strips to make breakfast migas (yay Tex-Mex, boo bleeding), so you put the unexpected urgent care bill on the credit card "just to be safe." Rent is due in three days and you just got a parking ticket, so you pay for it with a credit card "just to be safe." We also have a new villain, Buy Now, Pay Later, in which you can split your next social media splurge or weekly grocery bill into four payments over six weeks—say it with me—"Just to be safe." Safe from what, exactly? Yourself?

"Just to be safe" makes it very easy to overspend. Then, when you don't have the extra money to pay what you owe, your debts sit there and quietly grow, often at very high interest rates. A month or two later, your "just to be safe" justification happens again, and you slowly dig yourself deeper. Debt begins to eat up more of your budget and erode your personal spending power. And if you have too much debt, it might affect your ability to get a car loan, personal loan, or mortgage in the future. Lenders look at your minimum monthly debt payments in comparison to your monthly income, a metric known as **debt-to-income ratio (DTI)**, when deciding whether they want to loan you money.

Personal finance has a lot of dense terms and jargon. So to help you along I'll give you a little callout box entitled "tea," queer slang for truth that originated within Black drag culture (because let's be real, most of today's queer culture came from Black ballroom culture, and much of our progress as queer people came from this community).

Graphic designer, spill that acronym one more time.

TEA

Debt-to-income ratio (DTI): A measurement of how much of your income goes to debt payments every month. If it's too high, lenders and landlords might give you the stink-eye and turn you away from loans or housing because they're not sure you'll be able to pay your bills.

Debt is one of those four-letter words that has many definitions and emotional charges, so we'll spend all of chapter 2 developing a plan for how to use it wisely.

THOUGHT PATTERN NO. 4: BINARY PERSPECTIVES

"You should have NO debt!" "You need SIX MONTHS of expenses in savings!" "THIS is the right way, and if you do it any other way, you're a SUCKER!" Personal finance culture is often binary—"Do this, not that"—and personal finance personalities even more so. But our lives are not binary. They're multifaceted, with many circumstances and other people to consider. Be skeptical of personal finance thought leaders who only ever speak in binary terms.

We think in binary because it's easier. It lets us make quick snap judgments, often without context, and move on. If I told you I spent $60 on lunch . . . what's your snap judgment of me? Am I bad with money? Sloppy? What if I was a business owner and took two important clients out to lunch? What if I had my kid with me? What if I simply *wanted to*—and had budgeted the money to do so? When we think in binary, we lose the nuance, the very quality that helps us create the life we want for ourselves.

Nuance becomes helpful when unexpected financial situations arise. Sure, it's easy to save money when you're in a cushy job. But what about when unexpected medical debt shows up? Or you have to move to a different city or state because new anti-LGBTQ legislation is being enforced? These are real scenarios that queer Americans grapple with every day.

Be thoughtful and fluid with your personal finances so that *when* your money situation changes, you can remain *Cirque du Soleil*–flexible.

THOUGHT PATTERN NO. 5:
"I'M A STARVING ARTIST, THIS IS JUST HOW IT IS"

I know this money martyr mindset well because I lived it for a long time—and loved it. I chose to study classical music in college because doing so symbolized freedom of expression at a time in my life when I wasn't yet out of the closet. I viewed creative autonomy as a critical component of my queer expression, and any career alternative was absolutely out of the question.

"I'm all about the MUSIC!" I would exclaim to the man sitting across from me while on our first date, neck vein throbbing while I spoke, as he nervously drank from his coup glass to try to mask his

reaction. Changing careers felt like selling out. I saw it as my martyred destiny that, as a person working in a creative field, cereal for dinner at the end of the month in order to make rent was as good as life was going to get.

As I got older, and became more grizzled, my queer identity became less about what I *do* and more about who I *am*. The ship had mostly sailed on me becoming America's next top horn star, and my barely-making-ends-meet lifestyle in the meantime felt increasingly unaligned with the kind of life I wanted to live. So I changed careers.

To my surprise, financial security *increased* my creativity because I was no longer preoccupied (consumed) with the stress of how I would pay my bills. I was able to find other outlets in life that let me scratch the creativity itch. Eventually, my queer identity became multifaceted enough that I decided to sell my instrument. I had a little phantom limb at first, but got over it (especially knowing my French horn had gone to a teenager who would learn music with it), and I got some sheet music tattooed on my forearm to commemorate a special time in my life.

Still unconvinced? How about this: Science confirms that being in a chronically stressed, pissy mood stifles personal expression. In the book *Thinking, Fast and Slow,* the late author and psychologist Daniel Kahneman describes an experiment in which people in bad moods were less able to access their creativity and intuition on command. Eliminating money stress might help you unlock your most fulfilling, inspired work yet.

Changing careers was my solution, but it doesn't have to be yours. If you're a full-time creative, and want to continue being one, chapters 5 and 8 will help you get paid what you deserve.

THOUGHT PATTERN NO. 6: COMPARISON CULTURE

Comparison culture is nothing new—"Keeping up with the Joneses" began as a comic strip in 1913—but it's especially mainstream these days. Entire Bravo franchises have been built brick by brick on comparison culture, really. And while a little healthy competition can be motivating at times, it can also drive us to spend beyond our means.

Expensive bridesmaids' dresses. Tickets to every new show that passes through town. Those summer gay-cations and parties that can sometimes feel like an audition. Comparison culture hijacks your good times because it makes the core social motivation less about sharing joy and more about feeling wanted or asserting social status.

Mikey, 31, California: *Summer is the worst for this kind of pressure. It feels like every week there is either a trip or a party you just HAVE to go to. Whether it's for Pride or just the pressure to go out, it can add up quickly. I am pretty good about resisting that desire to spend, but it does become difficult. We all want to belong. Sometimes you get caught up in the moment, and the next thing you know you have thousands of dollars' worth of trips planned.*

Queer people are more susceptible to comparison culture because our hearts and souls are starved for acceptance. Growing up, we turn ourselves inside-out to fit in with the crowd, often at the expense of our own self-expression. Later, when we do find "our people," we seek a sense of belonging and want to fit in. When we see other queer people posting thot pics or vacation selfies (or the ultimate jab-hook: thotty vacation selfies) on social media, our first instinct is to compare . . . and perhaps despair.

Release aspects of your life that eat up time or money but aren't actually authentic to who you are. When you free yourself from these thought patterns, you stop spending yourself into oblivion just to prove to people (or faceless online profiles) that you're on their level and worthy of their attention.

THOUGHT PATTERN NO. 7: "MORE IS BETTER"

Who clocked comparison culture early on, then used it to their advantage? Corporations, of course.

In psychology-based advertising, more is always better. I know this because I worked as a copywriter for years and was part of the problem, convincing people to buy all kinds of shit via the written word. Marketing, a career field in which manipulative homosexuals like me excel, tries to convince you that (1) what you currently have is not enough and (2) the only way you'll be happy is to be, do, and have *more*.

When you're shown that which you do not yet have, then close the gap by spending money, your body releases dopamine, the feel-good chemical, which reinforces the behavior and motivates you to repeat it in the future. This soon becomes an unconscious pattern: You see something, buy it, and let the temporary high wash over you. The *behavior* is what's getting reinforced, which can turn into a problem. Even when you have everything you need and want, your mind still fixates on the thing you *don't* yet have. You're never satisfied. Your queer joy gets stolen—it's homophobic.

It's not our fault we're like this. Consumerism has been gaining momentum for decades. By the early twentieth century, most Americans already had what they needed for their households. This was bad for supply chains because all these big-ass factories had just been built during the Industrial Revolution (they were giving werk, but at scale). Corporations needed a way to keep demand propped up, so they began to sell products not just on their features, but also what *feelings* the products stirred up in us, and what having those products *represented*.

Fast forward to today and it's completely normal to spend some or all of your money toward reaching an aspirational identity. Watch any luxury car commercial to see this moody inspo in action; it's like an Enya music video, but with our Celtic chanteuse swapped out for a Land Rover (or a Ford pickup truck, whichever your car kink). Psychology-based advertising reinforces gender norms, societal perceptions, and shared aspirations by making certain ideals attractive and other ideals unacceptable. It affects queer people in more ways than one.

An antidote to consumerism is to define "enough." Until you define what is enough, your default will always be that more is better, and discontent will become your personality (ick). When you define enough, you give yourself purpose and direction.

SOCIAL MEDIA, YOUR DOPAMINE DOM

Lots of opinions out there about social media and comparison culture, so let's align on the facts.

No causal link to depression or anxiety. Surprising, right? Multiple peer-reviewed studies have found no causal link between social media and mental health disorder. Social media can exacerbate symptoms for some users based on *pre-existing* mental health, but it hasn't been proven to cause new depression or anxiety.

It's free, and everything else is expensive. *Of course* users worldwide spend an average of 143 minutes a day on social media: It's inexpensive entertainment.[4] To see why social media persists, just look at what the economy has done to our other leisure options (whoever gave bowling the overpriced gastropub makeover, I'm mad at you).

Still has warts. The negative side effects of social media come with the territory. Most commonly, they include low self-esteem (from comparison culture), cyberbullying, and lost sleep, so watch out for those. Social media feeds create a feedback loop in which every swipe of your thumb gives you another spanking of dopamine, so if it gets to be too much, the safe word is "airplane mode."

Pros outweigh the cons for queer people. Social media is a haven for queer people to organize, learn, laugh, and bask in queer joy. This is especially true for rural LGBTQ+ people, who may not have access to an in-person community. One meta-analysis of twenty-eight peer-reviewed studies concluded that social media can be positive for queer people because it lets them explore their identity and connect with peers.[5] (Also, how will I know which drag queens are performing this weekend?)

Money defines so much of our lives. We associate financial status with being competent and worthy. But we're also told to stay in the shadows about our struggles and not admit to the world or ourselves what's really going on. So we suffer in silence, compare ourselves to others, and numb through mindless spending until we feel better. Refreshing your thought patterns is step one to mastering your money.

° ° °

To sidestep all this thought pattern–building machinery, start being more aware and intentional. Instead of relying on outside billboards, feeds, or our own habits to guide our financial lives, we must reflect on what matters to us in life, look at our money, and make a plan to have the two work together in harmony.

TIME TO START LOOKING AT YOUR MONEY

"Wait, what? *Now?!* I'm not ready!" Well, you knew this was coming. It's just coming sooner than expected. Kinda like my not-coming-out coming out, where I had a subscription to an indie queer magazine my freshman year of college, then canceled it before I moved home for the summer, but the mag didn't get the memo, so the issues got forwarded to my childhood home. ("Really, Mom, I have no idea why this is addressed to me," as I held up the June issue, the cover of which was just one giant manspread.)

We cannot manage what we cannot see. Therefore, we must first know what we are earning and spending. We don't have to get super-granular at this point—we'll look more closely at *why* you buy what you buy in chapter 4—but we do need an approximate understanding of where we're currently at.

Resist the urge to skim this chapter and avoid looking at your accounts. That's not awareness. We're cultivating judgment-free awareness, remember? We're also going to do this exercise manually, even if you use an online budgeting tool, because it's important you feel the feels as you look at your money.

THE "FOUR BUCKETS" BUDGET

Either get out a pen and paper or open up a spreadsheet (I use Google Sheets). Make a total of eight rows and two columns. (If your earnings fluctuate a lot from month to month, make five columns.) Also leave some space off to the side for chicken scratch as needed.

1.	
2.	
3.	
4.	
5.	
6.	
7.	
8.	

The four buckets budget exercise has three steps.

1. Calculate your disposable income.
2. Map your expenses into four buckets.
3. Reflect.

STEP 1: CALCULATE YOUR DISPOSABLE INCOME

First, we want to calculate how much money you're working with in a given month. This is known as **disposable income**. It's your gross income (the big number, the one before all that other stuff gets taken out of your paycheck) minus taxes. Disposable income is also *before* things like retirement account contributions or health insurance premiums are taken out, so if money gets taken out of your paycheck for those programs, disposable income includes that money.

TEA

Disposable income: Your gross income minus any taxes withheld. This is how much money you have to work with each month.

Disposable income is different from taxable income, which is how much of your income you actually get taxed on. No need to think about that until chapter 7. For now, just focus on figuring out disposable income.

If you have a day job, you can find your gross income and employee taxes paid by looking at a past pay stub. Take your gross income and subtract anything under "employee taxes withheld" to arrive at your disposable income. (You might also see employer taxes, which are the taxes your employer paid on your behalf; ignore these for now.) Here's a mock-up of how a past pay stub looks for me, as someone who lives in California:

EMPLOYEE GROSS EARNINGS

Description	Rate	Hours	Current	Year to Date
Regular Hours/Hourly				
TOTALS				

EMPLOYEE TAXES WITHHELD

Employee Tax	Current	Year to Date
Federal Income Tax		
Social Security		
Medicare		
CA State Income Tax		
CA SIDI		

EMPLOYER TAXES

Company Tax	Current	Year to Date
Social Security		
Medicare		
FUTA		
CA SUI		
CA ETT		

If you're doing freelance work or a side hustle, you likely won't have a pay stub. Taxes aren't being taken out when you receive this money, so I would *strongly* encourage you (beg you, really) to put some of it aside for when taxes are due. This rate is a sliding scale, based on how much you expect to make in a year, and readjusts every year; you can find the most up-to-date scale on the IRS's website or at https://nickwolny.com/book-resources.

To help cement ideas throughout this book, I've added some composites of queer people navigating hypothetical money situations. These composites were developed from testimonies, other interviews with LGBTQ+ Americans, and publicly available economic information. You and I will look at them together (on the couch, with some salty snacks nearby) to see money concepts in action. Once you feel clear on the exercises, repeat them for yourself.

Raye

Raye is a 22-year-old non-binary person starting a new job as a junior engineer. By day they're analyzing projects; by night they're opening cans of whoop-ass online playing *Super Smash Bros*. They're making $60,000 year in gross income, which comes out to $5,000 per month.

1. Monthly gross income	$5,000
2. Total taxes withheld	$825
3. Monthly disposable income	$4,175

According to their pay stub, about $825 is taken out per month for federal, Social Security, and Medicare taxes. Therefore, Raye's disposable income is $4,175 per month.

Action: Determine your monthly disposable income, based on either a past pay stub or your earnings from the last month. Write down monthly gross income, taxes withheld, and monthly disposable income in the first three rows of your budget sheet. (If you have a fluctuating income, do this for each of the last three months, putting your numbers in columns 2, 3, and 4. Then calculate the averages and put those numbers in column 5.)

STEP 2: MAP YOUR EXPENSES INTO FOUR BUCKETS

Feelings check-in: Are you already annoyed at having to do this manually? If the answer is yes, that's money malaise and avoidance starting to creep in, and you now have a reference for what it feels like. We are overwriting your "it's too complicated" money thought pattern in real time.

Now go through the last full month of expenses you have on file (each of the last three months if income fluctuates). This will require looking back at past bank statements and categorizing what you spent. Find those logins, open up those bank statements (just sign up for the damn paperless statements already while you're in there if you still get the snail mail), and create the clearest possible picture you can of all the money that came in and went out last month.

Go through your expenses one by one, using the chicken scratch section of your sheet of paper as needed. Plot each expense into one of the following four buckets listed below:

1. **Essential expenses.** What you spent on the essentials, including housing, food, transportation, and so on. Baby diapers. Utilities. Gas for the car. (To confirm: Poppers are not essential.) Log the expenses you need to reasonably function. If you have health insurance or other insurance through your employer, also include the cost of that here.
2. **Minimum debt payments.** Locate the minimum required monthly payment for all of your debts. You might have automatic payments set up that are higher than the minimum requirement. Look up what the minimum is and put it in this bucket; you'll need these amounts for the next chapter. If you have no debt, put zero.
3. **Fun money.** This bucket includes all the money you spent on nonessential items. Streaming services. Camping gear. Vintage gay magazines (this is one of mine). *Pokémon* trading card packs. Christina Aguilera memorabilia. Vapes. OnlyFans subscriptions. Houseplants. I don't care what the expenses are; I only care that you track them and categorize them into this bucket.
4. **Net worth contributions.** This bucket is for all money contributed to accounts or investments that increase your **net worth** (how much money you have in life minus how much you owe). Include any money you've put toward savings, investments, or additional debt payments. (Include the pre-tax contributions from your paychecks, too, like retirement contributions or health savings account contributions. If you don't know what those are, don't worry about it; we'll hit 'em in chapters 6 and 7.) This bucket might be empty, and that's okay—now we know!

Also, a little foreshadowing: We'll be "queer journaling" about these expenses in chapter 4, and it's gonna be revelatory (think ayahuasca, but less vomiting). Consider listing these expenses in an organized way now to save yourself from going back through bank statements later.

Plot these amounts in your chart in rows 4, 5, 6, and 7. Then, subtract these expense buckets from your disposable income to see what's left. That number will be your over/under, which will go in row 8. This number might be zero, and that's okay. It might also be a negative number. If that's the case, you're currently spending more than you're making.

Let's go back to Raye, our composite, to see an example.

Raye

Essential expenses: Raye keeps their living expenses low by living with a roommate (Rent and utilities: $1,600/month for Raye's portion). They and their roommate do grocery shopping and some meal prepping together each week ($700/month for Raye's portion). They also put in this bucket two haircuts a month ($100), gas for the car twice a month ($100), car insurance ($100/month), and occasional new clothes ($100/month). Total = $2,700

Minimum debt payments: $70/month on a small student loan, $30/month on a credit card (which is on a zero-percent interest rate for a few more months because they did a balance transfer), and $300/month on an auto loan. Total = $400

Fun money: Raye's fun money includes latté trips to the coffee shop a few times a week ($75/month), dinner out or drinks out once a week ($200/month, with dates taking the priority), and a big box gym membership ($75/month). Total = $350

Net worth contributions: Their net worth contributions are $250/month to a savings account and $300/month to a Roth IRA retirement account. (If that sentence made no sense to you, don't worry, we're gonna cover it later.) Total = $550

Raye typically ends the month with about $175 left over, which they put into a separate savings account for vacation money.

3. Raye's Monthly Disposable Income	$4,175
4. Essential expenses	$2,700
5. Minimum debt payments	$400
6. Fun money	$350
7. Net worth contributions	$550
8. Leftover (Over/Under)	$175

Action: Plot your last month's expenses into one of four buckets. Then, subtract each of these numbers from your disposable income to determine your over/under for the month.

STEP 3: REFLECT

Okay, so how was that? Eye-opening? Painful? Surprising? All of the above? I hope so.

At first glance, this awareness exercise might have helped you realize you're spending more than you thought in certain areas of your life, or that your gig money isn't stretching quite as far as you thought it would, or that you're still paying for subscriptions you stopped using long ago. We love a quick win, so please don't wait on me to make any obvious initial money-saving changes.

The bigger reason we start with this exercise is to expose the impact your existing thought patterns might be having on your money. I'm talking about money malaise, avoidance, and numbing that, if left unchecked, will continue to show up in your bank statements, sabotaging your future. Can't hoe out a weed if you can't see it, which is why it's critical that you start looking at your money on a regular basis. Look at your money often, at least once a week, and ideally once a day (apps make this easy); looking at your money builds the habit of awareness.

We'll revisit this exercise in future chapters, so keep your work in a safe place until then.

Action: Reflect on your four buckets budget sheet with the following questions.

Where do I spend more money or less money than I originally thought?

What feelings came up during this exercise?

Are there any easy wins I can take action on right now?

EXTRA CREDIT, BECAUSE QUEERS LOVE EXTRA CREDIT

This is a book on how to pattern *new* habits into your life. Habits like paying down debt, moving money into savings, fishing for a better salary, understanding your benefits, and investing for a better future. For extra brownie points with the instructor (me), consider these other action steps to give yourself a running start.

Get a budgeting app. If you don't use an online budgeting app or website yet, I suggest you sign up for one. Many of these are free, and they let you connect all different types of accounts, from checking and savings accounts to student loans to credit cards to retirement accounts, so you can see all your activity in one place. If you found looking back through past bank statements annoying (and who doesn't?), an online app will reduce a lot of the mental friction and make it easier to build new habits around money. If you want a recommendation, check https://nickwolny.com/book-resources to see my most updated picks.

Be kind to yourself during this process. Speaking of reading, judgment is sometimes a main character in LGBTQ+ culture. And while it's often done in jest, when we're dripping with judgment toward others, we might be less willing to turn that critical eye on ourselves. Be willing to look inward without adding your mental voiceover of one-liners, put-downs, and slams. For some, this will be the most challenging assignment of the chapter. Money stress is right up there with super glue in terms of stickiness; don't let your unwillingness to address it ruin your life.

Do a no-spend challenge. Oh, you want *extra* extra credit? Okay, try this: Pick a specific category of spending and abstain from it for a predetermined length of time. This could be something like a week without Starbucks coffee, or a month without buying anything off an Instagram ad. For a variation, go one day without spending money on *anything*. What thoughts come up? What thought *patterns* come up?

∘ ∘ ∘

The four buckets budget exercise is rigorous enough that you become familiar with where your money is going, but not so granular that you want to give up before we've even really started. It gets you out of avoidance and into awareness.

Remember to take a beginner's mindset with this stuff. It's possible (probable, if this book is doing its job!) that you will learn new context and strategies for various aspects of money, strategies you had not considered before or had written off, that have the potential to transform your financial situation and life. Reading is fundamental, and in this case we do mean that literally.

This mindset will serve us well as we take on one of queer people's biggest money thorns: debt. With new awareness in tow, let's start taking action around your money.

2

DEBT

Slay the Stress and Death Drop Your Deficits

"No, Nick—don't answer the phone."

I heard this a lot while growing up in rural Illinois in a single-parent household, back in the landline days, when phones had cords, so you had to get up and walk across a room when they rang. I once pushed my luck and picked up when someone was calling. The bill collector on the other line asked to talk to my mom, so I handed the phone to her, and she yelled at me afterward. Only later did it make sense: We were in debt collection.

Money was a taboo topic growing up. It was one of the main reasons my parents had gotten divorced, and I never learned much about how to manage it. Like a lot of closeted gay kids in rural America, I saw college as a way out, so I took out student loans without really understanding what my income or repayment would look like after I graduated. As I navigated the working world and began living on my own, setbacks like flat tires would pop up here and there. I didn't have any savings, so I'd bail myself out with credit cards "just to be safe," without being able to pay them off. And because I didn't really understand how debt worked, I was easily swayed by things like signup bonuses and cash-back offers.

This seemingly rational reasoning of "just to be safe" can be quite destructive because it creates drag (the physics principle, not the queer art form) on your whole financial situation. I call this phenomenon **debt drag**. It's the inertia you feel when part of your monthly budget is going toward things you bought months or years ago. Some of these expenses have long-lasting value: a good pair of steel-toe boots, a computer, gender-affirming care. Other expenses, maybe not so much.

Debt drag prevents millions of Americans from living free, autonomous lives. The average consumer with a credit card has a balance of nearly $6,000. Gen Z consumers are taking out credit cards at faster rates than millennials did at the same age, and one in seven Gen Z credit card holders have already maxed out their limits. Average credit card interest rates are now well past 20 percent, with retail credit card interest rates nearing 30 percent. Since the end of a three-year pandemic-induced pause on student loan payments, nearly three in ten borrowers were already behind on their monthly minimums.[1]

For queer people, it's worse: Research from the Federal Reserve found that LGB people (sexual orientation was measured, but gender identity wasn't) were more likely to have both student debt and credit card debt, and were more likely to have taken out alternative debt like a payday loan.[2] We take on debt, then make painfully slow progress paying it off, and soon find ourselves taking a mud bath in it (frightening, Super Mario quicksand-y mud, not exfoliating spa mud). Many young people never get a chance to experience a debt-free adulthood before being drowned by the sticky, sludgy money mud that is chronic debt.

But to summarize the scenario as "debt = BAD" is too binary. In some cases, debt is leverage. Debt is how millions of Americans afford a home in the form of a mortgage. Debt helps young people purchase a car, which can enable better job prospects and social autonomy. Debt is how some of your favorite coffee shops and small businesses got off the ground and built community. A debt like a small business loan can help you outsource production for that gay cross stitch kit side hustle of yours that's taking off (if you have a gay cross stitch kit business, please contact me immediately). In these examples, debt can be a tool, like a knife, or for my horror lovers, a chainsaw: effective when used properly, destructive when used improperly.

Debt can sabotage your financial future, and it has been expertly engineered to be extremely sticky. As long as there is high-interest debt in your life, it's hard to find momentum on any other money goals. By understanding the various external and internal forces that sink us into debt, you'll be better equipped to make a plan, slay the stress, and put yourself on the path toward a better financial future.

Why You're in Debt

1. Not enough money to cover essential expenses
2. Really profitable for banks and lenders
3. Credit score culture
4. The costs are confusing
5. Separates the act of purchase from payment
6. Not enough in savings

REASON NO. 1: WE SOMETIMES NEED DEBT TO COVER ESSENTIAL EXPENSES

"Shouldn't have spent the money to begin with!" That's the usual armchair commentary we hear when we talk about debt. It frames having debt as being irresponsible or frivolous, which might apply to some people's financial circumstances, but isn't accurate as a blanket statement.

Debt is prevalent because, for many, essential expenses are outpacing earnings. When you look at today's household incomes compared to ten, twenty, or fifty years ago, jobs certainly pay more *dollars* than they used to. But our *purchasing power* hasn't necessarily gone up that much, because expenses experience inflation, too. (This is why your grandpa complains about how a Snickers bar cost a quarter back when he was a young whippersnapper, while also conveniently leaving out that he was making two dollars an hour.) Inflation happens for many reasons and can turn into a rabbit hole, so we won't get into it any more than necessary to understand the basics. For now, just know that some expenses like housing have inflated faster than earnings recently, which is why life feels so expensive these days.

One-time financial setbacks can also lead to debt. For example, no one expects medical debt, yet twenty million people in America have it. For three million of those people, the medical debt is over $10,000.[3] Despite working hard, living frugally, and going to church (drag brunch) every Sunday, millions of Americans still struggle to make ends meet. We then use debt to close our budget gap every month, which makes our situation increasingly worse.

Let's look at a different composite from the previous chapter's four buckets budget exercise.

Marek

Marek, a 25-year-old man, works at a marketing agency for $21 an hour, which is slightly above the median US hourly wage in 2022.[4] (Remember that median is different from average. Median separates the upper half from the lower half. This means about half of all workers make this amount or less.) His salary is $42,000 a year, which makes his disposable income (income after taxes) $3,000 per month. Marek's four buckets budget exercise looks like this:

- **Essential expenses:** $2,340/month for rent, groceries, transit, basic toiletries, and clothes.
- **Minimum debt payments:** $600/month, including $125/month to cover minimum payments for three credit cards and $475/month toward student loans.
- **Fun money:** $250/month, which covers streaming services,

restaurants, nights out with the gaggle, and the occasional DoorDash or Uber.

- **Net worth contributions:** No saving, but he puts an extra $100/month toward his credit card to at least feel like he's trying. This is futile, because he's already overspent for the month.

Marek's Monthly Disposable Income	$3,000
Essential expenses	$2,340
Minimum debt payments	$600
Fun money	$250
Net worth contributions	$100
Leftover (Over/Under)	**-$290**

Marek's good intentions to put extra money toward his debt aren't working because more money goes out than comes in every month. This scenario summarizes many Americans' current money situation. Make it your goal to understand your monthly cash flow so you can escape the debt machine and not let it wield power over you anymore.

REASON NO. 2:
MEANWHILE, DEBT IS PASSIVE INCOME FOR BANKS AND LENDERS

Banks, lenders, and retailers want you to use their debt products (things like credit cards and loans) because the interest collecting on your debt is easy money in their pockets. When you use credit cards and loans, banks and corporations make passive income off you in the form of interest, and if you fall behind on your payments, they bring in a collections agency to do the dirty work and start making your life hell.

"But I'm getting points/rewards/3 percent cash back!" Yes, but you're sitting on a credit card balance that has a 22 percent interest rate, boo, so you're losing money in the long run. Credit card providers like to bamboozle you with points and rewards because they're effective in getting new customers to sign up. Retailers get in on the action, too; they partner with credit card companies to entice you with a discount, then take a cut of the interest payments (in 2023, store credit cards represented 8 percent of retailers' gross profits, on average).[5]

It's true that if you pay off your credit card every month, you'll scoop up the perks without paying interest on your debt. But only about half of Americans do this successfully. The business model of credit cards depends on you not paying your balance in full each month, and the odds are fifty-fifty, which for them is pretty good.

REASON NO. 3: HOW YOU HANDLE DEBT DETERMINES YOUR "WORTHINESS"

You can't just peace out from the debt machine, though, because your track record on paying off debt is what determines your creditworthiness.

Each of us has a creditworthiness rating called a **credit score**. This number is important because it helps you secure important loans, like a mortgage or auto loan, and can affect your ability to secure housing. Like you, lenders prefer to loan money to people who are likely to pay it back, so they use your credit score to assess your track record for paying bills on time and determine what terms and conditions they want to offer you.

The three main credit bureaus that measure credit scores are Experian, Equifax, and TransUnion. There's also a score that combines all three of these bureau ratings, **the FICO score**, which is what is typically checked when applying for something like a loan or a credit card.

The FICO score ranges from 300 to 850, credit bureaus' scores have similar ranges, and they're all calculated through five criteria:

- **Payment history** (35 percent of score): Your track record of making payments on time.
- **Amounts owed** (30 percent of score): How much you owe, compared to how big of a line of credit you have. This is called utilization. If you owe $5,000, and your line of credit is $5,000 (100 percent utilization), that's considered bad; however, if you owe $5,000, and your line of credit is $50,000 (10 percent utilization), that's considered good.
- **Credit history** (15 percent of score): How long you have had your accounts. This is one of those quirks where closing an old, dormant credit card account for the sake of having a clean spreadsheet actually hurts your credit score.
- **Credit mix** (10 percent of score): Having a mix of debt accounts can help your credit score, but this is a small slice of the pie; don't feel like you *have* to have many different types of debts.
- **New credit** (10 percent of score): If you opened too many lines of credit too recently, that might be seen as a red flag.

Your credit scores and FICO score determine whether you get approved for a car loan or a mortgage, as well as what the interest rate will be on those offers, which can add up to thousands of dollars saved over the life of a loan. Credit scores also get checked by insurance companies before determining coverage, and they even get checked by employers. Your credit score takes time to build up, after which you can mostly coast, so it's good to be aware of it in the background as you work on your money goals. A score in the 600s is considered good, and a score in the 700s or above will usually get you the best rates.

A recent theme has emerged in which queer people avoid creating a credit history as a way to protest this scoring system. Don't do that. Yes, credit scores have a sketchy history; before there were scores, bureaus kept individual files on people, which included written opinion-based evaluations of a borrower's character (translation: probably discriminatory AF). But if you never take out any lines of credit, your lack of credit history will make you "credit invisible," and it can affect your ability to get housing, a car, or insurance. This is another reason our system is messed up: The people who've been working and paying in cash all their lives are perceived as not creditworthy.

TEA

FICO score: A credit score that blends ratings from the three main credit bureaus. Don't pay to look it up; you can make an account at myfico.com to check it for free. Relevant for us because LGBTQ+ people are twice as likely to report having a low or very low credit score, and 35 percent of LGBTQ+ people who applied for credit were turned down (versus 21 percent for non-LGBTQ+).[6]

Credit score culture feeds the consumer debt machine because young people are encouraged to obtain products like credit cards and use them to get a credit history off and running. One educator I interviewed for an article shared with me how she taught financial literacy classes to high schoolers. She said the students with credit cards had received them from their parents, but had "no idea" how to use them.

Learn how to work with debt strategically so that you can build up your credit score without digging yourself into a hole.

REASON NO. 4: THE COST OF HAVING DEBT IS KIND OF CONFUSING

As we'll get to in a moment, debt itself isn't what's spiking the punch. The poison is how fast your debt grows, based on its interest rate, as well as how frequently this interest rate gets applied.

The minimum monthly required payment on a credit card is typically between 1 and 4 percent of your balance (or a flat fee; it depends on the card terms). Credit cards are advertised as having an **annual percentage rate (APR)**. In the second quarter of 2024, the average APR on credit cards with balances was 22.78 percent, but that interest rate doesn't get applied annually. *Parts* of the interest rate get applied to *every* billing cycle, which makes it a pain in the ass to do the math in your head.

To calculate your credit card interest this month, you'd need to divide your card's APR by 365 days (366 if in a leap year), then multiply that rate to your credit card balance at the end of *every* day—but *not* add it to your balance until the end of your next billing cycle. No one's gonna do this on a regular basis, and credit card providers are counting on that so they can leech more money out of you in the form of interest.

Credit card payments often go toward the newly accrued interest first, so you might not be making as much progress as you think. Let's look at an example together.

Antonio

Antonio is a 42-year-old bisexual cis man with a penchant for good house music, working in hospitality with a mix of gigs and hourly-wage jobs. He has an average daily balance of $8,000 on his credit card at a 21 percent interest rate. His minimum payment is 2.75 percent of his balance ($220). His billing cycle was thirty days. Let's also say he makes no additional purchases on his card in the month, to make the math a little easier.

Antonio would see 1.73 percent interest (22% APR / 365 x 30 days) applied to his $8,000 balance, which comes out to $138.40.

Statement balance	Monthly minimum payment	Interest applied	New balance
$8,000	$220	$138.40	$8,138.40

Seems reasonable. But the $220 payment isn't going toward Antonio's $8,000 principal. It first goes toward this new interest. Only after that's cleared away does the rest of his payment get applied to the principal.

Monthly minimum payment	Current balance the payment is applied to	New balance
$220	$8,138.40	$7,918.40

See the problem? Antonio put $220 toward his bill, but only made $81.60 in paydown progress. All the rest went to interest. This is one of the more measurable effects of debt drag. Antonio spends hours of his life every month making money that then goes into his lender's pocket, rather than going toward what he owes.

Keep an eye on big interest rates, particularly if you end up in a pinch one day and need to secure a payday loan or other high-interest debt, and do your best to pay off this debt quickly.

TEA

Payday loans: Loans that don't involve a credit score check and are often a solution for desperate consumers. They're also famously predatory, having APRs around 400 percent (not a typo). In one report from 2023, 9 percent of queer respondents had taken out a payday loan within the last year.[7]

REASON NO. 5: DEBT SEPARATES THE ECSTASY OF PURCHASE FROM THE AGONY OF PAYMENT

Debt is a slippery slope because it removes the obstacle of cash flow in the short term. Buying things with money you don't yet have is a normalized behavior for many Americans. It's also fertile soil for thought patterns like money malaise and numbing because the thrill of the purchase is separated from the pain of parting with your hard-earned coins.

Thanks to technology, the *ability* to spend money has gotten much faster and easier. Digital wallets keep your credit and debit card information saved on your computer or smartphone, and you can approve transactions simply by clicking a button or scanning your face. No more analog checkbook-balancing nonsense, like what my mom would do when she'd take me with her to JCPenney as a kid to purchase a new microwave and put it on layaway (which probably only took a few minutes, but for an 11-year-old gay in 1998 wanting to get back into the mall to go leer at the Abercrombie storefront, this felt like an eternity).

Since everything is more digital now, balancing the checkbook is a thing of the past. The new shopping mall lives within your smartphone, and it's the perfect catalog, well-curated and available to you whenever you want, even when you're under the covers at the end of the night. It's also right next to social media, which we scroll for hours a day, and which LGBTQ+ people use more frequently.

Milo, 19, California: *Something I want older queer people to know is that TikTok helps young queer people understand who they are. The algorithm is addictive, but it can also pick up on how long you watch queer content, even if you don't search for it, and this will also happen to people who are just finding themselves. I spend a lot of time on social media, and there are ads for a lot of things I want on there. Since the pandemic, I've been doing a lot more online shopping.*

In recent years, another slippery debt product called Buy Now, Pay Later (BNPL) is presented as a convenient alternative to credit cards. Simply split the cost of your transaction into four payments over six weeks, with no additional fees (but a fee of up to $65 if you accidentally miss a payment). And so, "just to be safe," you spread out your payments, because it feels better in the moment to keep more money in your bank account. Except, uh, when is that next payment due again? The "play it safe" card enables you because it lets you skate by without knowing how much money is coming in and going out each month, and the more financed transactions there are to juggle, the harder it is to stay on top of everything.

One Bloomberg report found that a third of BNPL users owed over $1,000 on the service, and a substantial percentage had missed a payment.[8] BNPL makes your cash flow messy, no matter how many sponsored posts you see from your favorite drag queens, so avoid using this service as much as you can.

REASON NO. 6:
NOT ENOUGH IN SAVINGS

"But Nick, I don't *have* much in savings to fall back on." I know! This is true for millions of people! Fifty-six percent of Americans say they couldn't pay for a $1,000 emergency expense from savings, and 27 percent report having no emergency savings at all.[9]

When you don't have any money in savings, the debt dragon is always looming over your shoulder, ready to strike the moment you get into a fender-bender or get hit with a surprise tax bill. Even if you're diligent about not using debt, it often becomes the most viable and immediate solution when you don't have a savings cushion to absorb a setback.

Cholopat, 23, California: *I never really feel like I have enough for an emergency fund. Like, I save. And an emergency is what savings is for. But when I moved here from Boston, and had to move all my things, I definitely underbudgeted. It's scary how things can go over budget in a flash. If I have an actual emergency, I'm dead—all my assets would be drained.*

Debt drag weighs you down month after month, as we saw earlier. It's mentally draining, holds a vise grip on your psyche, and eats away at your peace of mind. Debt can even affect your physical health; research from the National Institutes of Health found that people who believe they had higher levels of debt also had higher diastolic blood pressure, which is associated with a greater risk of hypertension and stroke.[10]

To get debt-sober, or just sober-ish, we must build up *other* financial resources so that you can steadily wean yourself off. An overarching theme of this book is to follow step-by-step strategies that build a savings cushion and help keep money stress at bay.

TEA

"Can I just not pay my debts?" Much like that one friend deprived of their Celsius energy drink for too long, these debt collectors can get nasty real quick. If you stop paying your debts, lenders can send your bill to a collections agency to start hounding you. From there, they can escalate further and take legal action, garnish your wages, seize your assets, or get a bank levy, which lets the lender take the money it's owed directly from your bank account. Do everything you can to make those payments.

○ ○ ○

Remember the 7-word plan for building wealth: lower expenses, increase earnings, invest the difference. When you increase the gap between income and expenses, you can then use that money to pay down debt from the past, finance your queer life in the present, and prepare yourself for the future. This strategy lets you ignore the fancy spreadsheets, influencers with get-rich-quick solutions, and politicians' pie-in-the-sky promises that may or may not come to fruition (#studentloans).

It kinda feels like coming out, really. When you stop hiding your financial secrets from yourself and confront your money situation head-on, the initial discomfort gives way to a new, more fulfilling way of life. We want that to be a life where debt is no longer weighing you down, so let's formulate a plan to get rid of it once and for all.

HOW TO SLAY YOUR DEBT

Not all debt is toxic. What makes a debt good or bad (or, more accurately, cheap or expensive) is its interest rate: how much interest gets added to your debt or loan, as well as how frequently the interest is assessed.

Most of the debt we've mentioned so far refers to credit cards, which have very high annual interest rates. Let's call debt that has an annual interest rate of more than 10 percent **high-interest debt**. In contrast, we'll call debt that has an annual interest rate between 4 percent and 10 percent **medium-interest debt**, and we'll refer to debt with an annual interest rate below 4 percent as **low-interest debt.**

High-interest debt creates the most debt drag, so it's usually best to chip away at this debt first. Meanwhile, medium-interest debt and low-interest debt have a bit more optionality to them. Yes, we want to pay our debts off, but it might be beneficial to start working on other financial goals concurrently. Splitting your efforts between lower-interest debt payoff and savings is a good idea so that, if one of those unexpected expenses flares up again, you won't tumble back into high-interest credit card debt.

Personal finance purists are aghast right now. "How DARE you tell these people to not pay down their 10-percent-interest-rate debt as quickly as possible?!" Okay, but what if the state, city, or neighborhood you live in suddenly becomes more hostile because of anti-LGBTQ+ legislation? Or a homophobic/transphobic neighbor starts making your life hell? Or awful job prospects leave you unemployed for several months—or longer? You might want to move. You might *need* to move. And you can't put down a deposit on a new apartment with your slightly-more-paid-down student debt or auto loan. You need cash for that. Cash is opulent—own it.

Ricco, 22, Missouri: *We've etched out a little queer life here at home. As we look for a place to live together, one of our big thoughts is whether we stick around in a rural area that's not accepting. I'm all for defending myself, and I'm not going to let someone come in and try to dictate my life. But the change in presidency has me worried. If it's going to get dangerous around here, do I really want to stay?*

This also answers the very common money question of whether you should prioritize paying down debt first or building up savings. The *mathematical* answer is usually debt paydown so that you pay a little less in interest overall. The *practical* answer is to do what makes sense for your life to cultivate feelings of stability and peace. You're *supposed* to fully prioritize the debt paydown, per the finger-wagging spreadsheet. But that spreadsheet isn't a queer person living in America, whereas you are, so we must approach our debts with a sense of both responsibility and safety.

AVALANCHE METHOD, SNOWBALL METHOD

Arranging your debts from highest to lowest interest rate and paying them down in that order, like what was described above, is known as the **avalanche method**. You pay the minimum on each of your debts each month, then put all the remaining leftover money you have toward the highest-interest debt, since that is the one that is costing you the most to maintain.

The counter to this is that, if the debt you're prioritizing payoff on is really big, it can be hard to stay motivated because the payoff drags on and on. An alternative debt payoff strategy, the **snowball method**, trades math for motivation; it advises that you pay down the debt with the smallest *balance* first, because doing so will give you a feeling of momentum. I don't know why we decided to use similar wintry names for these debt paydown methods, because it makes them easy to mix up (gays in marketing would have never approved this). A helpful memory trick I use is this alliteration: "Snowball Starts Small."

Snowball method enthusiasts see momentum as more valuable (and tolerable) than saving a few hundred bucks over the course of their debt payoff journey. Both strategies work. You might find yourself drawn more to one or the other, and that's fine.

YOUR DEBT PAYDOWN PLAN

Get out a pen and paper, or open up another tab in your spreadsheet, and put two lines down the middle so you have a total of three columns.

Your debt paydown plan has three steps.

1. Identify all your debts and their interest rates.
2. Arrange your debts either by the avalanche method or snowball method.
3. Apply additional debt paydown funds to your debt in your chosen sequence.

STEP 1: IDENTIFY ALL YOUR DEBTS AND THEIR INTEREST RATES

Remember: We cannot manage what we cannot see. Find those logins, rustle up those passwords (stop wasting time, just use the damn "Forgot your password?" button as needed to get it taken care of), and write down each of your debts' current balances and interest rates.

For each of these steps, look at how our composite Marek would do it, then repeat for yourself. If writing on paper, do this in pencil or off to the side, since you might be rearranging the information from step to step.

Marek

Marek pays $125 a month to cover the minimums on three credit cards, two of which he took out recently. He also pays $475 a month on his student loans, split across a $162 monthly payment for federal loans at 6.8 percent and a $313 monthly payment on a private student loan at 9.5 percent.

Debt	Balance	APR
Bank credit card	$500	21%
Retail credit card 1	$4,500	27%
Retail credit card 2	$1,000	32%
Federal student loan	$60,000	6.8%
Private student loan	$24,250	9.5%

Action: Identify all your debts, their current balances, and their current interest rates.

STEP 2: ARRANGE YOUR DEBTS EITHER BY THE AVALANCHE METHOD OR SNOWBALL METHOD

Queer people *love* arranging things, so this step should feel both productive and satisfying.

Arrange your debts in payoff order, based on the debt payoff method you have chosen. A reminder of your options:

- Avalanche method: You arrange the debts from highest interest rate to lowest interest rate. This method is better for saving the most money overall.

- Snowball method: "Snowball Starts Small." You arrange the debts from smallest balance to largest. This method is better for people who have a lot of separate debts and want to build momentum from seeing the small wins stack up.

Marek

Marek decides on the snowball method in order to nip these new credit card debts that are seeping into his life. He arranges his debts by balance, from smallest to largest, because Snowball Starts Small.

Debt	Balance	APR
Bank credit card	$500	21%
Retail credit card 2	$1,000	32%
Retail credit card 1	$4,500	27%
Private student loan	$24,250	9.5%
Federal student loan	$60,000	6.8%

Action: Decide whether you want to approach your debts using the avalanche method, the snowball method, or a combination of both. Then, arrange your debts in payoff order, based on your chosen method.

STEP 3: APPLY ADDITIONAL DEBT PAYDOWN FUNDS TO YOUR DEBTS IN YOUR CHOSEN SEQUENCE

Go back to the buckets exercise from chapter 1 and locate your "net worth contributions" bucket. This was the bucket where you had savings, investing, and retirement contributions, along with any additional debt payments. You may find that seeing your debt payoff plan in front of you has inspired you to adjust these numbers up or down. Also note if you had money left over in your over/under calculations; you might want to allocate some of this toward debt payoff, too.

Then, jot down some ideas on how you can make this debt payoff plan work for your life. This might mean refinancing certain debts, adjusting other expenses, or brainstorming ways to make more money (more on this in chapter 5).

Marek

At $42,000 a year in gross salary, Marek has just $3,000 a month in disposable income to work with. He needs to inventory his options for both making more money and lowering his expenses.

On the income side, he could (and should) look for a job with a higher salary and consider a change in industry in order to achieve that if needed. He could also take on a side hustle, either online or in-person, to help bring in some bucks.

On the expenses side, Marek might be able to refinance his private student loan to a longer term, which would lower his hefty $313 monthly payment. He might also be able to trim on fun money here and there, but his budget is already pretty lean.

Combined, these efforts should help him increase the amount of money he has left over each month in the four buckets budget exercise. With these extra resources, he can focus on paying down his debts using the snowball method, from smallest to largest.

Action: Reference your net worth contribution bucket from the four buckets exercise to see if you are allocating any money toward additional debt paydown. Also reference your over/under to see if there are additional funds there. Then, put all of these extra funds toward the next debt in sequence, based on whether you're following the avalanche method or snowball method.

LAST RESORT OPTIONS

Debt Consolidation, Debt Settlement, and Bankruptcy

Real talk: There may come a point at which your debt becomes too overwhelming. You have options. And you don't have to call the greasy dude in the infomercial to get more information about them. I'll run down the list for you right here and now.

Debt consolidation: This is when you take out one new debt to then pay down your other debts (yes, solving a debt problem with more debt—so on-brand for America). Debt consolidation can help you become more organized because you'll have just one debt payment and monthly due date, and you might be able to get a lower overall interest rate that would save you money long-term. Debt consolidation is a blanket term that refers to any of the following:

- **Personal loan.** Take out one loan, pay off most or all of your other debts, focus on paying the loan each month.
- **Balance transfer credit card.** Some credit cards offer a zero-percent APR for an introductory period. You can transfer a balance to this credit card, then pay it off before the intro period ends, which would save you money on interest. As of this writing, some cards offer a zero-percent interest period of up to eighteen months.
- **Home equity loan/home equity line of credit (HELOC).** If you own a home, you can put up your property as collateral, then borrow against it, either for a lump-sum loan (sometimes called a second mortgage) or a tappable line of credit. I don't love this option, because if you suddenly can't make your payments, you risk losing your home since that's what you put up as collateral. But it is a source of financing for those who own property.

Debt settlement: In debt settlement, you negotiate a lower total payoff plan with your lenders. Your lenders get their money back sooner, and you pay less overall, but you have to negotiate with the lender. There are debt settlement companies that can do the negotiating for you. Settlement companies may tell you to stop making your payments while they're negotiating, which means your credit score will take a hit. Settlement is also risky, because if the negotiation doesn't go great, the late fees and money you'll have to pay the debt settlement company might cancel out a lot of the benefits. If you're really stuck, though, debt settlement is an option.

Bankruptcy: This is the big one for when you're completely underwater. But it's really not the end of the world. Over 260,000 Americans filed for Chapter 7 bankruptcy in 2023 alone; debt really is this quiet monster that secretly impacts many people's lives.

Most individuals will file Chapter 7 bankruptcy (there are other chapter types for businesses and farms that we won't get into here). In this approach, you plead your case in bankruptcy court and show why you have insufficient income and/or savings to pay your debts. If you pass a "means test," which means you've shown that your income and assets are insufficient to pay off your debts, the judge declares you bankrupt, which means you stop rolling the dice to move a dog figurine around a game board (the more you think about it, the more effed up Monopoly really is). Alimony, child support, and federal student loans aren't dischargeable in bankruptcy.

Once you're bankrupt, your credit score will crater, and the bankruptcy will remain on your credit report for ten years, which might affect your ability to get a future mortgage, loan, or job. Excess assets must be sold, but you're usually able to keep your essentials, such as a car and a place to live so that you can get to and from work and be a productive member of society.

Reed, 52, California: *The woman who's now my ex-wife came from a family that had money. Very quickly, the message from her family* *was "You're not taking care of her the way in which she is accustomed." I thought, "I'll show you." So I lived in the cycle of credit cards and payday loans throughout my late twenties and early thirties. We had the Lincoln and the Cadillac in the driveway, the big SUV, the fancy vacations and the best clothes. We lived in the prettiest house on the block. We were that Mormon couple.*

Eventually, I had to declare bankruptcy. God, that I feel such shame when I say that. I know what it's like to have to drive two cars down to a repo lot and leave the keys under the mat. I know what it's like to show up at bankruptcy court and stand in a courtroom full of people and declare bankruptcy. We divorced after that.

It was horrible rebuilding my credit back up from a 400 credit score. It took years. But doing so has helped me live an honest, up-and-up life as a gay man in the decades since.

A softer category of bankruptcy, Chapter 13, helps you create a payoff plan for your debt over the next three to five years. Your credit score will still be torn down to the studs, but you'll have the option to keep some of your nonexempt assets.

No matter your financial situation, there are ways to get help; don't feel like all is lost.

TEACHER'S PETS: ASSEMBLE

Where my "extra credit essay" people at? (*Raises and shakes hand excitedly*) To get your debt payoff fire burning a little brighter, calculate the payoff timeline for each of your debts.

Go online and search for a free debt payoff calculator (searching "debt payoff calculator" did the trick for me). These calculators take into consideration your current balance, interest rate, and monthly payment. Look for a calculator that will give you a paydown schedule, where you can see month by month how your debt is progressing. If you get stuck, visit https://nickwolny.com/book-resources for my latest resource recommendations.

Calculate how long it will take you to pay down that first debt with your additional payment amount factored in. Then, for your next debt, calculate what the balance will be *after* paying the minimum during that first timeline, and calculate the paydown timeline of this debt using the same calculator (add this timeline to the first timeline to get your total paydown schedule).

Example: Say you have two debts, the minimum payment on the second debt is $50 a month, and you'll get your first debt paid down in six months. Plan to have paid $50 a month on the second debt for those first six months, then put all the money you were putting toward the first debt toward your second debt thereafter to figure out your overall timeline.

Also distinguish your high-interest debts from medium- and low-interest debts as you go. The lower-interest debts might be less urgent to pay off in your overall financial plan, as we'll establish in the next chapter. For example, if you have $100,000 in student loans, it's going to take a while to pay those down, and you might want to use some of your net worth contribution bucket to bulk up savings or start investing instead.

Extra credit: Mark which of your debts are high-interest, medium-interest, and low-interest debt. Then, calculate the paydown timelines for each of these debts, based on your overall debt paydown method.

○ ○ ○

You might have no debt at all. Or you might have a lot of debt, so much that it feels insurmountable and might stay with you for the rest of your life. I was the latter for many years, and I'm here to reassure you that (1) you, too, can escape the debt machine and (2) its weight doesn't have to ruin your life in the short term. Debt is far more prevalent in the LGBTQ+ community than you might think. You are not alone.

What makes talking about personal finance tricky is that everyone has different earnings, different expenses, different family dynamics, and different priorities. So to help us calibrate and get on the same page, we're going to focus on one metric that can always serve as your North Star throughout your money journey. Her name is saving rate, she's fabulous, and she's going to help make your financial life a whole lot less stressful.

Let's give her the spotlight now.

3

SAVING RATE

Your Step-by-Step Roadmap to Building (and Redefining) Wealth

Popping a squat had never hurt so bad.

I was 33. I had just moved to Los Angeles. I began going to a gym down the street that offered strength training classes (so butch!). One day, about fifteen minutes into the group session, I felt a shift in my lower back while warming up on a barbell squat, followed by sharp and immediate pain.

Uh-oh.

Although I had thrown my back out several times before, the tweaks had been easy to shake off using an ice pack, a secret family recipe (ibuprofen), and a night on the couch watching reruns of *Law & Order*. But this time, the pain kept getting worse. Various physical therapists concluded that I didn't need an MRI, but the sciatica persisted, which meant I had severe, shooting pain all down my glute and leg, continuously, for months.

I'd seen and heard plenty of influencers say the phrase "health is wealth" before (often while hawking an expensive supplement—consumerism!), but this was the first time I really believed it. Y'all, the pain monster was everywhere. Standing was painful. *Sleeping* was painful. Free time, which could have gone toward exploring the new city I lived in, was no longer usable or enjoyable.

"I'm too young for this," I thought to myself in Tammy Faye ugly-cry voice. I became moody and difficult to be around. And since I was self-employed at the time, this physical pain stunted my work output, and therefore my income. Poor health wasn't just robbing me of time and happiness; it was draining my bank account, too.

Eventually, I found a physical therapist who helped me get better without having to resort to surgery. My back pain is mostly gone now, and in addition to my renewed mobility and mental clarity, I also have a broader, more holistic definition of wealth that includes health. I budget for a trainer, a yoga studio membership, and an occasional massage (expenses most personal finance fanatics would sneer at) because keeping my body functional is a priority. Health is a part of my definition of wealth, and it might be a part of yours, too.

The problem with personal finance culture is that its definition of wealth is overly weighted toward numerical assets. Since our lives are lived outside of a spreadsheet, there is often a mental tug-of-war between saving for the future and the visceral experiences of the present. Avoidance, numbing, and money malaise make us feel better in the short term, but we never really feel *that* good, because there's always a cloud of paranoia and despair about the future hanging over our heads. At the opposite end of the spectrum, all work and no play looks great on paper, but it could result in feelings of regret when your realize some of your most adventurous years passed you by. Don't be one of these rich, lonely queers who drops dead having never tipped a death drop.

Why not have both, with ease? Why not throw out the "either/or" binary and instead create a plan that lets you have a great quality of life in the present while also feeling confident and optimistic about the future? There's a way to do that, you know, and in this chapter we'll explain how.

The best part about this approach is that *you get to stop thinking about money all the time*. You know exactly how much you're saving, where that money is going, and why, often on autopilot. You'll think about money less, yet feel more confident, a paradoxical one-two punch that works wonders for both complexion and self-esteem. You'll feel reassured that what you're saving is enough, and that you don't need to restrict your budget and save more if you don't want to. You'll also begin to detach from the world of "shopping is bad" and other money perspectives that are oversimplified. And if you find you *do* want to start saving more aggressively to build financial wealth, you'll know how to work toward that, too. (We talk more about these financial independence strategies in chapter 9.)

In this chapter, we'll go over a magic metric called saving rate and how to use it to set meaningful goals that align your wallet with your values. Then, in Part II, we'll dig deeper into how to cultivate queer wealth in every area of your life. Your money, health, chosen family, time, mental wellness, and sense of purpose will begin to work together in harmony.

Before this magic metric can take root, however, we must first reframe our idea of wealth to be more holistic . . . and more queer. Take my hand, let's frolic.

Reframing Wealth

1. Wealth is more than just money
2. Building financial wealth may not require making a lot of money
3. Many rich kids will blow it
4. Lifestyle creep erodes wealth
5. Opulence and frugality can coexist
6. Independent wealth cultivates activism and safety
7. Your wealth-building efforts can be a boring side character

REFRAME NO. 1: WEALTH IS MORE THAN JUST MONEY

I already gave you my sales pitch on why health is wealth for me personally, and perhaps you have a similar perspective. But your definition of wealth can include many other things, too. Wealth is time. Wealth is mental clarity. Wealth is relaxation, strong social connections, education, space to binge *Housewives* franchise reruns whenever you want, and the freedom to be and show up as who you really are. Your energy and mental health are currencies, too.

Because money is numerical, it's easy to micromanage it with spreadsheets, formulas, and account balances. When we do this, we lose sight of some of the other indicators of a high quality of life. In chapter 4, we'll adjust how we approach these numbers; for now, think about what some of the qualities of a fulfilling queer life would be. Go beyond the superficial stuff. Is the goal really going to Mykonos with friends just so you can be in the photos and get the likes . . . or is it *having* friends in the first place?

Reflect on what a wealthy life means to you. That means figuring out what would put you at ease and bring you a deep sense of purpose and fulfillment.

REFRAME NO. 2: BUILDING FINANCIAL WEALTH MAY NOT REQUIRE MAKING A LOT OF MONEY

It can sometimes feel like you have to bring in dump trucks of money to build any kind of meaningful monetary wealth. Not true. To illustrate, let's lean back into our queer composites for some examples.

Kai

Kai, a 32-year-old trans man making $64,000 a year, opens up an investing account. He sets up a bank transfer that puts $250 a month into investments. The investments grow in value by an average of 8 percent per year. He maintains this contribution for the next thirty years, even as his work situation ebbs and flows over time.

Kai has *contributed* $90,000 over thirty years. But since his investments grew by 8 percent each year, they're now worth $352,138. He earned the other $262,138, the majority of his account, *without doing anything else.*

Here's a bar chart that shows how much money he contributed versus how much he has now. Don't panic at the sight of a chart. Just notice how much of his money he put in versus how much total money he has by the end.

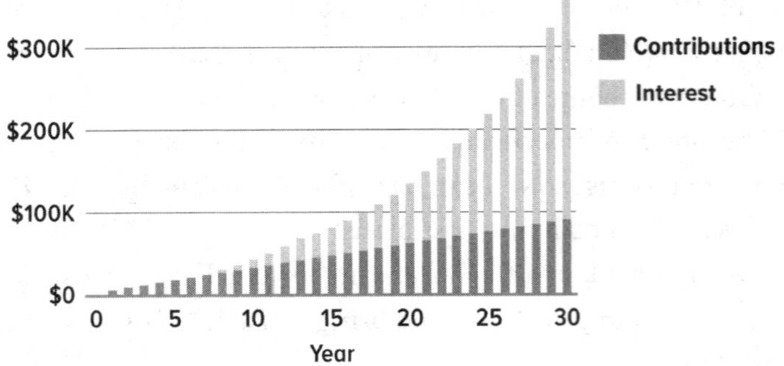

Kai's path to a more secure future at 62 doesn't involve magically winning the lottery or having a $352,000 inheritance drop into his lap. It comes from building a life now in which he can spare $250 a month for investments consistently, and still have enough left over for current life priorities that give him meaning. He gets top surgery. He starts his own business on the side. He gets married and becomes a dad. He is able to pursue these life priorities while also securing his future. Knowledge and patience are two of your BFFs for building financial wealth.

Raye

Raye, who is ten years younger than Kai, decides to take a similar approach. Same $250, same account, same rates of return. With ten extra years on their side, Raye's $120,000 in contributions will become $805,270 by the age of 62, and $685,230 of that came from no additional work. Same habit, extra ten years, more than double the yield.

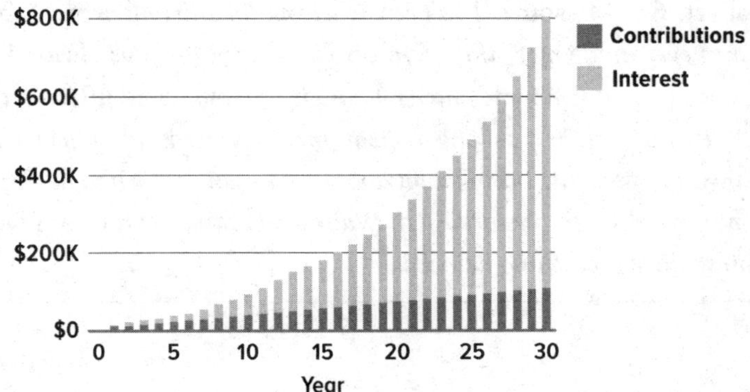

This growth is known as **compounding**. It's when your *money* starts making money, and like that super tall girl in that one season of *America's Next Top Model* (*loudly interrupts* it was Ann in season 15 and she had best photo the first FIVE episodes in a row), once she gets warmed up she's a force to be reckoned with. Compounding is something financially wealthy people understand about money. They work jobs and take home wages, but the money they have saved and invested is also quietly generating income at the same time.

Personal finance influencers love these little word problems about compounding ("See?! Can you SEE the difference?! *Invest!*") because they're straightforward anecdotes that fit nicely into a social media post and demonstrate the power of investing. But our lives aren't this predictable, and neither is the stock market, so there are other factors we're not considering yet that could influence these results. We'll get to them more in chapter 6.

What I want to sell you on for now is that, although a bigger salary does make building wealth easier, it's not the only solution. Your earnings could be meh and still lead you toward a life of financial security. Find ways to use the power of time and compounding to your advantage.

Robert, 60, Missouri: *I've been teaching for thirty-four years and have never made more than $70,000 in salary. But I've always kept a good eye on my money. I haven't paid interest in about fifteen years. I'll never be rich, but as long as I can meet my needs and a few of my wants, I'm content. I think a lot about "old man me" when he's 80. I don't want him to be working at Walmart because he has to. I want him to have everything he needs.*

REFRAME NO. 3: MANY RICH KIDS WILL BLOW IT

While we're on the topic of wealthy people, I have a side note for all my fellow petty Bettys.

Some people are financially better off than you because they have generational wealth, and that's just how life goes. But not all rich families stay rich. The reason? Financial literacy, of course.

The kids and grandkids who swipe their parents' credit card for a BMW on their sweet sixteen often continue to live above their means and eventually spend down the family purse in adulthood. (Side note: The most popular statistic attributed to this phenomenon says that 70 percent of wealthy families lose their wealth by the second generation and 90 percent by the third generation. But that stat is wrong; the study referred to the rate of *family businesses* being passed on, not wealth overall, and a better study in 2011 showed that many family businesses actually *are* carried on successfully. Just another example of how information often gets exaggerated and distorted over time to fit a narrative.)[1]

Still, the meltdown is common enough that rich families will factor it into their estate planning (estate planning is end-of-life paperwork on how money and assets get transferred, and we cover it in chapter 10).

When you have a good grip on how money is made, saved, and compounded, you build financial independence and confidence, and this confidence gets bolstered further when you start to see your numbers go up.

REFRAME NO. 4: LIFESTYLE CREEP ERODES WEALTH

Pop quiz: Queer person A feels immense satisfaction and fulfillment on a salary of $72,000 a year. Meanwhile, queer person B makes $300,000 a year in a high-stress job that requires corporate travel three weeks a month, and that they cannot quit, because the mortgage payments for the home they're rarely even at are too high. Who is more "wealthy"?

The answer depends on your definition of wealth. And really, we can't give a definitive answer because we need more information on these two people's spending and saving habits. For all we know, person A has been diligently saving for years and can retire soon, whereas person B doesn't have a dime in the bank and is one layoff away from going completely broke and losing the condo.

There's a term for this phenomenon—Parkinson's Second Law—but that's a little academic, so the gays in marketing came up with a sexier name: **lifestyle creep.** In lifestyle creep, expenses tend to go up as income goes up. Although making more money does bring more resources into the picture, it's very easy to turn around and spend all that extra money, often as a reaction to pent-up money malaise or wanting to blow off work stress. Look at how many celebrities made millions in their prime, only to declare bankruptcy years later. Lifestyle creep can be destructive when left unchecked.

Our consumerist society encourages lifestyle creep. It wants you to pursue making more money not for financial security, but because doing so means you can buy more stuff. Part of your goal should be to develop good financial hygiene with the money you currently have.

REFRAME NO. 5: OPULENCE AND FRUGALITY CAN COEXIST

I sometimes wonder if we took Junior LaBeija's opulence coaching in *Paris Is Burning* a bit *too* literally (mandatory queer homework to go watch that documentary if you haven't yet seen it). The notes were for a competitor preparing to walk in a ballroom category. *The dog was wearing a pearl necklace.* It was about fantasy. The witty satire of categories is wonderfully enmeshed into queer culture, but when we blur the lines of fantasy and reality too much, it's easy to slide into financial self-sabotage.

Our collective reaction to queer oppression is to be out, loud, proud, visible, and free. When the credit cards are maxed out, however, it's hard to feel at ease. Escapism isn't as fun when reality sucks. There are ways to express your full queer self sustainably. There are also ways to cultivate frugality without feeling inhibited.

Think of frugality not as being cheap or lower-class, but rather as being resourceful, a way to cultivate self-sufficiency and craft. Example: At the time of this writing, RuPaul is probably richer than some of these Saudi princes, and yet he's out here on social media teaching us all how to change a car tire. Self-sufficiency is really important for LGBTQ+ people. Frugality teaches us this self-sufficiency, and it helps us build confidence.

When you detox from consumerism, you'll have more time and energy to do things for yourself, from decorating to cooking to exploring new creative endeavors. These activities are a nice break from scrolling all day long, and the money you'll save along the way is an added bonus.

REFRAME NO. 6: INDEPENDENT WEALTH CULTIVATES ACTIVISM AND SAFETY

Yes, there's a lot of inequity in our country. The wealth gap is widening, wage gaps persist, and queer people are getting priced out of their own neighborhoods. We see ourselves as othered and are ready to protest.

Unfortunately, screaming "To hell with capitalism!" when you're prompted to tap or swipe your card during self-checkout at the grocery store isn't a method of payment (at least not yet). Yes, activism is a great way to channel money malaise and get energy moving. But if you spend *all* your energy protesting a system that has had an up-and-down track record for enacting change, you risk burning yourself out along the way.

Make self-preservation a high priority at work, at home, and in other areas of your life. There's a reason they remind you in the airplane safety briefing to put your oxygen mask on first (it's to cover the airline's ass from liability claims . . . but also for your safety, which I guess they care about, too). Yes, we need reform, but that reform might take a while, so we must learn how to operate within capitalism and utilize it to our advantage in the meantime. Find ways to maintain independence over your money so that you don't become stranded or unsafe when new stressors emerge.

Keli, 42, Missouri: *My financial journey is largely tied to my queerness. I married a woman in 2005, before gay marriage was legally recognized, so in order for us to do things like rent a one-bedroom apartment as two adult women, we had to really enmesh our finances together. That was a dangerous situation for me, because it later came out that she was an addict. She took control of our money in a financially abusive way. Eventually she left one day and just didn't come back. I no longer had any savings, and I no longer had any money in a checking account, so I couldn't get an apartment—everything was drained. It was devastating. I had to move in with a* *couple friends and live on an air mattress in their living room for a few months while I started rebuilding my life.*

For queer people, self-preservation is critical. Don't just get mad—get paid, and ensure you maintain control over what you earn.

REFRAME NO. 7: YOUR WEALTH-BUILDING EFFORTS CAN BE A BORING SIDE CHARACTER

It sometimes feels like money has to have this dramatic narrative and take up a lot of our time and attention. So I want to be clear: The goal of this book is to help you automate and simplify your money so you can spend *less* time worrying about it and *more* time doing fun queer stuff instead. Your money doesn't have to get the same character arc as a *Housewives* cast member or an A24 villain. It can be a boring side character, one that has an important role in your story, but gets little screen time and none of the good zingers.

We're so used to consuming drama that we start to seek it out in other areas of our lives, and if there's no drama to be found, it feels like there must be something wrong. We avoid putting money in a savings account like it's the plague, but will call it future-thinking to invest in a cryptocurrency named after Netflix's *Squid Game* that has existed for mere minutes and later turns out to be a scam (this actually happened, by the way. In 2021, the creators of Squid Coin ran off with $3.36 million).[2] When it comes to money, being basic is a virtue, not a read.

Some of the most reliable paths to building monetary wealth are rather boring, and that's why I've been brought in to liven 'em up. I hereby give you permission to be basic with your money. When you get to the point where your money harmoniously hums along in the background while you live your best queer life, you'll be glad you did the work.

∘ ∘ ∘

Despite this broadened definition of wealth, money is still a means of exchange. So we want to track how well we're handling it. Rather than bombard you with line graphs and catastrophic financial headlines that just make you want to sweep it all under the rug, we're going to distill down your money efforts into one number you can look to at any point, no matter your income or debt situation, to determine whether you're on the right track.

YOUR METRIC FOR MONETARY WEALTH: MODIFIED SAVING RATE

To help reinforce new behaviors and habits, we're going to zhuzh up a common money benchmark known as **saving rate**.

Saving rate is the percentage of your disposable income that goes toward either savings or investments each month. The Federal Reserve, which is the central bank of the United States (translation: a big stone building that manages all the money supply), has been measuring our average saving rate as a country for over sixty years, and as one big group project, well . . . we're a hot mess right now.

From 1960 to 1985, Americans were consistently saving 10 percent or more of their incomes per month. As wages have stagnated and credit card debt has increased, this rate has steadily gone down. The average saving rate was 3.3 percent in 2022 and 4.5 percent in 2023, and one study from 2024 found that one in four Americans didn't save anything at all.[3] If you're not saving much or any money right now, know that there are millions of others in a similar situation.

I don't love saving rate as a metric because it doesn't include additional debt paydown, and as we discussed in the previous chapter, debt paydown is a productive activity that might be consuming a substantial portion of your budget. If Marek makes more money and starts putting hundreds of extra dollars toward his debt paydown each month, that wouldn't count toward his saving rate. He *should* be able to count that money, though, because it's money he's putting toward building wealth by reducing his debts.

I want to give you points for effort, so let's make up a variation of saving rate that includes additional debt paydown. We'll call it **modified saving rate (MSR).** And here's some good news: You already did most of the work to calculate this number back in chapter 1. The expenses in your "net worth contributions" bucket are what we will count toward your modified saving rate. Simply take that total number and divide it by your disposable income (which you also already found in chapter 1) to get your MSR.

TEA

Modified saving rate (MSR): Your saving rate *plus* any funds you're putting toward additional debt paydown, expressed as a percentage of your disposable income (and assuming you're not spending more than you're making each month).

Eventually, when you're no longer doing additional debt paydown, you can reallocate this money toward savings (or spend some of it—it's your life!), and your modified saving rate will be the same as the Federal Reserve's definition of saving rate.

Let's revisit Raye's numbers to see this quick math in action.

Raye

Raye's net worth contributions bucket was $550 a month. Their disposable income is $4,175 a month. $550 divided by $4,175 equals 0.13, or 13 percent. Raye's modified saving rate is 13 percent; they're putting 13 percent of their disposable income toward either savings, investments, or additional debt paydown.

Action: Refer back to your chapter 1 notes. Calculate your current modified saving rate by dividing the net worth contributions bucket by your overall disposable income.

WHAT'S A "GOOD" MODIFIED SAVING RATE?

Rather than give you an initial benchmark, I want to encourage baby steps and progress. So here's a goal for you: Calculate your current MSR, then aim to reach the next 5 percent threshold. For Raye, who is currently saving 13 percent of their monthly income, that would be 15 percent. For Marek, who is currently saving nothing, it would be 5 percent. By pursuing this goal, you will practice changing your saving rate on command by taking smart, sustainable actions.

"No, Nick. I'm an extra credit queer; you're gonna give me that gahdamned benchmark." Okay, okay, jeez: A strong modified saving rate to work toward is **15 percent**. Fifteen percent would give you a lot to work with regarding debt paydown and savings buildup. This will get you in the habit of setting aside income each month to cultivate financial stability, and for many people, having a number to aim for becomes a fun game, a target to hit and surpass. By holding or even increasing your MSR as your earnings grow, you'll protect yourself from lifestyle creep.

You can also certainly go higher than 15 percent. In Financial Independence, Retire Early (FIRE) culture, where people are hustling in order to retire years or decades ahead of schedule, a saving rate of 50 percent or more is not uncommon. Don't work toward this if it means sacrificing your best queer life, but know that, in chapter 9, you'll get a clear set of action steps to move in the direction of financial independence if it appeals to you.

Modified saving rate releases us from this idea that we must have a huge income or miserably tight budgets in order to pursue financial stability. It's a dashboard that shows you how you're doing in real time.

THE 7-WORD PLAN FOR BUILDING WEALTH

We've alluded to this 7-word plan a few times now, so let's calibrate on what it actually is and how it can help you transform your financial life.

There's a lot of bluster in the personal finance space. You can ignore most of it. You can ignore a lot of the acronyms and account types. You can ignore the crazy news headlines about the stock market, which are often sensationalized. Ignore the crypto bros, ignore the pyramid schemes, ignore 19-year-olds on TikTok telling you they've found a way to not pay taxes, ignore the haters, and ignore the people who call you a stick in the mud for choosing yourself and saving money.

To increase your modified saving rate, focus on widening the gap between income and expenses. Then put more of that extra money into your net worth contributions bucket. If we distill all the personal finance advice on how to do this down into its simplest form, it can be summed up in seven words: **lower expenses, increase earnings, invest the difference**.

LOWER EXPENSES

We start with expenses because it's the area of your money over which you have the most control. For some, the act of even knowing what you're spending your money on (and why) is transformational. This is why we like doing exercises manually the first time, even if you use an online budgeting app; manual review helps you see more clearly where your money is going.

Essential expenses have gone up in recent years because of things like strangled supply chains, labor shortages, and a splash of pandemic-induced global inflation. It's tough out there! We want to budget for these items and take actions that can help lower their cost. Lowering your expenses might mean negotiating a lower cell phone bill, getting a roommate, or just being more diligent with your allowance so that when you go out in the gayborhood it's a $50 night rather than a $250 night.

Our composite Marek's money situation was bleak. Here's how he could turn it around.

Marek

Humbled by the budgets exercise, Marek decides to move back in with his parents, with a goal to live there for one year and regroup. While this isn't the sexiest decision, it's probably a good move financially, especially since his parents live in the suburbs, which means he can still go see his friends in the city as he wants. With just $3,000 in disposable income per month to work with, his budget is already really lean, and not paying rent will save him $1,100 per month. Marek sets two goals for the next year: get a better-paying job that lets him work remotely and save three-quarters of the money he's saving on rent, which after a year would give him $9,900 to use as savings and/or additional debt paydown.

Diminishing returns are at play here, so be cautious of overdoing frugality. If you're miserable, money malaise and numbing behaviors can make you spend frivolously to feel better, and we want to ensure that behavior doesn't spiral out of control and wipe out all your other efforts.

We'll take a deeper dive into expenses in chapter 4.

INCREASE EARNINGS

If personal finance is a vehicle, your earnings are rocket fuel. Increasing your earnings is one of the most powerful and transformational things you can do for your life because more money lets you buy back your time, energy, and health.

In our 7-word plan, the reason we clean up expenses hygiene first is to ensure you don't blow all the additional money you start bringing in as you increase your earnings. By bringing more money in *and* keeping more of it at the end of each month, you'll widen the gap between income and expenses, which helps you increase your modified saving rate.

Your efforts to make more money fall into one of three categories:

- Make more money from your current main source of income.
- Make more money by finding a new source of income.
- Make more money by creating an additional source of income.

It's important for queer people to know how to go out and make more money in a variety of ways. LGBTQ+ people are statistically more likely to have a variable or unpredictable income because they often work as freelancers, contractors, performers, and artists. Because of this, personal finance advice that assumes a steady monthly income and budget can feel unhelpful (and can lead to more money malaise). By learning our way around the "income stream rainbow," then creating a step-by-step action plan, we become more facile at making money on command.

Here's a hypothetical example of this thinking in action.

Soraya

Soraya is a 37-year-old lesbian working as a licensed practical nurse and making $68,000 a year. She wants to progress in her nursing career, so she's working through a registered nurse (RN) program and studying for the NCLEX exam, which will give her the additional required credentials she needs. RN jobs in her area make anywhere from $20,000 to $35,000 more per year; her hope is that this bump would bring her salary above $90,000, extra income that will be very valuable as she and her wife prepare to start a family.

Education on how to make more money is worth reading about, and it might even change your life. It certainly changed mine. We'll take a deeper dive into all things income stream rainbow in chapter 5, then go even deeper with an introduction to entrepreneurship in chapter 8.

INVEST THE DIFFERENCE

Investing feels confusing because the messaging around it *is* confusing. It's increasingly driven by emotion and hype, and just like when your flight is delayed, it's damn near impossible to get someone to explain what's actually going on. Our chapter on investing will give you the fact-based foundation you need, and as we've already seen earlier in this chapter, investing money can help you build financial wealth faster.

We like investing because you can be as hands-on or hands-off as you want. Once you've set yourself up, investing requires little or even no maintenance, which frees up your time for things you enjoy in your present-day life. Anyone can invest; you don't have to be rich or have received generational wealth to start investing. Also, if you're over it with these big corporations, there are ways to ensure you're investing your money in other organizations or opportunities without compromising your values.

Here's how cutie composite Antonio might get started.

Antonio

Growing up, Antonio often overheard his parents being wary of the stock market. They never invested, so neither did he. At 42, he thought it was too late to start, but he now realizes that thought pattern isn't true. He's saved up a decent amount of money over the last few years, and he discovers that some of this money could be put into hands-off investments that aren't so risky. In addition to moving some of his extra savings into investments, he also sets up a monthly automatic transfer that invests his deposits for him so he doesn't have to think about it anymore.

I'm gonna do everything I can to get you excited about investing—quips, puns, sparklers, nipple tassels, you name it—because few concepts in life will give you a better return on a few hours of your time than learning the basics of investing. Chapter 6 is where I'll do this dance for you, so get those dollar bills ready.

YOUR SAVING RATE ROADMAP

Great work! Your money skeletons are out of the closet, and it feels great. Let's review:

- You've examined your thought patterns around money and had a few lightbulb moments.
- You've taken responsibility for your debt, had a stress cry and a slice of rainbow cake, and are now ready to move forward.
- You have numbers to look at, including a net worth contributions bucket and a modified saving rate, that tell you how much of your income each month is going toward financial well-being.

When it comes to the 7-word plan, there's so much more to say, which is why Part II of this book is dedicated entirely to becoming a fully evolved Charizard on each of these three strategies. I will be going full drag mom to help you build fluency and agility with your money so that you won't feel trapped if you get laid off.

But a lingering question remains: Where should I *put* the money I'm saving? There are many options, and it can be confusing, so I've created a roadmap for you that puts these options in sequence and tells you where to put your modified saving rate dollars to get the best bang for your buck.

It's called the **Saving Rate Roadmap**, and it categorizes your money priorities in a way that is financially advantageous, but also gives you space to choose your priorities based on your unique situation. (*Gives spotlight cue*) Behold!

THE SAVING RATE ROADMAP

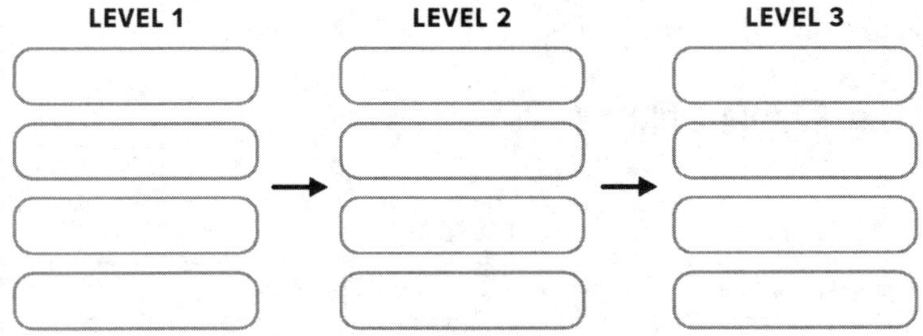

Like any good drag number, this roadmap has *reveals*. Can't show you everything at once, it'll ruin the suspense! Here's how the Saving Rate Roadmap works.

Every month, you'll take the money in your net worth contributions bucket and apply it to these steps in this order. For some steps, you'll allocate money to them until you've reached a certain goal, and for others you'll allocate money to them every month. Some actions are a higher priority than others, so I've bucketed them by levels. Level 1 actions are the highest priority. Start on Level 2 actions once your Level 1 actions are dialed in. Consider Level 3 actions only after you're moving and grooving on Levels 1 and 2.

For all you overachievers, something I want to normalize right away is that you may not actually get that far along in this flowchart with the money you currently have, and that's okay. I say this with love: If you're sitting on $50,000 in credit card debt at a 20 percent interest rate, day-trading stocks and agonizing over savings account terms are not the priority right now. The amount of debt drag you have is more than canceling out the benefits of these other boxes, so staying put with high-interest debt paydown, albeit tedious, is the better use of your money. This is about you, a queer person, cultivating a financial situation that can provide you with safety and stability.

In Parts II and III of this book, I'll give you the tools you need to keep moving forward in the roadmap. For now, here are the essentials to prioritize first.

INITIAL $2,000 CUSHION

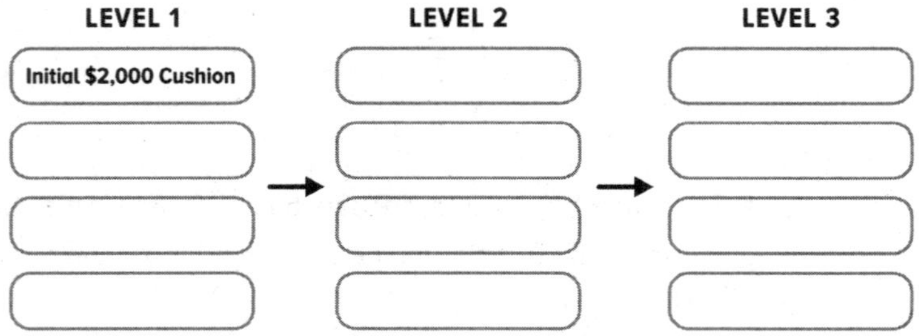

First, if you have little or no money saved, get an initial cushion established so that you won't have to fall back on credit cards or loans in the event of an unexpected setback. Your first few months working on your Saving Rate Roadmap should focus on getting this established as quickly as possible. I recommend $2,000, but this number can be higher if your circumstances require more cushion.

Consider putting this money in a **high-yield savings account** (HYSA). This is an account that pays above-average interest rates (free money!) but also keeps your money close, so you can pull it in a day or two if needed. Interest rates on HYSAs fluctuate with Federal Reserve rates, but as of this writing are above 4 percent—far better than the paltry national average of 0.46 percent for regular savings accounts. Check https://nickwolny.com/book-resources if you want my latest HYSA picks.

TEA

High-Yield Savings Account (HYSA): Savings accounts from online banks that came along and read traditional banks to filth. These savings accounts can see interest rates as high as 5 percent per year, with no additional effort and no risk of losing the money you've deposited.

If you already have at least $2,000 in a savings account, move on to the next box in the Saving Rate Roadmap.

EMPLOYER RETIREMENT MATCH

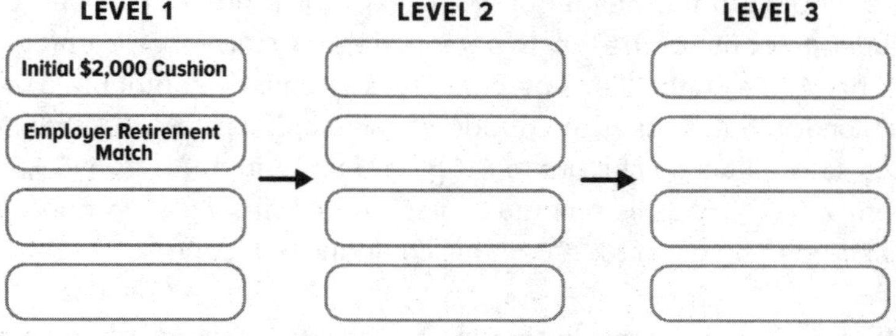

Have you ever been in a long line for the bathroom at an event, and then some kind stranger walks up and tells you that there's another bathroom on *the other side* of the lobby where the line is half as long? And you still get to go pee, get a drink refill and a churro, and make it back to your seat before intermission ends? It's me, I'm that kind stranger, and I'm jumping ahead in the book for a moment to tell you about a shortcut.

If you work as an employee, and your employer offers a match on retirement plan contributions, I want you to contribute enough to your retirement account to get this match. This is free money from your employer—think of it as a little extra allowance you're getting for good behavior—and opportunities like these are rare, so I need you to scrape these extra dollars off your employer whenever you can.

Depending on your employer's plan, your employer will match 50 or even 100 percent of your contribution, up to a certain point (usually between 2 and 6 percent of your income, before taxes). Even if you have to break into your employer-sponsored retirement account early (doing so before age 59.5 incurs a 10% penalty), you'd likely still come out a little richer as a result of taking this match.

Stop procrastinating, look up your employer benefits, and enroll in this match if you haven't yet done so. Here's what those numbers would look like for Marek, who's more excited to save now that he isn't underwater anymore in his monthly budget.

Marek

Marek looks up the details of his 401(k), which he hadn't been contributing to at all for the last two years he's had this job. His employer matches 100% on the first 3 percent of his income he contributes, so he signs up for that. It takes ten goddamn minutes. At his $42,000 annual gross salary, this comes out to $105 per month from his pay ($3,500/month x 0.03), and his employer also contributes $105. In one year, he's scraped an extra $1,260 off his company, ethically.

If you're already contributing to your employer-sponsored plan and getting the match, move on to the next box in the Saving Rate Roadmap.

DEBT PAYDOWN

Next, put your modified saving rate dollars toward paying down debt. Your debt payoff priorities will vary by interest level. High-interest debt paydown is a Level 1 priority because it's sucking away at your life force (and not in the hot vampire way). Medium-interest debt is a Level 2 priority. Low-interest debt, which we define as debt with an APR below 4 percent, is a Level 3 priority. You can wipe out debt completely if you want, but you can also punt the lower-interest obligations in favor of other money priorities we'll reveal in Part II.

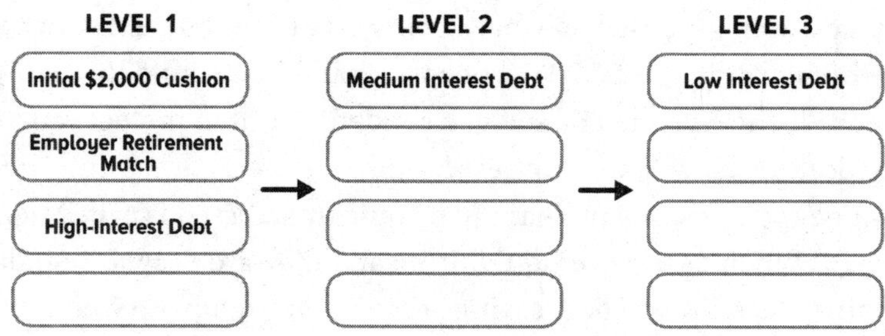

Marek

With an initial savings cushion in place, and his employer retirement match now automated, Marek turns his focus to his $6,000-ish in credit card debt. He calculates that he'll be able to pay off most of this debt by the end of the year, and if he gets a new job or a side hustle that increases his earnings, he can pay it off faster. Marek's Saving Rate Roadmap should slow down or pause here until he gets all his high-interest debt paid down.

Once you're either out of the high-interest debt jungle (avalanche method) or are down to your last debts that have longer payoff periods (snowball method), move on in the Saving Rate Roadmap.

LIQUID SAVINGS BUILDUP

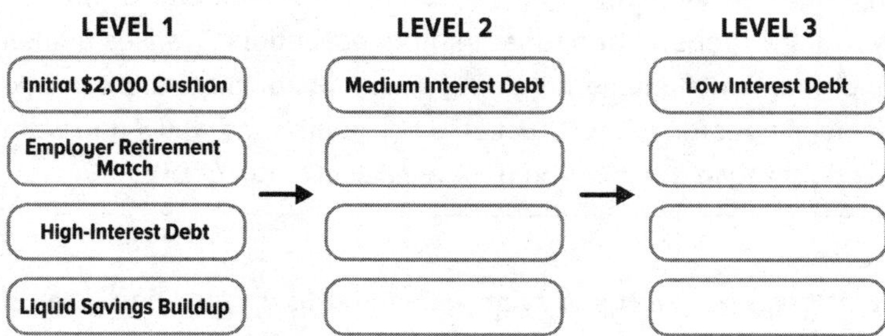

With these immediate tasks out of the way, we can move on to steps that have options, based on what's going on in your current situation. One high priority for LGBTQ+ people should be to build up savings, because if shit hits the fan and you suddenly need to protect yourself or relocate, cash will be your best friend.

Money you've saved up that can be quickly accessed is called **liquid savings**. When assets are liquid, it means they are easy to liquidate and turn back into cash. A savings account is usually very liquid because your money can be dumped back into your checking account with just a few clicks. In contrast, a house is not as liquid; you'd have to sell it to turn your asset back into cash, which will take time, depending on the housing market. Liquid savings is how you want to save your **emergency fund**.

Use the same account as your initial $2,000 cushion for this money. If you work as an employee and have a salary, I want you to concentrate on building up enough liquid savings that it could serve as an emergency fund and cover three months of expenses in the event you lost your income tomorrow. If you have a more volatile monthly income, consider a bigger cushion of six or even eight months in expenses.

TEA

Emergency fund: Savings that can be used to cover monthly expenses in the event you get laid off. To calculate a month's worth of expenses, add together your essential expenses bucket and your minimum monthly debt payments bucket. You can add some of your fun money bucket to this number as well if you want to count those expenses in your overall cushion goal.

It often takes months or even years to build up your liquid savings. That's okay, because you will develop the habit of saving along the way. Work on this concurrently with other financial priorities until you reach your savings goal.

Action: Map the money in your monthly net worth contributions bucket into your Saving Rate Roadmap. Prioritize a $2,000 savings cushion, an employer retirement match if you have one, high-interest debt paydown, and liquid savings buildup.

◦ ◦ ◦

There's more to the Saving Rate Roadmap, but you can't rush a reveal, darling. Before I show you where you can put your money next, I want to make sure you're doing everything in your power to increase your saving rate, both in terms of percentage and actual dollars. For that, we return to the 7-word plan–"lower expenses, increase earnings, invest the difference"—which we spend all of Part II covering in fabulously queer detail. You will have strategies. You will have templates. You will be that person at the function whose messenger bag has hand sanitizer, earbuds, and two packs of mint-flavored gum. The 7-word plan has the power to transform your money and life for the better.

As you track your modified saving rate, something magical will happen: You will become more confident and intentional with how you're approaching your money. The self-inquiry that comes with this work can be healing, because you will look at what influences are shaping and controlling your life. No more "I just don't get it." No more avoiding. No more money malaise.

Our queer ancestors wanted us to live confident, happy lives. Part II has the information that will give you this confidence, and it starts now.

PART II

IT'S GIVING CONFIDENT

4

BUDGETING

How to Spend Less and Save More, While Still Doing Opulent Shit

"Diets don't work," she said.

Fourteen people sat in a circle on the hardwood floor of the yoga room as I stood in the corner and observed. I was working at a yoga studio in my "odd jobs in my twenties" era, except that "eras" were not a trendy Taylor Swift colloquialism back in the 2000s, so it was just "doing what I could to make ends meet."

A local dietitian was facilitating a mindful nutrition workshop (this was before all the alternative health people went flat Earther on us, so it was fine). She explained to the attendees that most diets end up not working, because we inevitably focus on the foods we can't have. Instead, she suggested we start with eating *more,* sprinkling produce and fiber into our existing meals, rather than leading with restriction.

"Eat *more*? Oh, I *got this,*" I thought to myself. And sure enough, after a few weeks of putting more veggies in my belly, my desire for triple chocolate explosion ice cream began to recede. I realized that my habit of eating processed food three meals a day was the result of ongoing thought patterns, and that I could change this habit if I wanted to through intentional action and patience. As I began seeing results, like more energy and fewer mood swings, it got increasingly easier. I reconnected to what made me feel good, which improved my overall outlook on life.

I'm sharing this story because we've arrived at the chapter on budgeting. And since budget culture is only about four DNA strands away from diet culture, I must tread carefully to win your curiosity.

First and foremost: This is not a book about "being happy with less." You can certainly take the attitude of gratitude approach and be happy with less, and as personal finance pundits, we like it when you do that (mostly because it makes our jobs easier). But a lot of the new-age personalities telling us to be happy with less have never lived in an apartment that has roaches, or lost a home to foreclosure, or navigated the chronic anxiety of having no health insurance, or been stuck in a town with no other queer people and ongoing political rhetoric (or actual legislation) that makes life stressful. In those scenarios, more money *does* mean more happiness, because it can buy you time, rest, education, mobility, safety, and the freedom to be who you truly are.

More income will help you decompress your financial situation, which is why we dive deep into various money-making strategies in chapter 5. But if you don't do a little self-study on your own spending first, a devious debutante named consumerism will charm you into lifestyle creep. You'll blow your newfound cash and remain on the endless hamster wheel of chasing success until you burn out and have no energy left at all. This is why we work on budgeting first.

Detoxing from consumerism is hard because it's all around you, all day, every day. Consumerism is banner ads in subway cars, posters in elevators, and targeted videos on social media, all designed to create a satisfaction gap that you then fill with buying stuff. Consumerism robs you of queer joy, the kind of joy that comes with being different, yet worthy. And although you may have the same number of hours in a day as Beyoncé, you don't have her payroll, so cut it out with these productivity moonshots to try to reach the unattainable standards consumerism is selling you.

We noted earlier that one antidote to consumerism is to define "enough." Another antidote to consumerism is confidence. Confidence is looking at a price tag and being able to say "Yup, I want this, I have the money for it, I'm still taking care of myself, and I'm still protecting my future." When you do this confidence test, you discover which expenses really light you up versus which ones just numb you out. Some expenses will lose their luster and fade away. Others might actually go *up*, because you find they give you confidence and fuel your fire (which we want flaming). This is valuable work because you're discovering what gives you energy in life.

Once this grass-fed, preservative-free confidence starts flowing more freely, you'll have less FOMO about what others around you are doing and whether you should be doing the same to be happy. You will start to see spending money as an energetic exchange, a way to feel confident and energized, rather than depleted.

Let's go over common spending traps that trip you up, how to do this confidence test on various expenses in your own budget, and how to still enjoy those big, meaningful splurges without derailing your money goals.

Spending Traps to Avoid

1. Not planning for occasional opulent shit
2. Not looking at your numbers
3. Not planning for one-time and annual expenses
4. Letting retail therapy run rampant
5. Building a golden cage
6. Too much restriction

TRAP NO. 1:
NOT PLANNING FOR OCCASIONAL OPULENT SHIT

Money books typically shake their head no at you when you want nice things. "*Tsk, tsk—how shameful,*" says purity culture in a judge-y tone. My fruity take is that you deserve the nice things and experiences you desire, so you should make plans to have them.

Have an opportunity to go on an epic trip and create a lifelong memory with the people you love? Start that group chat. Want to buy the ultimate gaming rig because connecting with fellow gaymers for hours on end brings you enjoyment? Make the Pinterest inspo board. Then, open up a separate account for all your blow money so that, when it comes time to treat yourself, you can do so entirely in cash.

Financial advisors have a name for this account: the **sinking fund**. Since you're going to blow every dollar of this money on something fabulous, you don't factor it into calculations like net worth because the money's eventually going to go poof.

TEA

Sinking fund: A savings account that's excited to self-destruct. You don't factor this money into net worth, because you know you're going to spend it all one day on something fun. Also called a vacation fund or a treat yo' self fund.

Sinking funds are a hall pass to buy the most fanatic shit your heart desires. Jewel-encrusted crowns for Pride weekend? Do it. Trip to a different state or country for a music festival? Sign me up. Ultimate weekend at an anime convention in your best cosplay attire? Make it rain. By contributing money to a sinking fund each month, you make it easier to fund the things and experiences you really want, while also building healthy money habits along the way.

I found that when I started using sinking funds, the prospect of having nicer things and experiences crowded out my desire for smaller impulse purchases—much like the nutrition workshop experience I'd had years ago. Discipline got easier because I had something I was working toward, rather than just setting aside money for the sake of saving alone. Budgeting doesn't have to be about scarcity or cutting out the things you love; it can be about awareness, workability, and sustainability, all important ingredients for a wonderful queer life.

Stow your sinking fund money in a high-yield savings account. This keeps your money safe, and at interest rates near or above 4 percent, your money will compound a little, giving you extra souvenir cash.

TRAP NO. 2: NOT LOOKING AT YOUR NUMBERS

Avoidance is a very real coping mechanism. If your money is messy (stressful messy, not fun messy), the short-term solution is to sweep the mess under the rug. It's giving "still in the closet," which is not the vibe we want.

Look at your money every day. As we've learned from doomsday preppers and cult followers, what you look at on a regular basis shapes your perspective of yourself and the world. Taking a moment to look at your money each day helps you familiarize yourself with what's coming in and what's going back out. Money management will become more normalized for you because it will feel increasingly familiar.

A budgeting app makes all this much easier. I mentioned getting a budgeting app as extra credit in chapter 1, but it's becoming part of the regular syllabus, effective now. Budgeting apps are user-friendly and only take a few minutes to set up. You've spent entire days on the couch binge-watching horror classics before; I know you have time to do this.

A budgeting app makes it easy to do your daily money peep

during a commercial break or while waiting in line at the supermarket. And most apps track your monthly and yearly progress in the form of sexy line graphs so you can see your progress over time. Do some online research on budgeting apps, or peep my latest recommendations at https://nickwolny.com/book-resources to find one that works for you.

TRAP NO. 3: NOT PLANNING FOR ONE-TIME AND ANNUAL EXPENSES

We typically manage our budget in months because a lot of our expenses occur in monthly increments, from rent and utilities to streaming subscriptions. But not all expenses occur monthly. From holiday travel to summer vacations to car registration renewals, there are plenty of one-off expenses that take place throughout the year, and they can wreck your budget if you don't factor them in.

Know what months these transactions occur so you can set aside money for them and plan accordingly. Common one-time annual expenses include:

- Car registration
- Car maintenance
- Pet vaccinations
- Passport renewal
- Holiday or summer travel
- Copays for medical visits
- Birthdays and anniversaries
- Pride month
- Wedding gifts or funeral sympathies
- Warehouse club membership fees (examples: Costco, Sam's Club)
- Warehouse parties
- Professional certification fees
- Holiday décor

- Your very niche or slutty (or both) Halloween costume
- School registration and activity fees, if you have kids
- Taxes (more on this in chapter 7)

As you get better at budgeting and your cash flow improves, you might start thinking about your expenses annually instead of monthly. You might even opt for an annual subscription instead of a monthly subscription (okay adulting!), which usually saves you a few bucks.

There are also one-off expenses that occur only once every several years, such as buying a new computer or saving up for something you really want. This brings us to:

TRAP NO. 4: LETTING RETAIL THERAPY RUN RAMPANT

Ah, retail therapy, I know you well. When we feel emotionally down or hurt, the temporary endorphin rush that comes from shopping can make us feel better in the moment.

Retail therapy as a form of self-care isn't necessarily bad, and I'm not telling you to stop shopping (that would probably be career suicide for an LGBTQ+ author). If retail therapy is in your fun money bucket and you want to treat yourself, do it. The problem comes when self-care becomes self-destructive. You go overboard, spend way more than you expected, and throw everything on a credit card "just to be safe" (do I sound like a broken record yet?), which contributes to your debt drag and weighs you down in life.

"But the Beyoncé tickets sell out in five minutes!" Trust me, I know, because I went nonverbal at brunch to buy them on my phone the moment they went on sale. If you know there are experiences like these on the horizon that will require fast action, start putting money in your sinking fund now so you have what you need when the time comes.

TRAP NO. 5:
BUILDING A GOLDEN CAGE

The term "golden cage" refers to a scenario in which you have money, but don't have freedom, because you must keep working at your soul-sucking job to prop up your current lifestyle.

When you start making more money, you naturally want to improve the quality of your life and treat yourself. Making more money often comes with more hustle and more stress, so you want to blow off steam. When workload goes up and monthly expenses also go up, that's lifestyle creep in the flesh, and you have to run faster and faster on the hamster wheel to maintain it all. These days, lifestyle creep is trapping workers in upper-middle-class income brackets, too; one study found that 36 percent of workers making $200,000+ a year still felt like they were living from paycheck to paycheck.[1]

Sean, 27, California: *I have a career I'm proud of and have worked my ass off. Maybe this is too much information, but I make $175,000 a year and yet I still feel like I live paycheck to paycheck. I bought a condo, and my housing payment is 54 percent of my income right now, which is a high f***ing percent. I know what the salary bump of my next promotion will bring. But I'm wondering: Do I really want this life where I kill myself at work and am very unhappy, but just keep striving for the "more money, more problems" lifestyle? Or do I want to just say f*** it to the whole consumerism thing, have my friends and my health, and not want more than that? I think this is where the whole "masc for masc," pick-me vibe comes from. People want to be palatable; it's a natural state for us to be in. And what's more palatable than being successful?*

More income gives you the resources to live bigger, but when expenses drift too high, you lock yourself into a golden cage that robs you of another type of wealth: your freedom.

TRAP NO. 6: TOO MUCH RESTRICTION

This one's less common, but it does happen, and it comes from being *too* aware of your money. You stress out about saving as much money as possible as quickly as possible, and as a result you cut yourself off from living your life. When you're saving too much, you risk a life of lonely wealth in your later years, and if/when you retire you'll have no idea what to do with all your free time because you never explored your interests.

These feelings of scarcity might be from a past trauma or unpleasant experience. If that's the case, I invite you to work through them with a mental health professional or financial therapist.

REDEFINING BUDGET

Even the word "budget" can stir up emotions or feelings of restriction, so let's calibrate on a revised definition that feels more empowering.

A budget is simply resource management. It's the equivalent of making sure you have enough gas in the tank for the road trip, or drink enough water during the day that you don't develop a headache, or keep enough singles in your wallet so you can tip the go-go dancer if they're performing at the gay bar that night (oops, wait, that's me).

Budgets give us awareness. But most budgets only track numbers. They strip out the emotions and thought patterns, which we learned in Part I are the origin points for a lot of your spending habits. To properly review how we spend our money, we should take these emotions and motivations into consideration, too.

Recall our four buckets budget exercise from chapter 1. This was your first pass on budgeting; it gave you an initial sense of what was coming in and out each month so you could calculate your modified saving rate. We'll now go back through those categories and get curious about how your various expenses shape your LGBTQ+ identity and life. I call this exercise the **Bedazzled Budget**, and it's designed to give you more confidence.

For every purchase in a given month, I want you to know why you spent that money and whether it's working for or against you. You'll be interrogating your spending (and doing so without shame) and asking yourself questions that go deeper than spreadsheet numbers alone. The Bedazzled Budget is a journaling exercise, and its outcome is that you become more confident with how you spend your money.

THE BEDAZZLED BUDGET

Get out a pen and several sheets of paper, or open up a new tab in your spreadsheet, and create four columns. Make the third and fourth columns wider; you'll be writing in them. Label each column as follows:

Category	Amount	Relationship to queer identity (benefit/cost)	Action steps

Also have a separate tab or sheet handy for a forthcoming writing exercise.

The Bedazzled Budget has four steps: categorization, reflection, individual expense journaling, and action steps.

STEP 1: CATEGORIZE YOUR EXPENSES

Start by creating categories of known recurring expenses, as well as other areas of spending that matter to you. You'll be plotting individual expenses from your previous buckets work into these categories.

Within each category, you'll also distinguish essential expenses from wants. Include annual and other one-off expenses in these categories, but divide them into monthly increments.

Your budgeting app may have categorized many or most of these expenses for you already, which will give you a running start. Even if this work is already being done for you in an app, I still want you to do this exercise manually to encourage reflection and self-study.

Only fill out the first two columns for now. We'll go back down through the other columns in subsequent steps. Some common categories to consider are below, and you can certainly add categories of your own to get a clear spending snapshot.

FOOD

We say reading is fundamental, but that trophy actually goes to food. Food is our life force. Food gives us health, or can take it away. It's also social and cultural; food gives us a reason to gather. A bowl of chicken tikka masala hates to see me coming, because it knows the end is near.

Categorize the different aspects of food in your life. And avoid this binary idea that groceries are good and eating out is bad. If you spend $200 per month on groceries and $1,500 per month on going out to eat, and are plowing forward on all your financial goals with cash left over to spare, who am I to tell you what to do? We're creating *awareness*. For most of us, though, cooking at home is financially the more cost-effective option, and it helps ensure you're eating food that is nutritious and provides you with energy.

Food: Essential Expenses

- Groceries

Food: Fun Money

- Eating out
- Starbucks runs

- Saturday morning iced latté from the coffee cart guy near the entrance to the park (this is one of mine—$30/month)

As you plot, consider listing the category, then indenting the subcategory (essential or fun) and double-indenting the individual expenses, so that when you're done it's easy to find your way around your budget sheet. Like this:

Category	Amount
Food	
Essential	
Groceries	$850
Fun	
Eating out	$150
Starbucks	$40
Coffee dude	$30

HOUSING AND UTILITIES

A living space ensures your safety. This is vital for queer people. Your living space could mean renting the basement in someone's house, or it could be a 6,000-square-foot mansion in the suburbs because you, your spouse, your three kids, and your elderly parents who don't speak English all live under one roof (perfect recipe for a half-hour sitcom, btw).

For your housing category, include things like utilities, maintenance, and some money to save up for essential furnishings if you're young and still acquiring the basics. In many households, housing accounts for a substantial chunk of overall expenses, which also means there might be opportunities to save.

Housing and Utilities: Essential Expenses

- Rent/mortgage
- Housing maintenance
- Essential furnishings
- Utilities: electric, water, gas, trash, HOA fees
- Internet

TRANSPORTATION

Even if you don't have a car and don't need one for work, you still need to be able to get around town from time to time. Set aside enough money to cover the cost of a vehicle and/or public transportation and rideshare options. If you do need a car, know that new cars lose quite a bit of value the moment you drive them off the dealership lot, so consider a gently used car instead. Also aspire to own a car rather than lease one; once your car is paid off, you can usually get a few or even several more years out of your vehicle without having a car payment.

Transportation: Essential Expenses

- Car payment
- Car insurance
- Gas and maintenance
- Transit card
- Rideshare fares

HEALTH CARE AND WELLNESS

I know, I know—in the United States, health insurance is exorbitant. I personally did not have health insurance for several years in my twenties. I felt chronically paranoid that if something bad happened to me, medical attention would wreck my finances. Sadly, this sentiment is common; one poll found that 23 percent of Americans avoided calling an ambulance for a medical emergency because of the potential cost.[2]

Not taking care of yourself can be expensive and lead to discomfort and pain later (looking at you, dental health). And while we don't expect to get into accidents or contract a sudden devastating illness, the reality is that it happens, and it can saddle us with medical debt. Do everything you can to have health insurance, even if it's just basic insurance that covers you in the event of unexpected disasters.

Categorize expenses like hormone therapy and gender-affirming care as essential. Also consider including mental health care in your health expenses. When you're anxious, depressed, or overwhelmed, impulse control typically goes out the door, which can affect your money. I look at mental health care as an essential expense and apply the phrase "health is wealth" to mental health, too.

Health Care and Wellness: Essential Expenses

- Health insurance
- Mental health care
- Gender-affirming care

Health Care and Wellness: Fun Money

- Gym or studio membership
- Fitness activities (5K runs, softball league membership, etc.)
- Special workout gear (lifting gloves to keep those hands soft and supple)
- Self-care (one of my categories is a ninety-minute massage once a quarter for $150, i.e., $50/month)

CLOTHING

Clothing is a vehicle for personal style and helps you both express yourself and feel confident. It's also a category of spending that can be very susceptible to comparison culture because it's so visible.

This is a budget category in which the cheapest options aren't always best. For me, cheap boxer briefs feel like a tangled hammock between my legs (which is not my kink, to be clear), so I'll forgo something else in my budget to have better-quality underwear. Fast fashion also produces a lot of global waste; if being environmentally conscious is important to you, sustainably produced clothing is a way to exercise activism with your dollars. Think about purchasing items that make you feel good, are versatile, and will last a long time.

Allocate money in your budget for clothing each month so that you can slowly build up your wardrobe. Alternatively, treat your clothing budget like a sinking fund, contributing money every month but not necessarily buying things every month, and do a bigger shopping blitz a couple times a year. I do the latter, and I have found that shopping less often helps me have more control over spending temptations.

Clothing: Essential Expenses

- Seasonally appropriate clothes

Clothing: Fun Money

- Accessories and jewelry
- Reward shopping (Example: I'm lifting weights regularly for the first time in my life and getting bigger. Some of my shirts don't fit anymore. $100/month goes toward my new size-large wardrobe.)

DEVICES AND CONNECTIVITY

From smartphones to TVs to wearables to gaming systems and gadgets, electronics make our lives both functional and fun. For many freelancers and gig workers, a personal computer is a must-have device as well. If you plan to purchase certain electronics in the next year, add these to your budget.

Devices and Connectivity: Essential Expenses

- Smartphone
- Phone service bill
- Computer (if needed for work)

Devices and Connectivity: Fun Money

- Television
- Tablets
- Gaming gear
- Work from home items

ENTERTAINMENT AND LEISURE

Big, exciting category! And one of our most important categories, really. Live in queer joy now!

Entertainment can include going to shows, taking road trips to parks, or downloading new video games (which have so much more longevity than they used to back in the "blow on the cartridge to get the dust out" days). Or just create your own fun. Who cares if you don't have a couch yet? Invite a friend over for dinner, make some pasta, and play card games. Dabble online and connect with other queer people who have similar interests, too.

Your hobbies are an important aspect of who you are. Make investing in them a regular and normalized part of your budget.

Entertainment and Leisure: Fun Money

- Subscriptions
- Nightlife
- Sporting events
- Arts
- Hobbies and clubs
- Travel
- Vacation funds

FOLLOW THE FLIGHT ATTENDANTS

The Case for Travel as a Priority Expense

Many elders say they regret not traveling more when they were younger. Consider integrating travel into your life on a regular basis. You might discover something about yourself that reshapes your future money and lifestyle goals.

Queer spaces are more discoverable now (and hopefully, uh, it stays that way?), and many a travel blogger has published their best tips, experiences, and suggestions for planning out your next adventure. Here's the case for giving travel a little extra heft in your budget.

Travel exposes you to new cultures. You don't realize how much of your life is a product of environmental conditioning until you experience other cultures. Growing up, we never took family vacations or visited relatives. I started traveling on my own in early adulthood, first in music school to take auditions around the country and then later in adulthood to places like Mexico and Europe for leisure. It opened my eyes to different parts of the world, and I developed resilience and leadership skills, too. If you've ever navigated a public transportation system in another country, or explored a city where English isn't the primary language, you know what I'm talking about.

Travel opens your mind. You know who has strong opinions about how the world works? People who've never left the country, or even the county or state they grew up in. According to the Pew Research Center, 23 percent of Americans have never traveled internationally. (The main reason for this? Money, of course.) Just 26 percent of Americans were classified as "globe trotters," having visited five countries or more; for comparison, 88 percent of Swedes have this same classification. Travel gives us a break, reopens our hearts and minds to new perspectives, and makes us miss home, refreshing our appreciation for routine.

Travel can help you find community. For many LGBTQ+ people, travel lets us express ourselves in ways that aren't available at home, particularly if we live in a less welcoming community. From gay cruises to festivals, traveling to be around other people who are like us can be deeply fulfilling.

How to Seek Out LGBTQ+-Friendly Travel Opportunities

- Create a travel fund or vacation fund, using the sinking fund strategy we introduced earlier.
- Do research online. Read not only tourism websites, but also bloggers and creators for firsthand accounts and tips. Resist the urge to only do all-inclusive resorts. Immerse yourself in the destination so that you can experience the local culture.
- Keep an eye out for good travel deals. Utilize tools like flight price trackers to save money. Services like Google Flights let you bookmark an itinerary and receive an email when there's a price drop. Splurge on cultural experiences, rather than a first-class plane ticket that's only a small part of the trip. I once did an all-day private mezcal distillery tour in Mexico that was totally worth the economy-class flights and cheaper hotel.
- If visiting a foreign country, do some due diligence on that country's LGBTQ+ rights. As of this writing, it's still illegal to be gay in sixty-four countries. More countries have decriminalized homosexuality in recent years, but please don't let your wanderlust put you in an unsafe situation.

Travel is an investment in your personal development, and it doesn't have to break the bank. Reward yourself with adventure to keep your fire burning bright.

HOUSEHOLD AMENITIES

Consider the idea that investing in a comfortable space can help you save money down the road. You'll enjoy being at home more, and it's important that we cultivate and live our queer lives in Technicolor.

At one point in my twenties, I had an apartment with two roommates to try to save money. My space was uncomfortable, and as a result I didn't really enjoy spending time at the apartment. I spent most of my time out and about, which actually increased my expenses and cancelled out a lot of what I was saving from the lower rent payment.

Make your living environment a space where you enjoy spending your time. Outfit your kitchen and bedroom with the items you need to cook a meal and get a good night's rest. Set up your bathroom with items that let you do a facial at home while watching a movie. Remember, we're looking for ways to fend off feelings of chronic discomfort, because when you're chronically uncomfortable, financially destructive behaviors like avoidance and money malaise begin to creep in.

Household Amenities: Essential Expenses

- Cookware
- Bedding
- Bathroom essentials
- Cleaning supplies
- Toiletries
- Furniture

Household Amenities: Fun Money

- Decor (I'm becoming a bit of a plant daddy myself, personally. $40/month)
- Appliances

FAMILY AND PET CARE

If you have kids, or are caring for other family members, you have a whole other category of expenses to allocate for. This means additional expenses like childcare, school tuition, and activities. Family care might also include pets, for which you'll want to allocate funds for food, vaccinations, and pet insurance in the event Fido eats (another) one of your socks.

Family and Pet Care: Essential Expenses

- Childcare
- School tuition and activities
- Children's clothes
- Diapers
- Pet food
- Essential vaccinations
- Pet insurance

Family and Pet Care: Fun Money

- Toys and games
- Pet toys
- Pet daycare
- Dog walker

MINIMUM DEBT PAYMENTS AND NET WORTH CONTRIBUTIONS

You already documented these expenses back in chapter 1. Minimum debt payments are the minimum monthly payment you are required to make on your debts each month, so you should absolutely document them and make sure you're allocating money to them. You also documented money going toward savings, investments, and/or additional debt paydown. Track this money as well so it's accounted for.

List each minimum debt payment and net worth contribution as its own line item in your budget. If you did the work in chapter 1, this will be an easy copy-paste job.

Action: Go back through all of your expenses from the previous month. Map these expenses into different subcategories. Leave no expense unturned.

STEP 2: RECALL YOUR QUEER IDENTITY AND GOALS

By this point, you should have a long, customized list of tracked expenses that give you a snapshot of where your money currently goes, and what your life looks like as a result. Now—what do you *want* your life to look like?

The objective of this chapter is to align our money habits with both who we are as upstanding queer citizens and what we want (and deserve) for our lives. We want lives of stability and self-sufficiency, of purpose and meaning; that means we need to go beyond dollar amounts and do some reflection on why we spend the money we do.

Grab your separate sheet of paper or your separate spreadsheet tab, and jot down answers to the following questions:

What are some ways I can live and be that were not available to previous generations of LGBTQ+ people?

___

___

___

When am I my happiest? When is my happiness deeply satisfying and fulfilling?

___

___

___

What aspects of my life give me consistent peace of mind and satisfaction?

___

___

___

When do I feel most comfortable in my queerness?

___

___

___

What do I want for myself now? What do I want for myself in the future? How can these two categories of wants coexist?

____

____

____

If I no longer had to work for money, how would I spend my time and energy? What would I do differently with my life?

____

____

____

This work is deep, but also very valuable because it gives you life aspirations from which you can reverse-engineer your money roadmap.

> **Action:** Journal on questions that are not budget-specific to refresh your spirit on who you are, who you want to become, and what some of your current goals and aspirations are.

STEP 3: JOURNAL ON EACH INDIVIDUAL EXPENSE

With these insights fresh in your mind, go back to the top of your budget sheet and locate the third column. For each expense line, jot down a few notes on how that expense connects back to your queer identity and overall sense of purpose. Does this expense support the pursuit of your best queer life? If yes, how? If no, how does it hold you back? The purpose of this exercise is to develop a spending plan that is deeply integrated with your goals, dreams, and LGBTQ+ identity. For some expenses, you might realize that this spending is not moving you in the direction of the queer life you want to live, and that some or all of that money would be better allocated toward something else. Other expenses might be huge sources of energy and personal power, in which case it could be a priority to maintain or even *increase* these expenses.

This is very valuable work because it builds confidence about your current and future spending. The temptation to avoid or numb will quiet down because your financial goals are exciting and clear. Money malaise and unconscious spending sprees will be replaced by confidence, excitement, and perseverance.

Brendan, 34, Washington, DC: *I'm not going to adjust [my budget on] going out, eating out, or having fun with my friends. That feels like too much of a sacrifice to me. I'll cut back in other areas, but when it comes to enriching myself, those are the things I'm not really willing to compromise on.*

Action: Go back through your budget sheet and write some notes about how each expense in your budget relates to your queer identity. Write as little or as much as you want, but write enough to feel clear and confident on why that expense is in your life and whether or not it's really serving you.

STEP 4: IDENTIFY ACTION STEPS

Now go back to the top of the budget sheet and write down potential action steps in the fourth column. If you realized that an expense is working against you, list one or more action steps you can take to lower or eliminate that expense. If you find that an expense really serves you and brings you fulfillment, and you have money left over at the end of the month, consider increasing that expense in order to be, do, and have more of what you enjoy in life.

Some of these action steps can be implemented immediately. Others will require that you either develop a new spending habit or increase the amount of money you're bringing in every month, the latter of which we'll explore extensively in chapter 5. Others still will be big, one-time decisions that lead to saving hundreds of thousands of dollars over the next year. They'll be humbling at first, but worth it in the long run.

For each category below, I've listed a few money-saving action steps to give you a running start. Take the action steps that appeal to you and leave behind the ones that don't.

Food

- If you are able, shop for groceries at the store or your local farmer's market. This lets you leverage coupons, spot markdowns, and get produce in season. Put the rewards card in your wallet, attach it to your keychain, and keep a spare in your car. Tape the rewards card to your damn forehead if that's what it takes—it's easy savings.
- If your cash flow is good, consider buying your favorite nonperishable items in bulk. Portion and freeze proteins. Aspire to cut down on food waste.
- Embrace cooking. It's fun! Get cookbooks from libraries or used bookstores if you need a running start, or find recipes on YouTube and social media. Bonus: You'll also actually know what goes into your food.
- Make going out to eat a social experience. Preserve these funds for date nights, happy hours with friends, or family visits. Trim down on the spend, not the socializing.
- Consider investing in kitchen gear that will save you time and encourage meal prep, such as a slow cooker, a good knife set, or a set of glass containers for storing leftovers.

Housing and Utilities

- Consider either downsizing to a smaller place, getting a roommate, or relocating to an area with a lower cost of living. For many of us, this is the single biggest expense change we can achieve in our budget. Some of the best apartments in cities get leased before they're ever even listed; start asking around and let people know you're looking to move soon in the event something comes up.

- See if you can negotiate utility costs. Shop around for different providers to see if other services in your area have introductory sign-on offers or specials.
- If you have a mortgage, and the budget is still tight, consider refinancing to lower your monthly payments.

Liz, 37, Kentucky: *We moved to Louisville to be closer to my wife's relatives. I never thought I would leave Denver—it's progressive heaven—but houses were expensive, even in the suburbs, and when we looked at life with a kid and a goal to have more, finances were a sticking point. Daycare costs in Denver were nearly double those in Kentucky. We currently pay $1,500 per month in daycare; paying double that per child would have left us constantly stressed and scrambling to cover expenses. We wanted to prioritize our family life, not just working nonstop to make ends meet. The move helped us afford a 4-bed, 2-bath, 2,700-square-foot house in a fantastic liberal area of Louisville for $470,000, and our daughter's daycare is a block away, so we walk her to daycare every morning. We're living this really full life now, and living within our means.*

SHOULD YOU LIVE IN THE GAYBORHOOD?

A Simple Litmus Test

Throughout the twentieth century, queer people flocked to gayborhoods like the Castro in San Francisco and Boystown in Chicago to escape discrimination and seek out a sense of belonging. Gayborhoods were bastions of culture and hospitality, communities where LGBTQ+ people helped one another find work and housing without fear of discrimination, as well as a romantic partner and circles of friends.

As acceptance has become more mainstream (which is good!), it's become less essential to live in a gayborhood. Many city gayborhoods have become increasingly expensive and gentrified over the years, shutting lower-income queer people out entirely (*Another* gastropub? Really?). Here's a simple three-question test to determine whether you should make that gayborhood zip code a priority.

Do you need close physical proximity to the community? If being around gay bars and seeing queers holding hands as they walk down the street helps cultivate feelings of safety and belonging—and you were a mess during the COVID-19 pandemic quarantine because of all the isolation—you might want to make gayborhood living a priority. Your mental health and social wealth will potentially get a boost. If this physical proximity isn't a must-have or isn't available, be sure to create a plan for how you can cultivate a sense of community and belonging, both offline and online. Community matters.

Do you want to own a home one day? Homeownership is a big financial goal that involves a substantial down payment. With expensive condos increasingly becoming the norm in gayborhoods, it might make more sense for you to rent or buy property in a different neighborhood that is more cost-effective. If buying a home is in your future, saving toward a down payment would be a good idea. If you don't ever plan to own, or simply prefer the convenience and flexibility of renting, live wherever you want.

Is the commute tolerable? Multiple studies have shown that the longer someone's commute is, the less happy they are, particularly if that commute involves driving in traffic. Yes, it's fun to live in the cool, artsy neighborhood, but if it makes for an hour or more of driving each way to work, will you have any energy left over to really enjoy it? Weigh the pros and cons.

It's important that we continue to cultivate social connection with our community, secure safety, and give gay-owned establishments our patronage whenever we can. Maybe you need to live in the gayborhood to fulfill on this . . . or maybe you don't, because you can recreate most or all of these benefits on your own. If you do choose gayborhood living, be mindful of the fear of missing out (FOMO) and impulsive spending.

Whichever you decide, knowing about and connecting with your local queer community IRL is important. Do what you can to incorporate it into your life.

Transportation

- If you're leasing a car, consider saving up enough money to own one instead. Once paid off, you'll no longer have a car payment. (Cars do go down in value quickly, though, so if you plan to sell your car within a couple years of purchase, leasing might be the better option.)
- Prioritize car makers that tend to have lower maintenance and repair costs. A luxury car might be similar in price point to other models on the lot, but the difference in ongoing maintenance on the back end can be wildly different. No one wants to take their car into the shop and be suddenly hit with a quote for hundreds or even thousands of dollars in repairs. My Toyota RAV4 is big enough to hold the beach gear, but also manageable on the gas and maintenance costs.
- Consider a hybrid vehicle or electric vehicle. Lower carbon footprint aside, EVs have had tax rebates in the past, which can save you money. Those credits are at the discretion of the government and can be changed at any time, so be sure to review federal and state perk opportunities before making your purchase if that's the deciding factor.
- Learn your local public transportation routes, particularly if you live in a city. Make it a game to know where the nearest bus and train stops are from your current location. Leverage public transportation

when you can to cut down on parking and/or rideshare costs. Bonus: You can watch all the YouTube your heart desires on your commute when you're not the one driving.

- Consider whether you actually need a car. With your newly upgraded public transportation knowledge, you might find that you can navigate most or all of your day-to-day life without one.
- Clean and detail your car yourself. Put your favorite playlist in your earbuds, grab that spray bottle of interior car cleaner, and go to town.

Health Care and Wellness

- If paying for gym or studio memberships, ask if there are any work-for-trade options. Some local businesses are happy to trade a membership for an extra set of helping hands around the studio. Back when I worked at the yoga studio, I noticed the people who did this came from all different generations and socioeconomic backgrounds. It was seen as a win/win, not a haggle.
- Look for options for discounted classes. Stock up on class pack sales, which happen intermittently throughout the year.
- If you have health insurance, familiarize yourself with and use all the perks that are available to you. Most insurance policies will cover the cost of an annual physical and/or regular checkup. Some policies also cover nutrition or mental health consultations.
- Get your physical every year, have routine blood work done, and don't skimp on going to the dentist. Root canals hurt (I've had one). Keep those pearly whites shining, strong, and healthy.
- If you live in a city that has an LGBT center, go check it out. Familiarize yourself with the mental health and community resources that are available to you. If the area you live in does not have an LGBT center, research free online webinars and workshops you can attend to keep yourself informed.
- Explore your options for both in-person mental health and telemedicine.

- Reflect on your consumption of alcohol and other substances. How do they serve you, and how might they diminish your physical and mental health? How much do they cost each month? Can their benefits be replicated with a less frequent dosage, or something similar? Seek balance and moderation.

Clothing

- Consider checking out secondhand shops and other thrift stores in your area, which can be a great way to pick up essentials at a reduced cost. "But I don't know where it's been"—oh, please. Some of you let your dogs lick your entire face morning, noon, and night.
- Also consider cleaning out closets and selling items that you know you're not going to wear anymore. You might be able to bring in extra money for doing so.

TEA

For some easy minimalism porn, try the **reverse hanger trick**. Turn all the hangers in your closet around so that they hook onto the hanger bar from the back instead of the front. As you wear your clothes, hook them from the front moving forward. After a year or so, look and see what clothes are still hooked from the back. You haven't worn these items in a full cycle of seasons, so it might be time to consider trading them in or donating them.

Devices and Connectivity

- Do a price comparison of different phone bills. Check what your current contract says and when it ends so you know when you'll have the option to switch to a less expensive provider.

- If you upgrade your phone, look at the trade-in value of your previous device.
- Familiarize yourself with how to purchase refurbished electronics. Some refurbished electronics are scams, so ensure the product is refurbished with parts from the original manufacturer. Good refurbished electronics will give the option of a warranty. This can be an easy way to shave down the price of a new laptop or desktop computer, and the device often works like new.
- Check out garage sales, or shop on websites like Etsy for other gear. Often, resellers are simply trying to unload items they don't use or don't have space for anymore, which can be to your advantage.

Entertainment and Leisure

- Take a good look at those streaming subscriptions. Do you need nine streaming subscriptions? (If you felt attacked when I said that, you already know the answer.) Consider paring them down and rotating between different services throughout the year. This will give you *less* to choose from so that you spend less time surfing and more time actually watching. Nearly every streamer lets you unsubscribe and resubscribe as you please. Press a bunch of buttons on all of the unsubscribe sequences to see if you get offered a discounted rate for a few months to maintain your membership. If you accidentally cancel, just sign back up.
- Brainstorm ideas to trim down the cost of nightlife activities with friends. Double-fist on beverages by ordering a water along with your cocktail (you'll also feel better the next morning).
- If you like to travel, look into discount travel sites, subscriptions, or forums that can help you find good deals. Often, buying tickets at the right time can help you save money on your next trip.
- Look into free groups, events, and social nights in your area. Famil-

iarize yourself with where to locate this information so you can reference it when you want.

- Host a potluck or a picnic for a few friends. You'll get all the social fulfillment without breaking the bank.

Household Amenities

- Toiletries: Simplify to just the essentials that you need for health and beauty, and recreate services that you would normally go and pay for at home instead. For example, I bought moldable teeth whitening trays and vials of whitening gel online (then wore them while writing this book, so the longer I sit here agonizing over my silly little jokes, the brighter my smile gets).
- Kitchen: Invest in a few multipurpose appliances that let you create a variety of meals. Examples include a Dutch oven or a pressure cooker. When you cook, make enough to also have a couple days of leftovers if the meal keeps well. You can also freeze the leftovers so you don't burn out on the same meal in a given week and throw food away.
- Décor: Look for inexpensive frames at secondhand shops. Visit local plant shops; plants can be inexpensive and add vibrance to any décor. Experiment with inexpensive smart lights, which can create a variety of moods and options for a fraction of the price of expensive lighting fixtures.

Action: Identify action steps you can take to lower expenses. Prioritize lowering the expenses that are not contributing to your best queer life over the next sixty days. Then, either put that money toward additional net worth contributions or increasing spending in the expense categories that really light you up and give your life fulfillment and purpose.

FAT, FEM EXTRA CREDIT

This budget work is deep and transformational, and you only need to do it once. As you start making changes to your spending habits, you will discover new things about yourself. If you want to go above and beyond, consider returning to this exercise every four to six months.

Revisiting your Bedazzled Budget will help you see where you are and aren't making forward strides in your money management. It also makes you return to past journal entries and action steps to see if they were true. Maybe you decided to cut a video game streaming subscription, but have discovered that you miss your online community and want to resubscribe. Maybe you allocated funds to join a gay sports league, but realize you don't care about that sport enough to buy all the gear and travel to all the tournaments, and would rather drop in at a run club instead. Nothing is permanent in this process. It's your life; make it one that you truly enjoy.

By occasionally revisiting your budget, you ensure that the way you spend your money is aligned with how you want to live your life, rather than just being driven by money malaise and unconscious numbing. With that foundation in place, you'll keep more of the money you earn. This means we're ready to turn our attention to one of the most exciting topics in this book: how to make more money, and all the different ways you can do so without burning yourself out.

5

INCOME

Your Action Plan to Navigate the "Income Stream Rainbow" and Collect More Cash

Money is way more fun to learn about when you have some in the bank.

The first money book I ever purchased was Suze Orman's *The Money Book for the Young, Fabulous and Broke.* "Ooh, look, it's me, I'm all of those things," I thought to myself, 23 at the time, emphasis on the broke part. "And Suze's a lesbian—bonus!"

I learned about what a credit score was and how to make a budget. I learned a bunch of stuff about personal finance, valuable information I had not received during my upbringing or college education. But there was still a problem: I didn't really *have* any money to be able to work on a lot of the things the book (and many other financial books) talked about doing. "Look at me, I saved 31 dollars this month!" I would desperately affirm to myself, before the interest on my credit card debt vaporized all my progress days later. My salary was a little over $40,000 at the time, I was trapped in the land of the dreaded 3-percent raise, and now I had personal development blue balls, too. I felt stuck.

Fast forward a few years, and my money situation was very different. My income had nearly doubled. I didn't have to be as surgical with my budget in order to survive. I had spending money for fun stuff, like traveling to new parts of the country and world, and I was also making faster progress on my saving goals because *I had more money in the picture to begin with.* I had resources to explore and define my queer identity, and I felt more in control of my destiny.

What changed? Rather than follow the career path that had been presented to me at work as my only option, I unlearned what I thought was the "right" path forward, then replaced those beliefs with actionable knowledge about other ways I could make more money.

First, I took a job with a high-commission pay structure, a win/win arrangement that increased my annual earnings by 50 percent. Later, I began working for myself, using my same skill set to service clients directly and setting my own rates. Being self-employed the next several years gave me flexibility to take on clients either full-time or on the side as my work situation ebbed and flowed. It didn't make me rich; socioeconomically, I was middle-class. But I had more financial freedom and time freedom than I ever imagined possible as a young LGBTQ+ adult, and this space gave me room to learn about myself and discover what I truly valued and cherished.

Career skepticism has gained traction in our increasingly imbalanced economy. Wage growth for lower earners has lagged for decades. Office politics often take precedent over actual skills when it comes to who gets a promotion. Staying at one job for your entire career, a concept shaped by pension culture and loyalty as a path to retirement, is increasingly old news; baby boomers had had an average of 12.7 jobs by age 56, whereas millennials have already had 9 jobs by 36, according to data from the U.S. Department of Labor.[1]

For queer people, our identities can create additional career inertia. Casual microaggressions might be the norm at your workplace. Transgender and non-binary people may encounter additional obstacles, such as a background check outing them by revealing a dead name. And although gender discrimination is currently illegal, you know how some of these corporations are: rainbow logos during Pride month in the front, cutting checks to anti-LGBTQ politicians in the back.

Americans are also increasingly coloring outside the lines of a normal job to meet their financial goals and needs. In 2024, 36 percent of Americans reported having a side hustle, an effort that produced an average of $891 a month in additional income.[2] As we've illustrated in previous chapters, this amount of extra money can mean the difference between flailing in debt and securing a financially independent future.

A healthy dollop of skepticism (it has zero calories, lay it on thick) helps you evade corporate propaganda and puts your earning potential back into your own hands. More income can immediately improve your quality of life because it lets you pay down debt faster, save for big goals that excite you, and buy back your time in the interim. Or you can aspire to make the same income by working fewer hours at higher pay, giving you space to catch a yoga class, visit a farmer's market, or clack the fan at drag brunch.

Remember the 7-word plan for building wealth: lower expenses, increase earnings, invest the difference. We began this plan with lowering expenses because expenses are more within your control. After you take those initial cost-cutting actions, though, there's not *that* much more whittling you can do. You'll reach a point at which your willpower will be better spent increasing your take-home pay each month instead. And had I been given a blank slate in the art direction of this book, I would have put "INCREASE EARNINGS" in all caps, in gold foil, bordered by money-bag emojis and muscle-boy pin-ups, because for most people increasing your income is the single most powerful thing you can do to transform your financial future.

As queer people, we must broaden our understanding of income so that we know all the different ways to bring it in. Once you have this more diverse perspective, you'll be better equipped to make more money without giving up so much time and energy along the way.

In this chapter, we'll address the fixed mindsets about income that might be holding you back, the many flavors of the "income stream rainbow," and the actions you can start taking today to increase your earnings.

Income Traps to Avoid

1. Thinking that more money won't make you happier
2. Missing opportunities to transfer skills
3. Doing what you love instead of doing what you are
4. Tolerating an anti-LGBTQ+ work environment
5. Undervaluing your time
6. Overlooking other aspects of compensation
7. Letting your career become too much of your identity

TRAP NO. 1: THINKING THAT MORE MONEY WON'T MAKE YOU HAPPIER

Some science drama for ya: Remember that happiness study from 2010 that said happiness from more money tops out at $75,000 a year?[3] Both the media and self-help gurus had a field day with this number when it came out, and still do to this day, even quoting the same $75,000 salary point, despite the fact that $75,000 in 2010 is more like $108,500 in 2025 dollars.

Later, a different happiness study of 33,000 participants, published in 2021 from a different researcher, found that well-being *does* continue to rise with income, even beyond the $200,000 mark, directly contradicting previous "happiness tops out" conclusions.[4] Escándalo! Rather than scream it out *Dance Moms*–style, the two happiness researchers decided to work on a new round of research together (they called it "an adversarial collaboration," which also describes me when having to breathe the same air as anyone who dislikes Robyn), and in 2023 they found that well-being does indeed continue to rise with income.[5]

The newer study found that, for the 20 percent of respondents who reported feeling really unhappy, their feelings of unhappiness steadily diminished up to the $100,000 salary mark, at which progress plateaued. The researchers mutually concluded that the data point from 2010, which had previously been interpreted as happiness topping out, actually measured the threshold for unhappiness *bottoming out* (for people whose unhappiness and discomfort could be relieved with more money). To summarize: As long as your income growth is sustainable, and not leading you toward burnout, more money will indeed increase your well-being, according to the most up-to-date science.

Money won't fix the problem if you haven't worked on your baggage, though, and the scientists' collaborative research backed this up. For respondents who were rich and still miserable in life, more money made no difference.

TRAP NO. 2: MISSING OPPORTUNITIES TO TRANSFER SKILLS

Consider that your same skill set could be more valuable (i.e., lucrative) when applied to a different industry.

If you were an audio-visual production lead for music festivals, do you think you could run the audio for a tech conference? If you worked as a kitchen manager or host, could that skill set carry over into project management for a startup? If you're a genius at kissing ass because you work in nonprofit development, would that same energy put more money in your pocket working in commission-based sales? Sometimes, the company or even the entire industry you're in just doesn't pay that great, no matter how hard you work. Weigh the pros and cons of making a pivot.

When I decided at 24 to not pursue classical music professionally, it was terrifying. Music was all I had known and all I had worked toward for years, and my orchestra audition skill set ("I am highly proficient at playing fanfares from the 1700s in an audience-less blind audition setting!") felt way too niche. As it turned out, music school gave me several transferable skills, like how to perform under pressure, absorb and synthesize information quickly, and uphold the discipline necessary to take feedback, practice, and improve. Once I realized these skills could transfer, and learned how to articulate my skills in ways that were valuable to companies, I branched out into new industries, an action that totally changed both my professional purpose and income.

When you look at your employability through the lens of skill set rather than industry, you might uncover new opportunities. Consider digging around on LinkedIn and doing a search on job searches by the name of the skill to see what comes up.

CONTENT WARNING: THE FOLLOWING TESTIMONY INCLUDES DESCRIPTION OF THE AFTERMATH OF A MASS SHOOTING AT A QUEER ESTABLISHMENT.

Aly, 43, Florida: *I didn't love practicing law. I was burnt out as a business owner, and I didn't know what the next step looked like for me. One of my clients was the Pulse nightclub here in Orlando. When the shooting in 2016 happened, I had to be there the morning after and do the walkthrough with the insurance adjusters and be very heavily involved. Emotionally, it was a low point for me. But I got to see the resiliency of our LGBTQ+ community firsthand. The event triggered something in me where I was like "I can't keep doing something I don't like doing anymore." When an executive recruiter reached out about a job in private wealth management, I went for it, and my wife supported the decision. I always liked the clients part more than the law part, so it was a perfect career change for me.*

TRAP NO. 3: DOING WHAT YOU LOVE INSTEAD OF DOING WHAT YOU *ARE*

"Do what you love and you'll never work a day in your life," they said. This advice means well, but in today's world it can ruin your passions because the work you're paid to do as a cog in someone's machine can be a slog at times. People don't move up in their careers and make more money because they love their job more, they move up because their strengths and skills align well with the task at hand. Don't do what you love; do what you *are*.

I didn't have that skill transfer mentality in early adulthood, so I *thought* I was doing something I loved after music school when I worked in retail for a fitness apparel store. I liked being around fitness products and other fitness enthusiasts, and got to wear stretchy pants to work every day (this was huge back in 2011). But I didn't enjoy the work itself, which mostly consisted of talking to strangers all day with an upbeat disposition (kiss of death for an introvert).

Meanwhile, there were other managers who could talk to strangers effortlessly, all day, every day, and sure enough, they began to pass me up for promotions. "Doing what I loved" was both burning me out and keeping me broke. As I learned what came to me naturally—organizing information and ideas—I pursued work that focused more on those skills, changed careers, and got paid more while also feeling less burnt out because the job was a better match for my personality.

Focus on jobs that lay well with your strengths and natural gifts, the things that come easily to you but that others find challenging. Also seek out work environments that you'll thrive in, rather than settle for ones you come to dread.

TEA

Try this: Journal on what skills come naturally to you. Some prompts to get the pen moving:

- What do people say you're good at?
- What do you find straightforward that others find challenging?
- What tasks do you naturally gravitate toward?
- If you had to choose, would you rather talk to a person or tinker with a spreadsheet?
- What tasks energize you?

TRAP NO. 4:
TOLERATING AN ANTI-LGBTQ+ WORK ENVIRONMENT

The thesis of this entire book is to live out and proud while also cultivating financial independence. If your workplace is making that impossible, whether it be leadership or some shitty person in the cubicle next to you, it's time to go, and my hope is that this book gives you the knowledge and tools you need to go make that happen.

Unfortunately, workplace discrimination protections based on sexual orientation or gender identity were only established in 2020, and it's not clear how long that precedent will remain. Even with these protections in place, we know that discrimination still happens, and it can eff with both your headspace and your paycheck; the LGBTQ+ wage gap is 90 cents on the dollar. This queer wage gap varies based on race and gender, and it mirrors the variations in how often various demographics report LGBTQ+ discrimination in the workplace.[6]

TEA

The LGBTQ+ wage gap: It's 90 cents on the dollar overall, but it varies greatly within the community. Here are the cents on the dollar made by queer people compared to the typical worker, according to a survey and analysis by the Human Rights Campaign in 2021.[7]

- Asian and Pacific Islander workers: $1.00
- White queer workers: $0.97
- Latine queer workers: $0.90
- Black queer workers: $0.80
- Native American queer workers: $0.70
- Queer cis male workers: $0.96
- Queer cis female workers: $0.87
- Trans male workers: $0.70
- Trans female workers: $0.60
- Gender nonconforming workers: $0.70

If you are in an anti LGBTQ+ work environment, or even just a toxic work environment in general, I want you to get out of that situation ASAP. Enduring a discriminatory workplace environment can have a negative effect on your mental health, which leads to avoidance and numbing behaviors that sabotage your money, relationships, and more. Health is wealth, and that includes mental health; protect your shine however you can.

"Sara" (pseudonym), 31, Florida: *I was one of a few queer people in a team of about 200 at the corporation. My husband is trans, we live in Florida, and we knew that basically no other company here was going to offer gender reassignment surgery [as a benefit], which is why*

I stayed so long. It was like a carrot on a stick for them: "Aren't we so cool for offering this?" Meanwhile, the pressure at work to conform was suffocating, from how I dressed, to how I talked, to how I wore my hair. They were always dropping hints. I felt like I couldn't bring any of myself to work. After my husband got his top surgery, I came back for one day, just long enough to give my notice.

WORKPLACE DISCRIMINATION AND WHAT YOU CAN DO ABOUT IT

Issued in 2020, the Supreme Court case *Bostock v. Clayton County* found that, in Title VII of the Civil Rights Act of 1964, the phrase "discrimination on the basis of sex" also applies to sexual orientation and gender identity. *Bostock* applied to three separate court cases:

- ***Bostock v. Clayton County.*** Gerald Bostock was a county employee fired for mentioning at work he was interested in joining a gay softball league.
- ***Altitude Express, Inc. v. Zarda.*** Donald Zarda was a skydiving instructor who was fired for mentioning to a client that he was gay; he died in 2014, but his family continued the legal battle on his behalf.
- ***R.G. & G.R. Harris Funeral Homes Inc. v. Equal Employment Opportunity Commission.*** Aimee Stephens was a transgender woman who was fired after telling her employer she would return from vacation identifying and presenting as female; she died one month before the Supreme Court decision was announced.

If you're experiencing workplace discrimination because of your sexual orientation or gender identity, here's what to know and consider.

- **Seek legal advice.** Lambda Legal, a nonprofit focused on LGBTQ+ civil rights, has a help desk you can contact for free initial guidance and a library of legal resources.
- **Documentation is important.** Document incidents in writing, including date and time they occurred. Also document who witnessed the interaction, in case these witnesses need to be contacted later to help corroborate an incident.
- **Go to HR.** If your company has an employee handbook, there will likely be a protocol for how to submit a discrimination claim. If there isn't, refer to free legal resources on how to report incidents to a manager or owner.
- **Know your power regarding retaliation.** Retaliation is when you start being treated unfairly *because* you filed a complaint in the first place, and it's actually the most frequently alleged form of workplace discrimination. Retaliation against protected workers is illegal. If you file a complaint, and the way your workplace treats you changes for the worse, document this shift factually and diligently.
- **If nothing moves, you might be able to file a claim with the government.** Previously, this could be done through an organization called the Equal Employment Opportunity Commission (EEOC), and you would file the EEOC claim within 180 days of the most recent incident. At the time of this writing, the federal government has halted processing of EEOC claims related to sexual orientation and gender identity, but this may change again in future administrations.

Last, think about protecting your peace. Movies and TV shows dramatize lawsuits, but the reality is that legal action can be a time-consuming, expensive, and mentally draining process. Leverage the skills you learn in this chapter and others to seek out a new workplace so you're not having to navigate a difficult situation for years to come.

Later in this chapter, I'll give you the tools you need to find a better job (we're talking needle-nose pliers, cordless drill, hydraulic torque wrench, the works) and ensure you have what you need to make more money sustainably.

TRAP NO. 5: UNDERVALUING YOUR TIME

If we zoom way out—like, all the way out, until we're in outer space sittin' on satellites and sippin' rosé as we look down on planet Earth—any income you generate in the United States falls into one of two categories: earned income or investment income.

Earned income is money you earn through labor. This includes wages, which are the dollars you make as an employee, and it also includes non-employment income, the hodgepodge of money you make outside of formal employment. Non-employment income is the money you get from walking dogs on Rover, or delivering groceries on Instacart, or the 20 bucks your grandpa slipped you for mowing the lawn back when you were a teenager, or the fees you charge your customers as a masseuse or a graphic designer.

Since earned income requires our time, and time is very limited, we must ensure we're getting as much as we can out of every hour that we work. You can certainly make more money by working more hours, but you can only take that so far before you run out of hours and are on the verge of a meltdown (often accompanied by a money malaise–driven shopping spree). Instead, focus on making more money *per hour*, which increases your take-home pay without taking up more of your precious time.

In business, the metric for this is **effective hourly rate**. Companies measure productivity by determining how much revenue each hour of a worker's time produces, then adjust resources accordingly. It can be helpful for you to adopt a similar mentality with your own time.

TEA

Try this: Calculate your effective hourly rate. Look back at your budget or pay stubs to determine how much disposable income you made last month. Then, divide this by the number of hours you labored last month to make that income. (Include hours spent on commuting, shopping for work clothes, venting with your co-workers after-hours, and Sunday scaries.) This is how much money you're currently getting in return for an hour of your life.

Effective hourly rate helps ensure that you're being paid for the value, knowledge, and experience you provide. A plumber will charge you $400 to fix the leaky pipe in your kitchen sink, even if the job only takes five minutes, because they have the knowledge and skills to do so, and you deem those skills valuable at the time because you want to stop wearing galoshes in your kitchen ASAP. This exchange of money for skilled labor is how earned income works throughout our lives, and there are several strategies for increasing it that we'll cover later in this chapter.

There's also **investment income**, sometimes called passive income, which is money you earn without working (I'll take one in every color, please). In earned income, the money is generated from your time, but in investment income, the money is generated from your *assets*. Assets include things like investments, real estate, and intellectual property.

Personal finance culture encourages us to sock our money away in assets now, with the hope that these investments will increase in value over time (historically, they usually do) and provide us with a future source of income that doesn't involve working. In retirement lore, the ideal outcome is for your assets to produce enough investment income to cover all your expenses, eliminating the need to keep working for money.

There's plenty to say about both of these income categories, so we'll spend this chapter vibing on earned income to get the money rolling in, then spend the next chapter vibing on investment income so you know where to stack the cash.

TRAP NO. 6:
OVERLOOKING OTHER ASPECTS OF COMPENSATION

We love income. It's also only one component of compensation. There are other work benefits besides wages that can improve your quality of life.

Good health insurance is compensation. Fertility benefits are compensation. More paid time off is compensation. A professional development stipend is compensation. If your job has benefits, make sure you know what those benefits are and use them to your full advantage. Go back and actually bother to read your company's employee handbook (*gay gasp*), then sign up for all the perks and things that are available to you. Familiarize yourself with these perks so that, when you're negotiating a new job offer, you know what other benefits might still be on the table when the company tells you they can't come up any more in salary.

Alternative forms of compensation include:

- Annual bonus
- Performance bonus
- Additional paid time off
- A personal development stipend
- Volunteer time off
- Commuting allowance
- Remote workdays
- Other stipends for childcare or wellness

Example: When I changed industries and jumped from professional copywriter to media editor, I discovered I really enjoyed journalism. I was a little green on the technical parts of the job, though (translation: bad at grammar), so I enrolled in night school to improve my craft in writing and video editing. My company had a professional development stipend, so I asked my manager about it, then pitched HR on covering some of my tuition, explaining how I would bring my upgraded skills back to the job. We created agreed-upon deliverables, I took and passed my classes, and I got $1,500 of my continuing education covered along the way.

Take advantage of your work perks. Use up those vacation days and leverage every benefit that is available to you in your compensation package.

TEA

Try this: Look at all the aspects of your compensation beyond income. Then, consider some of the other aspects we've listed here. Is there an opportunity to request additional compensation other than income? Jot down some ideas now, and later in this chapter we'll go over how to make the ask.

THE REMOTE WORK RENAISSANCE

What to Consider

Remote work has been around for decades, but it was the work-from-home directives of the COVID-19 pandemic that really pushed it mainstream.

For some, a remote job is the top priority, because there's nothing better than still being in bed at 8:56 a.m., then arriving on time for a nine o'clock meeting (or maybe you're just allergic to open-concept offices). For others, remote work is a hard no because it's overly isolating. Pursue the work arrangement that aligns with your strengths and overall goals.

What to consider:

- **Kind of a compensation bump in that it saves you money.** There's no dress code from the waist down, you'll be less likely to eat out for lunch each day, and you won't have a commute.

- **Frees up more time.** You can get your laundry done during the day. You can work on a side project during your lunch break. Time that would have been spent commuting can be used for exercising, socializing, or relaxing. For many people, this extra time freedom is more compelling than a higher salary.

- **Might be more challenging to move up.** A study from 2023 found that remote workers were happier and less stressed than in-office workers, but also 24 percent less likely to be promoted.[8] If you work remotely, you'll need to make extra effort to be heard and seen as an emerging leader. Get that digital footprint up: Piss on every Slack channel, drop a thumbs-up emoji on every support ticket, and schedule those virtual coffee chats. Make your presence known.

- **Can enable more travel.** With remote work, you don't need to wait until vacation to see a different part of the world, and this perk might appeal to you. You can go visit family and friends and stay for a week or two while also getting your work done, which for many is a huge plus. If going abroad, check in with your company's HR department, as there might be some legal limitations on how long you can be working in another country without a visa.

TRAP NO. 7: LETTING YOUR CAREER BECOME TOO MUCH OF YOUR IDENTITY

Queer people often yearn for approval, and work can turn into an outlet to pursue this feeling. We sometimes overcompensate at work and make it a large part of our identity because we crave stability. It can then start to feel like we're stuck, especially if management is taking advantage of us.

CONTENT WARNING: IN THE FOLLOWING TESTIMONY, A QUEER PERSON DESCRIBES THINKING ABOUT SELF-HARM.

John, 35, Rotterdam (formerly lived in Maryland): *I had a boss in the Coast Guard who was a real piece of work. I managed 87 vessels and about 100 projects at any given time, and he wanted status updates for all of them—three times a day. It was high-stress, all the time. I slowly spiraled downwards. I began feeling suicidal. I didn't know what to do because the person in charge of me was two ranks my senior and directly affected my ability to have a future in the Coast Guard. That whole situation made me realize that if you work for a large organization, they don't care about you as a person. They know you as an employee number, and at the end of the day you're the only one who can take care of yourself.*

When work is your identity, it means you're not actively exploring and defining your own identity for yourself. Your identity gets wrapped up in work, this thing you spend a lot of your time doing (which is also quite influential because it gives you money).

Eventually, it feels scary to seek out new opportunities or a career change, because doing so would mean abandoning a large part of your identity. Society further reinforces this; "What do you do for work?" is often one of the first questions we're asked when meeting new people, and our answer gives listeners context on how to relate to us. (Try *not* asking this question the next time you go to a social function and see if it feels unusual or different.)

The problem with making work your identity is that your company probably doesn't give a shit about you. Employees come and go, we're cogs in someone else's machine, and at nearly every company the goal is to get as much work out of employees as possible for as little money as possible, because that's capitalism 101.

You might be rewarded for your loyalty with promotions or moving up the management ladder, but it's important that you not let a company's culture become *your* culture. (And if you want to create a machine of your own one day, I take you through the basics of entrepreneurship in chapter 8.)

We like queer ambition, so please focus on doing the tasks that you were hired to do. But don't let your current job become so much of who you are that it bleeds into your free time (which is also wealth) and close yourself off to future opportunities.

YOUR "INCREASE MY INCOME" ACTION PLAN

There are five different categories of income all LGBTQ+ people should know about. Even if all of your income only comes from one category, it's important to have a foundational understanding of these other categories to protect yourself from misleading advice. A great money tip for one person might be totally irrelevant to you, because we all make money in different ways and have completely different lives.

We want to get an overview of what categories of income comprise your monthly earnings, along with what action steps you can take to get those numbers up. Get out your trusty notepad or spreadsheet and create seven rows and three columns. Give yourself plenty of space, as you'll be writing in the second and third columns. For now, label the columns as shown on the next page:

Income Category	Sources	Current Monthly Income	Action Steps
TOTAL			

To better understand all the income options available to you, I've organized this full spectrum of moneymaking possibilities into something I like to call the **income stream rainbow.**

The income stream rainbow buckets income into five stripes. Two of these stripes are **earned income**, which is money you make from work. The remaining three stripes refer to **investment income**, which is money you make from assets. Some people build monetary wealth solely through work, and some solely through assets, but for many of us the winning formula is to cultivate both earned income and potential investment income throughout our lives.

There's a lot to say about earned income and investment income, so we'll spend the remainder of this chapter focused on developing an action plan for your earned income, then focus more on the investment income side of the income stream rainbow in chapter 6.

STRIPE NO. 1: WAGES

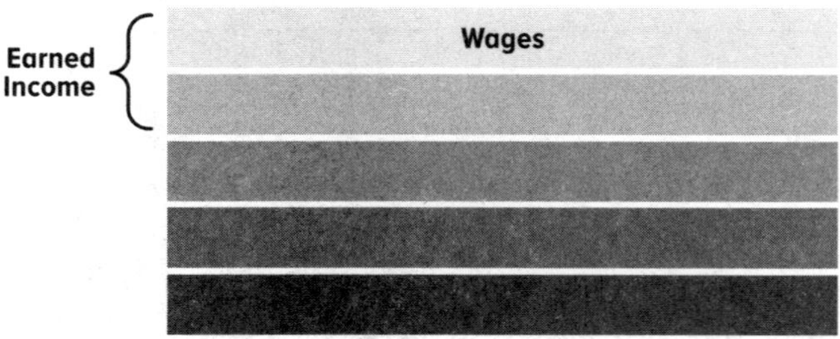

Wages refer to any type of employment income. This is money you were paid by an employer in the form of a salary, hourly rate, tips, commissions, or bonuses. Wages are the most common income source; they're how three in five working Americans get paid, according to a McKinsey survey from 2022.[9]

To be clear, "employee" isn't a mood. It's a worker classification. If you're an employee, your company covers part of your taxes, you're eligible for benefits like health insurance and vacation time, and you receive a W-2 tax form at the end of each year.

Action: In row 2 of your Action Plan, in the Income Category column, write "Wages." In the Sources column, write down the sources of your wages. In the Current Monthly Income column, write down how much money these sources currently bring in each month.

When you want to increase your wages, the most common strategies for doing so are to either get a raise or land a better-paying job.

OPTION 1: MAKE MORE MONEY AT YOUR CURRENT JOB

If you have a job, and you like it (or are neutral about it, that's fine, too), I want you to explore your options for more compensation at that existing job first.

The most straightforward path to achieving this is through promotion or a raise. What's the next role at the company, and what is required to be promoted to that role? (And . . . do you *want* that job?) If the answer is yes, have an honest conversation with your manager about your goals and ask for their help developing an action plan that will get you there.

If the company has career planning resources, look up your current role as well as the next role up in the food chain. Pay attention to the key responsibilities of your role, and document how you've delivered on these throughout the year. Make it undeniable that you've not only delivered on your current job description, but you are also already exhibiting behaviors that are a part of the next job description. You're making the case that you are the right person for the next role, and when that role becomes available you should be the person moved into that position (and compensated accordingly). Do this rigorously but also dispassionately to ensure your overcompensation triggers don't turn your pursuit of a promotion into your entire personality.

TEA

If you have a common job title, look up online what the typical salary range is for your title. If your current compensation is well below that range, you might be able to use it as negotiating leverage.

This approach serves a great litmus test to determine whether your company has your back or not. You'll see firsthand whether your company develops and promotes employees like it says it does. If the next job turns into a dangling carrot, or seems like it won't happen anytime soon, it's time to move on.

Sometimes there isn't a clear path to promotion—for example, working at a small business that doesn't have or need multiple layers of management—so you'll have to get scrappy, ask directly what it would look like to increase your compensation, and perhaps pitch a win/win solution. Resist the urge to threaten ("Pay me more, or else I'm leaving!" and then flipping the table reality TV confrontation–style would be a no-go); by sharing your goals, you're already gently telegraphing that you're not satisfied with your current earnings. It's expensive and annoying for employers to replace employees, so if your employer values your loyalty, it might be willing to work with you.

Negotiating is one of the most effective ways to increase wages throughout your career. Even a one-time salary negotiation of a few thousand dollars can make a big difference in your overall budget and wealth-building efforts (and there's nothing a career coach loves more than talking about the cost of *not* negotiating, usually in a LinkedIn post). It can also be nerve-wracking, but that's a discomfort worth leaning into: Research from CareerBuilder found that 73 percent of employers would be willing to negotiate salary, but that 55 percent of employees never ask.[10] Of the ones who do negotiate, a separate study found that 85 percent of employees got at least some of what they asked for.[11] As LGBTQ+ people, we sometimes don't negotiate because we don't think we're worth it, another homophobic thought pattern that holds you back from earning what you deserve.

It's typically tougher to negotiate at an existing job (we'll get to negotiation tactics for new job offers momentarily) because it's easy for HR to say "Sorry, not in the policy!" and then throw cold water on your money goals, ice bucket challenge–style (but not on video, so you don't even get the social media oohs and aahs). Instead, pitch a set of benchmarks that are a win for the company and would merit a bonus or salary bump for you. Outline a scenario in which you've helped the company achieve a financial or operations goal that wouldn't have happened otherwise, then reverse-engineer how you'll get there.

A few tips:

Financial gain is the easiest pitch. Connect the dots for your employer. Explain how your proposed additional effort would result in more money for the company (it has to be something above and beyond your job description). Illustrate how your efforts will more than cover the cost of your compensation bump.

No money to spare? Pitch other forms of compensation. If the company budget is already locked down tight, focus on other ways you could negotiate more compensation. Some extra vacation time? A continuing education stipend so you can acquire new skills and improve on the company's dime? Refer back to the compensation items we listed earlier in the chapter for inspiration. One reason you might find success here is that larger companies tend to regulate their salary bands carefully for equity reasons, but might be more lax with stipends or bonuses for their star employees.

Negotiate title. If you're not getting anywhere, see if there's an option to negotiate a better title. By doing this, you're laying groundwork for your next job. "Director" gets more recruiter eyeballs than "Manager," even when candidates have similar skill sets and work histories. Silly, but true. If you plan to be an employee for a while in your career, resist the urge to make up titles; employers get confused when your résumé says you were "Chief Sugar Rush Officer" at an ice cream shop for eight months. Being boring and direct with titles can help you make more money in the long run.

Action: Assess your options for making more money at your current job. If you see an opportunity, identify steps you can take to pursue this opportunity and list these steps in the Action Steps column of the Wages row of your grid. (Leave space in this box; you'll also put your action steps from the next option in the same spot.)

OPTION 2: GO GET A NEW JOB

If you're not currently employed, or your job sucks, or you've realized your current job is a compensation dead end (and not a cute, cul-de-sac dead end with good landscaping and a roundabout; more like an "unfinished road" dead end), your quickest path to making more money is to go get a new job with a different company. Consider this strategy if one or more of the following statements is true:

- Your workplace isn't welcoming to you as an LGBTQ+ person.
- Your work, people, and/or commute are draining to the point of money malaise (don't coddle yourself here; this is different from work being boring or having an annoying coworker).
- You'd have to take on way more work and responsibility to make more money and have decided that's not how you want to define wealth.
- You're already in "final boss" position because the company has no higher roles.
- Your company has been stringing you along on opportunities and it's not worth it anymore.
- You know you're getting paid less than you should be for your position, based on market averages.

"Sara" (pseudonym), 31, Florida: *I was constantly told I was getting promoted. "It's happening." "It's coming." "We should not have hired you as low as we did." "Hold on one more year." By the time I left, almost every other person on my team had been promoted, or they* *had hired an external person significantly above me. I was publicly beloved, and would be given workplace awards, but was weirdly still isolated. I was like "I can't do this anymore."*

There's a reason job hopping has become mainstream career advice: It works. A Pew Research Center study found that 60 percent of workers who had moved to a new employer in the last year reported a real wage increase ("real wage increase" is your wage growth after inflation gets factored in), compared to 47 percent for those who had the same job.[12] Job hopping also helps you pinpoint what you like and don't like about your industry, which helps you gravitate toward work you're good at and enjoy doing. And if another company will pay you thousands or tens of thousands more per year to do a similar job . . . why *wouldn't* you go after that? Consider that your next job might leverage your skills for a totally different industry, and that's okay.

Ironically, successful job hunting involves a whole set of skills that are often unrelated to the actual job. Three in five job openings are found through networking, not online.[13] For larger companies, many résumés are put through applicant tracking systems (ATS), which use software to give résumés an initial score based on factors like keywords. And in a job interview, the interviewer usually forms their opinion of the candidate from the first few responses. Sharpening up your networking, résumé, and interviewing skills can help you get more job offers.

JOB HUNTING IS BASICALLY A PAGEANT NOW, SO PUT ON A SHOW

At any given time, millions of Americans are looking for new jobs, and things can get pretty cutthroat out there (not quite "sudden death vogue-off to snatch the trophy at the function" cutthroat, but close). We want to ensure you have plenty of tricks up your sleeve to crush this catwalk. Know and improve these "job-getting skills" so you can grow your salary and career over time.

Listings and networking. Many job openings don't ever get listed online. Ask people in your network if they know of anyone who is hiring (do this on the DL if you have a job currently to avoid awkwardness) and get on the radar of recruiters whose entire jobs are to find great candidates for companies.

Résumé and/or portfolio. Your résumé is not a summary of your past work experience; it's a marketing document. Through outlined bullets and boring fonts, your résumé should tell a story—the amazing, Oscar-winning story that you and this company have intersected in this exact moment and found love. Tailor your résumé to fit the job, and if you're not getting traction, consider hiring a résumé writer who specializes in your industry (this is one scenario in which spending money has high potential for ROI). If you work in a creative field, get into the habit of documenting your best work somewhere online so it can serve as a portfolio.

Interview styles. Interview skills help you increase your effective hourly rate, and they're universal across many types of industries and lines of work. One increasingly common interview style to test for problem-solving skills is the behavioral interview. "Tell me about a time when you disagreed with a team member and how you resolved it." "Tell me about a time you juggled multiple projects and how you handled it." These are tricky questions that can catch you off guard if you're not prepared.

A popular strategy for navigating behavioral interviews is to use the **STAR method**, created by leadership consulting firm DDI.[14] It goes like this:

- **Situation:** Set the stage. What was the problem?
- **Task:** Explain the task you were given.
- **Action:** With the task at hand, describe the actions you took. (This walks the interviewer[s] through how you make decisions.)
- **Result:** Summarize the results of the actions that were taken.

Here's how Marek, who's hunting for a higher-paying job, might utilize the STAR method effectively in an interview response.

> "(S) Our team was down two people going into the busiest quarter of the year. (T) As the leader of our group, I knew it would be important to maintain week-by-week efficiency. (A) I closely tracked availability and time-off requests, then developed a plan for who would do what work each week. (R) We hit our goals for the quarter and also developed a better time-off procedure to keep our department running smoothly moving forward."

Don't give the first number. Sharing this as an interview skill rather than a negotiation skill because you might get asked what your salary requirements are in the very first interview. If the interviewer asks about your salary requirements, say, "I'd be more comfortable discussing that when an offer's on the table." Alternatively, if the company already listed a salary range in the application, position it that the higher end of their range overlaps with the lower end of what you're looking for.

For example, if the range listed is \$60,000 to \$80,000, say, "I'm currently interviewing for roles that have an annual salary range of \$80,000 to \$100,000." Yes, this is lying, and yes, I'm going to hell for endorsing lies, but according to some people's rules I'm going to hell no matter what for being gay, so let's at least get you paid more in the meantime.

If your job offer has a higher compensation package, well done! Just play it cool, boy . . . reeeeal cooool. (*Sings the jazzy* West Side Story *tritone riff*) Know that this moment is often *the best* window of opportunity to negotiate because you have the leverage. The new company wants you, and they probably want to get this position filled ASAP so that they can stop recruiting and start getting results. You have the upper hand in this moment—confront your fears and negotiate!

Ask for that salary increase. If all else fails, go for a signing bonus. This is one of the most common compromises, and it immediately puts some extra money in your pocket.

TEA

Phone a friend. If you're nervous about negotiating, and think you're getting close to a job offer, call a friend and roleplay the negotiation ask a few times to practice getting the words out. This can help you refresh on a skill you probably don't use that often, but can be very influential for your money and quality of life.

Action: Determine if you should start looking for a new job where you'll be an employee. If the answer is yes, identify what steps you want to take and which "job-getting" skills you should shore up, then document these action steps in the Wages row of your grid (the same place you put any "current job" action steps). It's okay to have both current job and new job action steps and be working on them concurrently.

STRIPE NO. 2: SELF-EMPLOYMENT INCOME

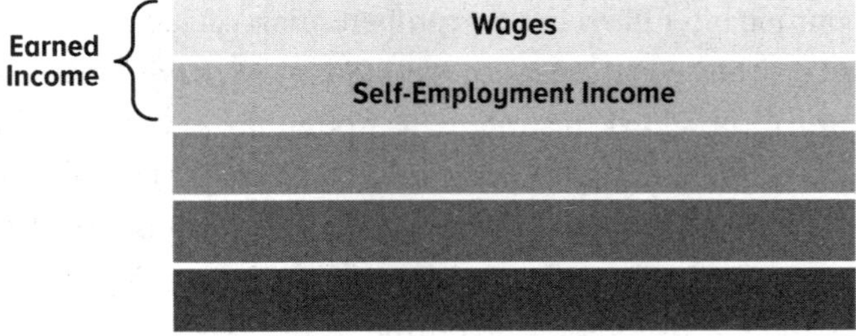

Self-employment income is an umbrella term that refers to two types of earnings: independent contractor work and sole proprietorship.

Independent contractor income refers to income you received from a company *without* being an employee. You wrote articles for a local magazine and were paid per story—independent contractor. You're a fire breather (omg, cool!) who gets hired by the state fair to do a number on stage before the concert starts—independent contractor. You sign up to drive for Uber or Lyft, safely shepherding queers from their social functions back to their neighborhoods—independent contractor. You post content on social media or a blog, which a company then monetizes against to make money and pays you a cut of the revenue—independent contractor. Independent contractors receive a 1099 tax form from a company by January 31 if the company paid them $600 or more the year prior.

There's also **sole proprietorship**, which refers to income you received directly from customers. You gave your neighbor's kid guitar lessons each week and were paid $120 a month via Venmo—sole proprietor. You made queer lapel pins and sold them on an Etsy shop—sole proprietor. You shoveled the snow off a little old lady's driveway for ten bucks and a ziplock bag of homemade chocolate chip cookies—sole proprietor. Sole proprietorship is a type of business, but it's also the default category the IRS uses to classify this money when you don't have a formal business set up yet. (Independent contractor work is technically categorized as self-employment, too, for reference.)

Sole proprietors might receive a 1099 tax form if they used a payment processor (PayPal, Stripe, Square, etc.) throughout the year to accept payments. Cash, meanwhile, is harder for the IRS to track and assess taxes on, which is one reason it's still common. I really don't recommend not paying your taxes (*IRS gorgon breathing down my neck as I type*), but the IRS can only tax what it can track, so I will let you decide how you want to interpret that.

TEA

Set aside some self-employment income for taxes. Giving you this tax tip now because I've watched too many people step in side hustle dogshit over the years. If you make money as an independent contractor or sole proprietor, remember that taxes are *not* being taken out—but you'll still owe tax on this money at the end of the year. Set some of your earnings aside for taxes throughout the year so that you don't find yourself in a hole when tax time rolls around.

Independent contractors and sole proprietors don't have the same cushy perks as employees, but they do have more creative control and freedom over their work. Interestingly, independent contractors in the previously mentioned McKinsey survey said they were more optimistic about the future, despite having less predictable sources of income. You can do independent contractor or sole proprietor work on the side for a few hours a week, or make it a full-time commitment, and if it's something you want to do consistently, you can always decide to officially form the business later.

Action: In row 3 of your Increase My Income action plan, put "Self-Employment Income" in the Income Category column. Name any sources of self-employment income you currently have in the Sources column. Then add up how much these sources bring in each month and put that number in the Current Monthly Income column.

HOW TO INCREASE SELF-EMPLOYMENT INCOME

If a day job isn't available, or it isn't providing you what you need, self-employment income can help you make more money. About fifty-eight million Americans work as independent contractors and sole proprietors in a wide variety of arrangements, but their work generally falls into three main categories: the gig economy, the creator economy, and products. As you read, decide if one of these categories appeals to you.

CATEGORY NO. 1: THE GIG ECONOMY

In the gig economy, you're offering a trade. A tradesperson is someone who has a skill and barters that skill for money. If you have existing professional skills, your hours are more valuable to certain people or companies, so you'll be able to charge a higher rate. I like to subcategorize trades based on how much work you're doing for your client; here are some distinctions between common terms.

Freelancing. You do the work on behalf of your client and provide the equipment necessary to do the job. If you're a photographer, and someone hires you to take photos at their event, you bring your camera, take photos, edit them, and deliver the finished product in exchange for money.

Consulting. Consulting is different in that you offer your client your expert opinion and recommendations based on their unique situation, then step out and let them implement. If you're a photographer and a small business doesn't have the budget to hire a photographer regularly, offer them a private lesson and recommendations for how their employees can do it themselves. You share your insights, but it's on your client to implement what they've learned.

Coaching and teaching. Coaching and teaching are similar to consulting, but with extra support and accountability. For many clients, the value of the service isn't just your expert knowledge; it's also about you keeping them accountable to reaching their goals. I pay the personal trainer once a week because, when left to my own devices, my motivation fades. I'll do one setup of bicep curls at the gym, then watch TV for ten minutes. Then I leave. But not before getting the smoothie from the juice bar (with extra peanut butter) on my way home.

If you don't have a trade or a skill, there are still opportunities to participate in the gig economy. Take surveys. Become a virtual assistant. Go participate in studies. Donate sperm or plasma. Offer handyman services. Be that sign-flipper on the corner of that busy intersection and throw in some spins and dips while you're at it. There are plenty of ways to trade time and labor for extra coins.

CATEGORY NO. 2: THE CREATOR ECONOMY

You also have the creator economy, which is all about monetizing *attention*. Creators develop and broadcast their ideas and opinions, and the subsequent audience they attract as a result becomes an asset. Here are the common ways this attention gets converted into income.

Ad revenue sharing. Platforms like YouTube give you the option to let ads play during your videos. As thanks for making and uploading the video, YouTube splits the ad revenue with you (as of this writing, 55 percent of the ad money goes to the creator, and YouTube keeps the rest). The more eyeballs you can get on your videos, the more the ads play, and the more money you make. You see this on blogs, too, when display ads show throughout the webpage. The more ads are shown, the more income gets generated, which is why some of these damn recipe sites feel like landing a helicopter in a hailstorm to get to the ingredients list.

Brand partnerships and sponsorships. Companies want to get their products in front of the right audience, but consumer trust in ads and commercials has been declining for years. When social media took off, companies capitalized on the ability to market to influencers' audiences directly, and influencers gobbled these dollars up (because if posing for a photo while holding a juice could cover next month's rent, you would probably do it, too). For several years, influencer marketing was the Wild West, with no real alignment on industry standards for what creators should be paid. Things have since become more structured with performance metrics beyond follower count, but creators are still very in demand. If you know how to attract an audience, that audience is an asset, and companies might pay you to work with you and get in front of your followers or subscribers.

Intellectual property and subscriptions. Is it hot in here, or are you just channeling your inner entrepreneur? (*Insert star-eyed smiling emoji*) Creators can also invite fans and followers to pay them directly, whether it be through merchandise, online courses, videos, or ebooks. This is called **intellectual property (IP)**, and it can be a great way to leverage your time, because you only produce the content once, but can sell it again and again. Since creators are pumping out so much content anyway, many of them sell copies of their best IP for money. Or they lease access to their best IP to consumers in the form of subscriptions. If you subscribe to a Substack newsletter, Patreon account, or OnlyFans channel, you're paying a fee for access to someone else's intellectual property, the platform takes a small-ish cut, and the creator gets the rest of the money.

Creator culture overlaps a lot with general entrepreneurship best practices, so we'll touch on it more in chapter 8.

CATEGORY NO. 3: PRODUCTS

Wares. Trinkets. Gear. Tchotchkes. Stuff. You make it, they buy it, you get paid. Products often require more skin in the game from day one. There might be upfront costs for materials and inventory, and then there's all the time you spend making the product itself. If you're putting in all this effort, and barely making any money on the back end, it's not an income stream; it's a hobby.

Keep these principles in mind when exploring craftsmanship as an additional income stream:

Cost of goods. How much is it costing to make the product? Know these numbers well. You might be breaking even or losing a little money at the outset, which is fairly common; as you gain traction, raising your prices can help you make more money.

Product-market fit. Do people want this product? Where are they currently going to get it? What makes you different? Do research so that you don't end up making a product nobody wants to buy.

Expenses tracking. Even if you don't have a formal business, you can claim self-employment expenses on your taxes, which will reduce your taxable income. Keep receipts and records of all your expenses so you can submit them when filing your taxes.

ONE SKILL, ENDLESS POSSIBILITIES

Taste the rainbow, baby: You can package and offer your skills in a variety of different ways. Let's look at how someone with a background in nutrition could leverage their extra time using each of the approaches described above to drum up some independent contractor income.

- **Freelancing:** You cook your client healthy meals each week, they swing by and pick the meals up, and they Venmo you for your service.
- **Consulting:** You give your client a private lesson, workshop, or consultation on how to do meal prep in their own kitchen (I actually purchased this from a personal trainer friend once and still use those cooking tips today).
- **Coaching:** You give someone your healthy meal prep blueprint, then connect with them once a week to see how it's going and keep them accountable.
- **Ad revenue share:** You start a blog and YouTube channel for your healthy recipes, then run display ads on the content to generate residual income.
- **Brand deals and sponsorships:** You partner with a brand and use their items in your videos. They get exposure to an engaged audience (your audience), you get money.
- **Subscriptions:** Someone pays a monthly subscription for your

Patreon, where you share your best videos and tips and do occasional livestreams.

- **Information products:** You publish a cookbook.
- **Physical products:** You invent the perfect avocado paring knife that will finally stop all of us from accidentally sending ourselves to the hospital.

Action: Brainstorm one or more ways to introduce self-employment income into the picture and write down action steps you see to take in the Action Steps column. Focus on approaches that leverage your resources, which might include time, knowledge, or experience.

HOW MUCH IS ENOUGH?

Exciting stuff, right? Let's make more MONEY! We want to make sure we're not overworking ourselves, though. As you do this work, consider also taking a moment to journal about what you're *not* willing to compromise on for the sake of making more money.

Would you take a $50,000 raise at a new job if it meant a two-hour commute each way, five days a week? Does the big promotion involve 70 percent travel? If taking a client meant not seeing your family during the holidays, would that be a deal-breaker—or a welcome distraction? The hustle for more money is intoxicating and measurable, but we want to make sure we're not sabotaging the other facets of what we call wealth along the way.

Challenge yourself to define your boundaries regarding work. Or consider giving yourself a cap on modified saving rate, the number we calculated in chapter 3, so that you don't forget to live a great queer life along the way.

∘ ∘ ∘

Income is the lifeblood of your money goals. And since work is one of the most time-consuming activities you do week in and week out, we should make sure you're doing everything you can to make this time commitment both lucrative and sustainable.

We've now given you sets of strategies to both lower your expenses and increase your earnings. As this gap between income and expenditures gets bigger, you'll have additional funds in the picture each month, and some of this money can be used to help secure your financial future *without you having to do anything else.*

That's the power of investing the difference, the last element of our 7-word plan, and it can make you money while you sleep.

6

INVESTING

Plump Up Your Ass(ets) and Secure Your Future

Hear ye, hear ye: You don't have to give a shit about the stock market to make money from it.

You can care more about who went home last week on *Survivor* than your investments. You can care more about your acrylics than your investments. You can care more about the color coordination of your furniture than your investments. The only catch is that you need to understand *how* investments work so you can leverage them and have more money in life.

Of course, no one told me this when I was younger, because no one told me anything about investing, or money at all, or being queer. Like many of us, I had to figure a lot of it out myself. And once I realized that my grandpa was probably wrong when he'd quip that the stock market is where people end up losing all their money, I walked into my local brokerage (this was in the flip phone days, banking apps didn't exist yet), opened an account, and began investing in individual stocks.

I then went on an obsessive fact-finding spree—think flashy montage, with dramatic orchestral music throughout. "What's the P/E ratio?" "When's the next investor call?" "Warren Buffett didn't eat a sausage, egg, and cheese at McDonald's yesterday; should I sell everything off?" I wanted to know everything about every company I invested in to maximize my chances of success. I'd check my balances obsessively, have all the confidence in the world when they went up, be in a pissy mood when they went down, and react to hype by buying high and selling low. Looking back, I would have made more money had I just put things on autopilot from day one and never looked at my investments again.

What financially independent working-class people understand is that it's tough to get rich through hard work alone. Your *money* needs to be making money, too. When we put our money into a savings account, or invest it in the stock market, or buy a rental property, our money becomes an asset, and as we discussed in the previous chapter, assets can be used to make you additional money without additional work.

As you lower your expenses and increase your income, you will begin to create surplus in your monthly budget. One of the things I recommend you do with this money is put it in places where it can generate investment income with little or no additional effort. This is investing in a nutshell, and it's fairly straightforward. The reason it *feels* stressful and confusing is because the stock market is endlessly overhyped in the media, often with an extra spritz of fearmongering to keep us freaked out. As LGBTQ+ people, we are sometimes more risk-averse when it comes to money and stability, but it turns out there's both a method and a motivation to this madness.

Remember the 7-word plan for building wealth: lower expenses, increase earnings, invest the difference. In this chapter, we'll cover the only math you need to know to get excited about investing, how to slice through the hype, and what you should do to make your money grow while you sleep.

Investing Traps to Avoid

1. Never starting
2. Letting the stock market's ups and downs stress you out

3. Buying on hype
4. "Investing feels like gambling"
5. Thinking retirement accounts are the only way to invest
6. "I need a professional to help me with this stuff"
7. "I don't want to help big corporations I don't believe in"

TRAP NO. 1: NEVER STARTING

The reason we personal finance people are so pushy about you investing is because the earlier you start, the more time your money will have to compound and grow. And it's okay if you have very little to start with. Even $5 or $10 a month is better than nothing. Our goal is to build new thought patterns and behaviors around money so that they become habits over time.

Recall from chapter 3 Raye's decision to start early and put $250 per month into investments. After forty years, they'd have contributed a total of $120,000, but since the investments increased in value by 8 percent every year, they now have $805,270. Most of this money came through compounding and required no additional time or effort.

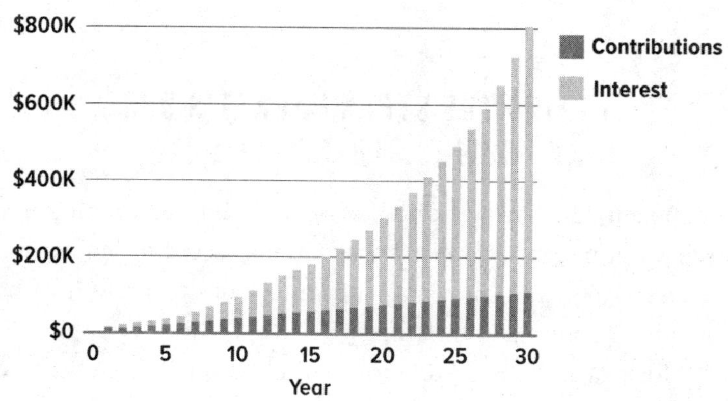

The earlier you start investing, the more time your money has to compound. The above example has a really long runway (forty years) for maximum drama, but investing would still be worth it if Raye had started later. They'd just need to contribute more than $250 per month to achieve the same results in the shorter timeframe. Here's what Raye would have to contribute to get to the same result of $805,270 by age 62 if starting later:

- Age 27 (35 years to compound): $375/month
- Age 32 (30 years): $560/month
- Age 37 (25 years): $885/month
- Age 42 (20 years): $1,410/month
- Age 47 (15 years): $2,375/month
- Age 52 (10 years): $4,450/month
- Age 57 (5 years): $11,000/month

Starting early is how lower- and middle-class people build monetary wealth. This is because their investments have more time to grow. If you can live a comfortable life in the present while also investing, you'll be building up an asset, one that can be a source of investment income in the future.

TRAP NO. 2: LETTING THE STOCK MARKET'S UPS AND DOWNS STRESS YOU OUT

No lies spoken, sis. The stock market is downright nauseating in the day-to-day, but in the long term it has a track record for going up, so we need a strategy that lets us take advantage of this growth without doomscrolling about it all the time.

Take, for example, the **S&P 500**, which is an index that tracks the stocks of the 500 largest companies in America. The S&P 500 goes up and down from year to year, but has grown an average of 10.27 percent per year since it was created in 1957. This is a pretty good return on investment for making a few transfers and then sitting on your ass the rest of the time, which is why we sometimes prioritize investing over other financial to-dos like paying off low-interest debt.

Stock market investing can be difficult to stomach at first, especially if you're not seeing the results you thought you would right away. In the long term, the odds get better and better that your money will grow. After one year, the chances of having a positive return on your money are about 70 percent. After five years, the odds go up to 80 percent; ten years, 94 percent; and after twenty years, nearly 100 percent, based on how things have gone in the past.

Despite these reassurances, money nausea often persists. So to remedy this seasickness, many investors use a secret weapon that puts Dramamine to shame: **dollar cost averaging**. In dollar cost averaging, you invest the same amount of money every month, regardless of whether the stock market is going up or down. This can help you opt out of the mental friction that comes with trying to time the market. If the stock market is up, you're happy anyway, and if the stock market is down, think of it as buying investments on sale.

TEA

Dollar Cost Averaging (DCA): Set it and forget it. In DCA, you contribute the same amount of money each month to your investments, regardless of stock market performance.

Dollar cost averaging helps you invest successfully without having to stare at charts and graphs all day. Many people have set up their dollar cost averaging once, dumped a slice of their income into investments year in and year out, never thought about it again, and become millionaires over time.

TRAP NO. 3: BUYING ON HYPE

The stock market has been a hype machine long before the internet ever came around. Part of understanding the investing landscape means understanding that investors are human, and humans are emotional.

Investor feelings can influence a stock's price, and sometimes these feelings are speculative, defining the stock's value by growth potential rather than actual profitability or market conditions. As a result, at any given time, some stocks are overvalued (aka overrated, as a sassy musical theater gay might say), meaning their price is probably higher than it should be given the company's performance. Other stocks are undervalued; they're hidden gems, durable and easy to understand, but lacking in bad boy rizz.

In **value investing**, investors focus on stocks or other investments they believe are undervalued, with the expectation that the price will go up later when others finally catch on.

TEA

Value investing: Great for people who love underdogs. In this traditional approach, you invest in companies or other opportunities based on performance, leadership, and market potential, with the belief that they're underhyped, and that other people will eventually see the light, too.

More recently, online forums and groups of users have gamed the market with a pump-and-dump strategy in which they collectively buy up a stock, inflate its price, then immediately sell it and run off (most commonly meme stocks and crypto scams). This leaves the investors who followed suit holding the bag as the stock price then craters. Resist the urge to invest your money on hype alone.

TRAP NO. 4: "INVESTING FEELS LIKE GAMBLING"

Although they might look similar on the surface, investing and gambling are different.

Gambling is designed for the house to win the majority of the time. That's the business model, and if it wasn't that way, casinos would go out of business. Gambling, like social media, relies on a rapid, dopamine-powered feedback loop to get you hooked.

Investing wouldn't be classified as gambling because the game is not inherently stacked in the house's favor. Investing is intended to be win/win. With stocks, if a company becomes more valuable, and you own shares (tiny pumpkin pie slices) of that company, it means your shares went up in value, too. With bonds, you're actually loaning money to the government or an organization, then charging interest on it. This interest pays out intermittently over the term of the bond, you get all your money back at the end of the term, and chances are low that the money you invested in high-quality bonds would be lost.

The reason investing *feels* like gambling is that there's potential for you to lose your money, and obviously no one wants that. We want to cultivate feelings of safety, and the risk that comes with investing can stress us out. Fortunately, it's easy to adjust your investments based on your appetite for risk.

TRAP NO. 5:
THINKING RETIREMENT ACCOUNTS ARE THE ONLY WAY TO INVEST

For many people, their first encounter with investing is when they get a retirement account, which is designed for setting aside money you ideally won't touch for decades ("You'll be glad you did this when you're in your sixties!" isn't the best positioning to get young adults excited about investing).

Retirement accounts are not the only way to invest, though. There are also brokerage accounts, in which you can buy a stock, sell it a year or month (or day) later, and put the money right back in your pocket if you want to. You can also invest in things like property or a business that produce additional income now rather than later. The goal of stock market investing is to grow a big stack of cash that can generate investment income later in life, but if you already have an asset, you might be able to start generating investment income from it now.

When you rent out an asset, like a house or a car, that cash flow is investment income. If you buy a Taco Bell franchise, and hire a staff to run it while you do nothing else, those profits are investment income (also, free Cheesy Gordita Crunches for life). For most, stock market investing has the lowest barrier to entry, so we'll give it extra attention in this chapter. Since our goal is to educate and empower LGBTQ+ people, we'll also briefly touch on other strategies along the way so you know what your options are.

TRAP NO. 6:
"I NEED A PROFESSIONAL TO HELP ME WITH THIS STUFF"

You don't! The category is confidence, remember? You can absolutely start investing today by yourself.

If you want to be totally hands-off, financial advisors and wealth managers can manage your investments for you. But despite their best intentions, financial advisors and wealth managers often don't do a better job than everyday investors, so they may not be worth the extra fees. You can do most or all of this selecting for yourself, and can automate your investing in just a few clicks, which frees up time to live your life. In recent years, "robo-advisors" have emerged as an alternative solution—simply tell the chatbot about your preferences and appetite for risk, and it'll pick out investments that align with your goals.

People are intimidated by investing because it feels like one more thing on your to-do list that will drain your time and energy. You really can automate this process, and later in this chapter I'll give you a hands-off approach that works for even the laziest investor (*raises hand*). This keeps you focused on what you can control, which is to maintain a healthy gap between income and expenses.

TRAP NO. 7: "I DON'T WANT TO HELP BIG CORPORATIONS I DON'T BELIEVE IN"

I hear you. A little due diligence on corporations' political giving can reveal whether an organization actually cares about queer people or not, and many of the largest publicly traded companies play both sides. It can feel out of alignment to invest in companies that are actively bankrolling anti-LGBTQ+ candidates or causes.

My advice is to channel your activism wisely. Publicly traded corporations are massive, and millions of people invest in their stocks every day. As long as we continue to live in a society powered by capitalism, these companies will be here to stay. Many people never start investing because the options they see in front of them are dissonant with their values. As a result, they miss out on personal finance engines that help you get more out of your money and work less in the future.

There's a way to do values-aligned investing, and we'll touch on it later in this chapter. First, let's go back to our Increase My Income action plan and pick back up where we left off.

YOUR "INCREASE MY INCOME" ACTION PLAN, CONTINUED

To review: Earned income is money you earn from work. Investment income is money you earn from assets. Now that we have more context about investing, we can revisit the income stream rainbow, talk about the different categories of investment income, and explain how they make you money.

Refer back to your Increase My Income action plan from chapter 5, which lined up with the income stream rainbow. By this point, it should look something like this.

Income Category	Sources	Current Monthly Income	Action Steps
Wages	Day job	$4,500	Negotiate WFH on Fridays Update LinkedIn profile
Self-Employment Income	Dog-sitting Donating plasma	$325	Create listing on Rover to sit more dogs
TOTAL			

Now that we understand what investments are, we can pick back up where we left off. Let's define each type of investment within the context of the income stream rainbow and look to see if you're currently generating income in any of these categories.

STRIPE NO. 3: INTEREST INCOME

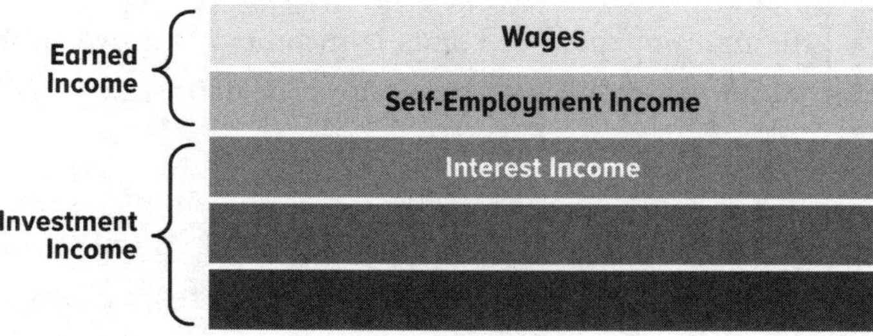

Interest income is income you make from money held in interest-generating investments. This is the most straightforward stripe in the income stream rainbow: The more money you put in the account and better the interest rate, the more income you produce. That's it!

Money can generate interest income when you store it in:

1. **High-yield savings accounts (HYSAs).** If you've been a good student and have stowed some cash in a HYSA, that money is making you money without having to do anything else. The money is FDIC-insured up to a certain amount (meaning you're safe even if the bank fails), and the bank pays you interest to keep it there. This interest counts as investment income.
2. **Certificates of deposit (CDs).** CDs are similar to savings accounts, but usually offer a better interest rate. The catch is that the money you deposit must be held for a set period of time, and if you withdraw your money before the CD matures, you'll pay a penalty that could negate most of your interest gains.
3. **Bonds.** If you're "grandma gave me a savings bond one year for Christmas" years old like I am, you might have heard the term "bond," but

not really understand what it is. A bond is when you loan money to a government or organization, and they promise to pay you back after a certain amount of time, with interest. That's right: IT'S DEBT (*death rattle sound effect*), but in this case *you're* the one collecting the interest. Bonds usually pay out interest twice a year.

Bonds have less growth potential than stocks, but they're also typically more stable, so they're a nice lower-risk option. Unlike stocks, the main purpose of bonds is income, not growth. Mainstream investing advice is to put more of your investments into bonds as you age to better protect yourself.

Action: In row 4, write down "Interest Income" in the Income Category column. Write down any current interest-generating accounts you have in the Sources column. Then, in the Current Monthly Income column, write down any income you are generating from interest each month (for example, the interest deposit you're getting in a HYSA at the end of each month). In the Action Steps column, jot down any actions you see to take.

STRIPE NO. 4: CAPITAL GAINS AND DIVIDENDS

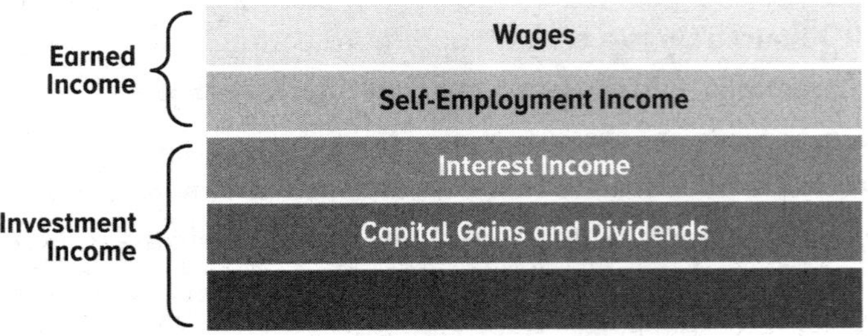

If you buy an asset, like a stock or a house, then sell it later for a higher price (which we like—that's the goal!), that difference is known as a

capital gain. The value of your assets can go up a little or a lot over time, but the capital gain doesn't technically happen until you've sold the asset. You get taxed on the capital gain the year you make the sale, since that's the year it's considered income.

If you bought a few shares of Apple or American Airlines (or Grindr, you do you, boo, the ticker is GRND), watched them go up in value, then sold them, that'd count as a capital gain. If you bought a house, lived in it, then sold it five years later at a higher price, that would also count as a capital gain. Collectibles are also considered assets, so if you bought first-edition *Pokémon* cards for three dollars a pack when you were a kid, then sold them today for thousands, that sale would be a capital gain (unless you're a dumbass like me and *threw all the cards away* during one of your temper tantrums about leaving your childhood behind . . .).

Some assets also pay **dividends**, which are when your assets share their profits with you from time to time.

TEA

Dividends: A strategy companies use to telegraph BDE (big dividend energy, obviously). When a company stock or asset pays dividends, it means the company distributes some of its profits back to you in the form of cash or additional stock. You can look up "stocks that pay dividends" for more information if this interests you.

In investing, there are your assets, and then there are also different types of *accounts* that can hold those assets. Let's now do an overview of both. First, here are the various assets that can produce capital gains.

1. **Stocks.** A stock is a tiny slice of a company. When you buy a share of a company, you, too, can say you own a microscopic, cell-sized

sliver of a corporation. If the value of the company goes up or down, your stock goes up or down, too. Publicly traded companies have to make their financial performance visible and available by law, which helps both Wall Street analysts and everyday investors like you and I make decisions.

2. **Bonds (again).** Wait—again? Yes, because outside of that interest income, the value of your bond might fluctuate a little, and if it matures or you sell it at a higher price than you bought it for, that's a capital gain. Bonds are a nice contrast to stocks because their prices are influenced by math, not investor tantrums, and there are limits as to how much they can fluctuate.
3. **Funds.** Ideally, we want to diversify our investments across a wide variety of assets, but it'd be quite the time suck to research hundreds of companies' stock performance. That's where funds come in: Funds are preset groups of stocks, bonds, or other assets that you can buy in shares. We love funds, because they provide exposure to many different types of investments all at once. Most funds come with fees, but for many of them the fees are minimal.

TYPES OF FUNDS

The most common types of funds are:

- **Index fund:** A fund whose holdings track a specific index of companies.
- **Mutual fund:** A fund that is more curated, so its entry fee is a little higher (it's like when drag brunch is ticketed). Mutual funds sometimes have investment minimums, higher maintenance fees, and sales fees.
- **Bond fund:** As its name implies, a bond fund holds various types of bonds from government and community organizations.
- **Target date fund:** A fund of stocks and bonds that is pegged to a target retirement date, and adjusts its holdings as you inch

closer to that retirement date. A true "set it and forget it" option that is popular for retirement accounts.

- **Exchange-traded fund (ETF):** A very popular option for individual investors—we're talkin' pink Power Ranger–popular. ETFs are traded on an exchange, just like a stock, and they tend to have lower fees.

  For example, if you wanted to put your money into the S&P 500 generally, without having to buy all 500 stocks individually, the Vanguard S&P 500 ETF (ticker: VOO) does that for you, at a very low fee of 0.03%. This is not an endorsement of VOO (I have to say that, legally). I just want you to know that funds like these exist, so if you don't want to think that hard, you can just invest in funds that are diversified, set up the automatic transfers, and get on with your life.

Funds are the easiest way to diversify your investments in the stock market, and you can start investing in them even if you only have $5 or $10 a month to work with at the start.

4. **Cryptocurrency.** The new kid on the block is cryptocurrency, which can be tough to get a handle on because it is both technical and wildly overhyped by extremely annoying people. Since some cryptocurrencies grew very quickly, their notoriety has attracted attention, particularly from queer people. One study found that queer people were less likely to have investing and retirement accounts, but were *more* likely to invest in cryptocurrencies than the general population (is it because of the *Matrix* vibes?), so let's calibrate on what the hell they really are.[1]

   Cryptocurrency is global digital currency. Crypto has become a popular way to buy things online without being tracked (similar to how you'd use cash offline to avoid being tracked), and users hold various **coins** in an account called a **wallet**. Enthusiasts call crypto "the future of money" because it imagines a world where banks and governments are cut out of the picture altogether. Critics say this is all hot air, that most cryptocurrencies fail the basics of value investing and have no actual worth, and that most or all of their pricing is based on hype. That certainly seems true at the time of this writing, because when crypto investors get spooked, prices plummet, but when they're confident, prices fly. Crypto gets flak for enabling illicit activities and emboldening cybercriminals, and it also gets flak for not being very green, since huge amounts of energy are needed to do the mining process.

Still, people were interested enough in cryptocurrency that they pushed to make it available on mainstream exchanges, and currently there are some funds that include Bitcoin. As the governance catches up, crypto will probably become increasingly mainstream. Prices are still quite volatile, so approach cryptocurrency with caution, with the understanding that the coins might be overhyped, similar to what happens with stocks.

5. **Real estate.** If you buy a home, it's an asset, and if you sell it for a higher price later, the difference between what you bought and sold it for is considered a capital gain. Since a home is an asset, it counts as an investment.

   The obvious perk of owning a home is that you can live in it. You can paint the walls (or knock them down and remodel) without the landlord losing their mind. Your mortgage payment will be the same each month, which can be attractive as inflation crawls along and rents across America continue to climb. Also, you can't throw a Halloween party in an index fund; a home is an investment you can utilize in your day-to-day life. The drawback is that houses can become money pits, both upfront and ongoing; things break, repairs take way longer and cost way more than expected, and that's just how it goes with homeownership sometimes.

   Can I say something? (*Reaches for talking stick again*) A *lot* of queer people have money malaise about homeownership. It feels too far away, like you need this stratospheric amount of money to get started. Look, I get that we can't buy homes as easily as our parents or grandparents could at our age. But if you follow the 7-word plan for building wealth, you're more likely to make and save the money necessary to turn your Zillow fantasy into reality. This also means making a conscious choice to kick your money malaise about it to the curb.

If you want to own real estate one day, your no. 1 priority should be to save up for a down payment. A common down payment for a house is 3 to 5 percent of the asking price. You'll also have closing costs, property taxes, home insurance, and, in most states, a real estate agent's fees. If your down payment is less than 20 percent of the asking price of the home, you'll need to pay for an extra insurance called private mortgage insurance (PMI), which is typically around $50 a month for every $100,000 you've borrowed (and continues until you've reached 20 percent ownership of the home). A lot of people take the PMI hit, though, because saving up enough money for a 20 percent down payment can take years. Your mortgage is a standalone loan; you don't need an investing account to have one.

Types of Capital Gains: Summary

- Stocks
- Bonds
- Funds
- Cryptocurrencies
- Real estate

Action: In row 5 of your Increase My Income action plan, write down "Capital Gains and Dividends" in the Income Category column. Then jot down what types of investments you have in the Sources column. (Leave some space in the Sources column; in the next part, we'll add more detail to this Sources box.)

"Great! So, uh, *where* do I put these investments? What buttons do I click?" Usually, investments must be made from accounts specifically designed for investing. You can't invest from a checking or savings account, and you can't go down to Wall Street shaking a $20 bill around and expect to buy something (except a hot dog, perhaps). Your investing money needs to be in either a retirement account or an investment account.

Here are the different ways you can hold these assets.

1. **Retirement accounts.** The 1970s were great for queer people: Harvey Milk became the first openly gay elected official in California, Divine ate dog shit on camera, and a new type of retirement account, the 401(k), was invented. The IRS wants us to save for retirement, so they offer tax perks within these retirement accounts, on the condition that you hold the money in the account until age 59.5. If you withdraw the money early, you pay a 10 percent penalty. (There are also ways around the age 59.5 thing, which we'll get to in chapter 9 if that is what's holding you back from saving for the future.)

   Common retirement accounts include:

   - **Employer-sponsored plans.** These are retirement plans that both an employee and their employer contribute to. They include the 401(k), 403(b), 457(b), and the Thrift Savings Plan. These plans transfer money from your paycheck into the account *before* taxes are taken out. The taxes are delayed, so instead of paying taxes on the money you earned this year, you'll pay taxes later when you actually withdraw the money (a withdrawal is called a **distribution**). Employer-sponsored plans have a cap on how much you can contribute each year, but the cap is high; it was $23,000 in 2024 ($30,500 if you were 50 or older), and any employer match doesn't count toward the limit. Consult https://nickwolny.com/book-resources for the most up-to-date limits.

- **Individual Retirement Accounts (IRAs).** If you don't have an employer, or your employer is a smaller business, it's no biggie. You can just open an IRA for yourself instead. There's the traditional IRA, the SIMPLE IRA, and the Simplified Employee Pension (SEP) IRA for self-employed people.
- **Roth accounts.** Plot twist: Employer-sponsored plans and IRAs have a doppelgänger called a Roth, in which you contribute after-tax dollars instead of pre-tax dollars. The trade-off is that, since you've already paid taxes on this money, you won't have to pay tax on future earnings. The **Roth IRA** is particularly special, and not just because Jujubee made a joke about it on television once. You can withdraw the money you contributed to a Roth IRA at any time, penalty-free, without having to wait until you're 59.5 years old. The Roth IRA has an income limit—it was $146,000 in 2024—but as mentioned, we have ways around this (legal ones, not sketchy mafia-speak).

Retirement accounts are good for building assets because their tax perks help you keep more of the money you earn, and while there is a penalty if you withdraw early, the long-term growth benefits outweigh these potential costs in most scenarios. If you change jobs, you can either keep your current employer-sponsored account or roll it over to your new employer.

2. **Brokerage accounts, investing apps, and crypto wallets.** As you can see, retirement accounts have a lot of rules and regulations since they give you tax breaks. But they're not your only option. You could also just let loose and start investing today using accounts that don't have any of these rules. These are the brokerage accounts we talked about earlier, and they're behind many of the investing apps we now see in our day-to-day lives.

Even if you've never used a brokerage account or investing app before, you've probably seen an advertisement for one: Robinhood, Acorns, Ellevest, Betterment, and Fidelity are a few of the most popular players. Opening a brokerage account is as straightforward as opening a checking account, and once it's live, you can deposit and withdraw money as desired, then use the funds in your account to buy and sell securities or cryptocurrencies.

TEA

Important: You have to invest the money that you deposit. If contributions go into your retirement or investment account and you don't invest them, the money sits there as cash instead of as stocks, bonds, and funds, so it won't grow. Don't make this mistake. Fortunately, it's easy to make both monthly deposits and monthly investments automatic, and most investing accounts give you clear step-by-step instructions to set this up.

When you sell investments for more than you paid for them, it's a capital gain, and when you sell for less than you paid, it's a **capital loss**, which sucks, but can be used to offset taxes on future years' capital gains. To encourage investors to hold investments longer and discourage market volatility, the IRS assesses different levels of capital gains tax based on whether or not you held an investment for at least a year.

3. **Tax-advantaged and tax-exempt accounts.** There's one other category of investing accounts to know about: tax-advantaged and tax-exempt accounts, which let your invested money grow tax-free as long as you spend it on certain qualifying expenses. They require a little more context on taxes, though, so we'll circle back to them in chapter 7.

Accounts for Capital Gains

- Retirement accounts (when you take distributions, though, that money is taxed as retirement distribution income at your ordinary income rate, not as a capital gain)

- Brokerage accounts, investing apps, and crypto wallets
- Tax-advantaged and tax-exempt accounts (more on these in the next chapter)

Action: Return to the Sources column in row 5 of your plan and specify which accounts you're currently holding investments in. If you've taken distributions from any retirement accounts, or sold assets from any of the other types of accounts, add those numbers together and write the total down in your Current Monthly Income column. Remember that capital gains are *only* considered income when you sell the investment, so if you're holding investments and not selling them, this number would be zero (and that's fine).

ALIGNING YOUR INVESTMENTS WITH YOUR VALUES

Earlier, we mentioned ethics as being a reason why people don't invest in Wall Street. The good news is you can still invest even if you don't want your money funding certain companies or industries. New ethically minded categories of investments have emerged in recent years; common names include "environmental, social, and governance (ESG) funds," "impact investing," "sustainable investing," and "socially responsible investing."

On the stock market, there are ETFs that focus on companies doing good for sustainability. In the bond market, there are green bonds, social bonds (which refer to socially conscious investments, not the warm fuzzies you have for your besties), and sustainability focused bonds. Just like how you use your dollars to shop local or visit a farmer's market, you can take a similar, values-driven approach with your investing efforts as well. (At one point there was even an LGBTQ ETF, the LGBTQ100, which screened companies to ensure they had pro-LGBTQ values, but it only operated for about a year.)

Since funds must actively screen their investments to determine whether they meet ESG requirements, they sometimes have higher fees. For many people, though, the extra fees are worth it for the peace of mind.

STRIPE NO. 5: OTHER PASSIVE INCOME

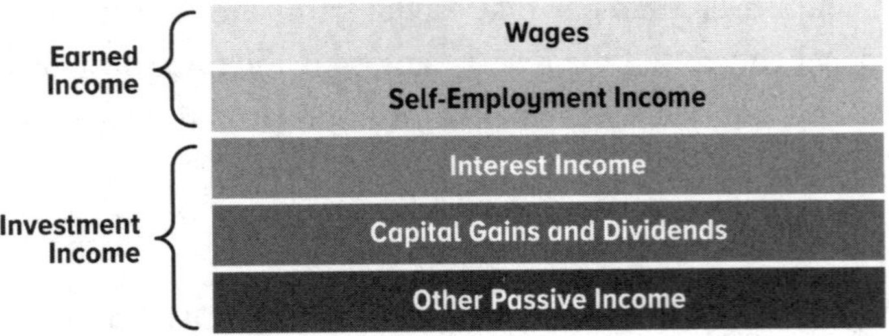

The last stripe of the income stream rainbow is a grab bag of passive income sources that don't fit into the above categories, but are classified as investment income.

Rental income. Think of rental income as "Airbnb for ______." Whether it's real estate or some other asset, the peer-to-peer (P2P) economy refers to renting out your property and receiving payments for it. For most, real estate comes to mind first: Buy a property, then rent it out. The pro is that you build wealth (and maybe even a little passive income each month) using someone else's rent payments. The con is that you'll have another job as landlord/landlady (landperson).

Rental property doesn't have to be real estate, though, and there's an Airbnb for everything these days. Turo lets you rent out a car. KitSplit lets you rent your camera stuff. BabyQuip lets you rent baby gear to families visiting town. The assets you already own can be helping other people and making you extra money when not in use.

Passive business ownership. If you own a business, but don't work in it on a regular basis, the profits that are coming to you are money you make from an asset without laboring, so that's investment income.

Royalties. If you own the rights to an artistic work, it's considered intellectual property. Musicians get royalties when their songs are streamed. Authors get royalties when their books are purchased (thank you). This also applies to licensing; if a TV show wants to pay an artist to use their song in the opening credits, they have to cough up the bucks to license it.

Action: In row 6 of your Increase My Income action plan, write "Other Passive Income" in the Income Category column. List any current sources of passive income and how much they're netting you per month in the appropriate columns, along with any action steps. Then, add up the current monthly income you're generating from all your income stream categories and put the result in row 7.

TEA

To be clear: Most people have very little or no investment income flowing today. That's okay! If you're putting zeroes in these remaining rows, you're not alone. The Increase My Income action plan helps you make more money by defining actions. But it also makes you aware of how much of your money is earned income versus investment income each month, and how the balance of those sources could change in the future.

○ ○ ○

Lots to consider! Know that a lot of this information is simply to give you awareness. There aren't any pop quizzes planned, so take your time absorbing and refer back to this section in the future as needed.

To keep things simple, we'll spend the rest of this chapter focusing mostly on **securities**, a blanket term for stocks, bonds, and funds. Securities are assets anyone can start building today, and they're assets that require little maintenance after initial setup, but quietly help you build monetary wealth over time.

PLUMP UP YOUR ASS(ETS)

Let's take a break from all the acronym chatter and get back to you and your money.

To get excited about something in life, we first need to see its potential, and the same holds true for investing. You already saw compounding in action earlier in this book when we talked about how Raye and Kai putting $250 a month into investments led to hundreds of thousands of dollars later in life.

I'm now going to teach you how to fish so you can replicate this excitement for yourself, using *your* numbers, so that this exercise can be about *your* future. You'll also be able to adjust the timetables and numbers however you want. Know that I'm first going to show you how to do this exercise manually, but will then explain how you can use a calculator to speed things up.

SEE IT, BELIEVE IT, START NOW

Create a new chart that has seven rows and six columns (sounds like a lot, but most of these boxes will be filled in by simple arithmetic, so it will go quickly). Label your table as follows:

Investments	Starting Value	Annual Growth	Annual Contribution	End of Year Value	Potential Annual Investment Income
Year 1					
Year 2					
Year 3					
Year 5					
Year 10					
Year 20					

We will use this chart as a forecasting tool, and based on the number of queer people who work as meteorologists, forecasting is already in your blood. Let's only look at row 2 to start as we define each column.

Investments	Starting Value	Annual Growth	Annual Contribution	End of Year Value	Potential Annual Investment Income
Year 1					

Starting Value: Put the current value of all your investments. This includes anything in retirement accounts, stock participation plans, brokerage accounts, and crypto wallets.

Annual Growth: This is where you *forecast* how much your investments will grow in the given year. The estimated annual growth we've been using throughout this book for investing is 8 percent, so I'll recommend that in our examples, but you can adjust as desired.

Annual Contribution: This is how much money each year you're putting into investments. Look back at your net worth contributions bucket as needed to see what this monthly effort is (only include investments), then multiply by 12 to get your annual number.

End of Year Value: Multiply your Starting Value by your expected Annual Growth rate (so, for 8 percent, you would do $X,XXX times 1.08). Then add in your Annual Contribution, and write this total down in the End of Year Value column. This is what we forecast your invested assets will be worth after one year. (I'm exercising a little restraint here, applying the Annual Growth rate only to the Starting Value and not to any mid-year contributions, for extra safety and to keep the math easier.)

Leave the last column blank for now; we'll get to it in the next step. For the Year 2 row, you would take the End of Year Value from the first row and use the same number as the Starting Value in the next row.

Here's how all of that would look for someone starting with $2,000 in investments who contributes an additional $100 each month.

Investments	Starting Value	Annual Growth	Annual Contribution	End of Year Value	Potential Annual Investment Income
Year 1	$2,000	8%	$1,200	$3,360	
Year 2	$3,360				

It's annoying to do this five or ten or twenty times to get those longer forecasts, though. Because I'm a cool mom, let me tell you about a shortcut.

If you do an internet search on investing calculators, you'll find plenty of free options that will model out this year-by-year growth for you. The one I like is at investor.gov, which is run by the Securities and Exchange Commission (the government agency that helps regulate investing). I recommend some others at https://nickwolny.com/book-resources. Simply enter your Year 1 Starting Value, Annual Contribution, and expected Annual Growth for whatever timeframe you want, and the calculator will spit back out a year-by-year breakdown of how your money will grow.

It's not cheating; it's efficient! As long as you understand *how* these numbers are calculated and what they mean, I don't care how you get it done. We're cultivating energy and inspiration; often, seeing the forecast of how your own money will grow is what will motivate you to make investing a priority.

Here's what happens over time when you start with $2,000 in investments and contribute another $100 every month. After twenty years, you'd have $64,236.27, whereas it'd only be $26,000 had you stuffed that money under the mattress instead. This would hold true whether your investments were in a retirement account, a brokerage account, or a crypto wallet.

Investments	Starting Value	Annual Growth	Annual Contribution	End of Year Value	Potential Annual Investment Income
Year 1	$2,000	8%	$1,200	$3,360	
Year 2	$3,360	8%	$1,200	$4,828.80	
Year 3	$4,828.80	8%	$1,200	$6,415.10	
Year 5	$8.128.31	8%	$1,200	$9,978.58	
Year 10	$18,983.08	8%	$1,200	$21,701.72	
Year 20	$58,366.92	8%	$1,200	$64,236.27	

Action: Complete the forecasting exercise to project how your investments will grow, based on how much money you plan to contribute each year. Choose both short-term and long-term timeframes to widen your perspective. We recommended one, two, three, five, ten, and twenty-year timeframes in this chart, but you can also do other forecasts if you like.

CALCULATE FUTURE INVESTMENT INCOME POTENTIAL

What makes investing tedious at times is that your investments are growing in value, but you're often not seeing these gains in your checking account. Instead, the gains are staying in the investments themselves so that they grow faster. It's easy to lose motivation when you're dumping money into these accounts for the future instead of buying cool shit in the present, so let's do one more forecasting exercise to keep excitement high.

Remember that, in investments like securities (stocks, bonds, and funds), the investments are the asset, and the *asset* is what generates your income, not work. A common rule to forecast how much income can be safely withdrawn from investments is the **4 percent rule**, so we'll use that here.

TEA

The 4 percent rule: A bunch of mathematicians sat around in a room with their calculators, stacks of research, and bags of snacks, and figured out that if you withdraw 4 percent of your investments a year, and leave the rest still invested, the odds of you running out of money after thirty years are nearly zero. As such, 4 percent is often referred to as a "safe withdrawal rate" for retirement planning. This rule has more lore than a *Housewives* franchise, so we'll circle back on it in chapter 9.

Go back to the top of your chart, and go to the last column on the right labeled Potential Annual Investment Income. This one's easy; simply take your end-of-year value from that row and multiply it by 4 percent (we only want the income this time, without adding it to the principal, so do $X,XXX times 0.04 instead of 1.04). Put that number in the far-right column.

If you stopped contributing additional money to your investments *right now,* and began treating them like an income-generating asset, here's how much you could plan to safely withdraw each year without eating away too much at the investments themselves.

Investments	Starting Value	Annual Growth	Annual Contribution	End of Year Value	Potential Annual Investment Income
Year 1	$2,000	8%	$1,200	$3,360	$134.40
Year 2	$3,360	8%	$1,200	$4,828.80	$193.15
Year 3	$4,828.80	8%	$1,200	$6,415.10	$256.60
Year 5	$8.128.31	8%	$1,200	$9,978.58	$399.14
Year 10	$18,983.08	8%	$1,200	$21,701.72	$868.07
Year 20	$58,366.92	8%	$1,200	$64,236.27	$2,569.45

Cool, right? Building wealth is fun. It just takes time. You'll never be younger than you are right now, so time is on your side; take advantage of it to secure your future.

Action: Calculate how much annual income your investments would produce if you were to apply the 4 percent rule now, then write this number down in the Potential Annual Investment Income column. Repeat this for each row.

REVISITING THE SAVING RATE ROADMAP

Saving Rate Roadmap—remember her? She's worked the room front to back and scooped up that first round of tips, so it's time for the next reveal.

Now that you have a PhD in the 7-word plan (lower expenses, increase earnings, invest the difference), it's time to go back to our Saving Rate Roadmap and decide what we want to do with the money available to us when we widen the gap between income and expenses. Again, these are not hard-and-fast rules, but instead are loosely prioritized levels, sequenced to financially benefit you based on things like interest rates and owing less in taxes.

Let's pick back up where we left off.

ROTH IRA

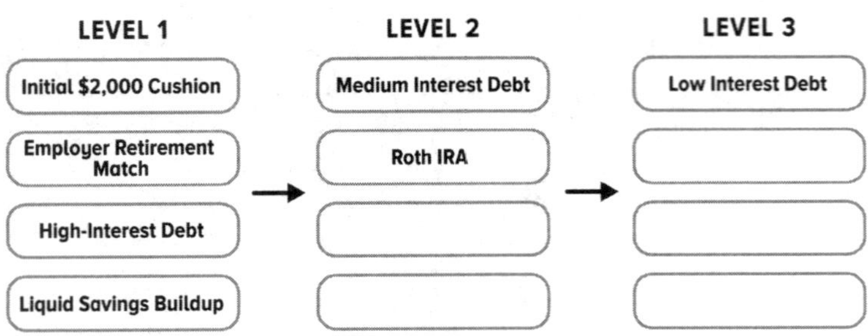

If you're just getting started with investing, I want you to prioritize a Roth IRA.

First, the Roth IRA gives you flexibility. Remember that typical retirement accounts like the 401(k) will charge you a 10 percent penalty if you take out either your contributions or investment gains before age 59.5. For the Roth IRA, this penalty only applies to the investment gains; you can sell and take back out the money you contributed at any time. The Roth IRA is a good option if you're ready to start dabbling in investing for retirement, but don't love the idea of getting penalized to withdraw the money you put in.

Second, the money you put into a Roth grows tax-free. You won't owe capital gains tax on these investments when you withdraw the earnings later in life, whereas you likely would owe capital gains tax on investments made in a brokerage account. Even if you had to break the glass early and tap into the investment gains in your Roth IRA, the 10 percent penalty might be offset by how much your investments have compounded over time.

Third, the amount of money you can contribute to a Roth IRA per year is limited by amount, timeframe, and income. You can only contribute a certain amount per year, and once the deadline passes, the jet bridge for that year's limit is closed, and no amount of bribing or pleading with the gate agent will help. You also can't contribute to a Roth IRA if your income is too high, so if you aspire to cross that salary number later in your working life, you should take advantage of contributing to your Roth IRA now.

If you're eligible to and have the funds, I suggest setting up an automated monthly transfer into your Roth IRA. To contribute the maximum for the year, take the annual limit and divide it by 12. For 2024, when the cap was $7,000 for the year, that came out to $583 a month (it's okay if you're a few dollars short of the cap; just don't go over). Also set up an automated monthly investment *within* the Roth IRA so that the money you're putting in actually gets invested. If it just sits there as cash, there's no way for it to grow.

The Roth IRA is a mutt—one with a good personality that also won't shit on your living room rug.

RETIREMENT ACCOUNT CONTRIBUTIONS

Technically, putting money into a Roth IRA counts as retirement contributions. I'm playing favorites, so I gave her a special shoutout.

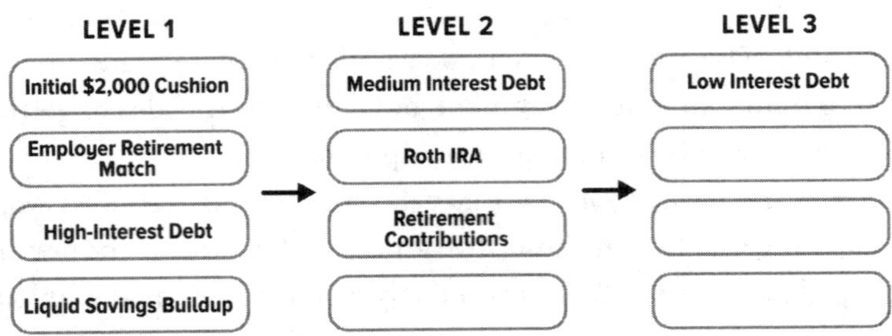

You can have both a 401(k) and an IRA, and these retirement accounts are quite good for growing your investments, so I'd recommend contributing to each if you can. Per level 2 of the diagram, consider pumping money into your employer-sponsored plan concurrently with Roth IRA and medium-interest debt paydown efforts. It's good to spread out your saving rate money across a number of priorities, but whenever you have extra coins lying around, throw them into those retirement accounts.

SINKING FUNDS

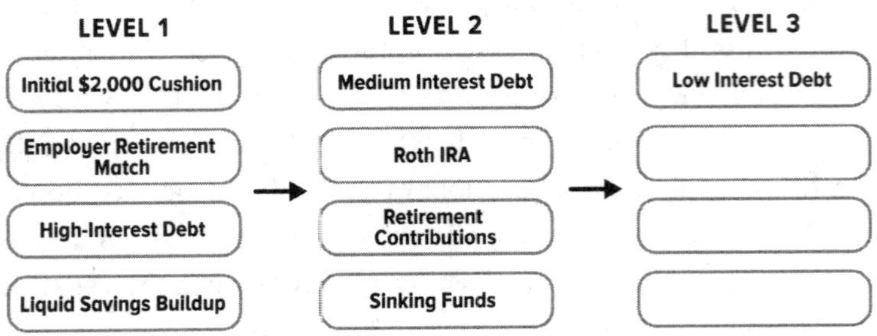

Money you put into sinking funds isn't technically going toward net worth, because you're going to blow it all down later. However, as you put all this saving machinery to work, I think it's important that you also enjoy some of the fruits of your labor and have fun. You'll positively reinforce healthy thought patterns and habits with your money, which is what we want in this book. Whether it be a big vacation, a wedding, saving for a home, or dropping a wad of cash on your next leather harness, sinking funds are for expenses you know are on the horizon.

Rule of thumb: If the expense is more than a few years off, you could put this money into investments to try to grow it. Investing inherently comes with risk—you might end up investing in a year when the stock market goes down—so proceed with caution. If the expense is less than a few years away, stow this money in something like a high-yield savings account so you don't risk not hitting your goal in time.

Also consider throwing money into a sinking fund for the sake of saving money. It's often a mad dash when those concert tickets go on sale (you certainly won't get eight months of runway to sock away the necessary cash), so if you know things like this will come up throughout the year, allocate money for them accordingly.

BROKERAGE ACCOUNT

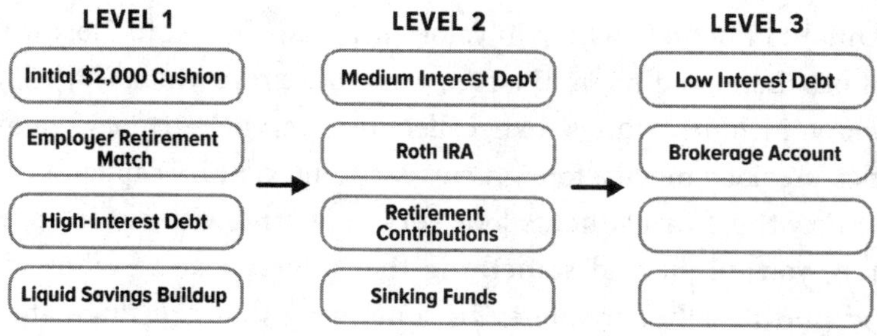

Brokerage accounts are investing accounts that have no deposit or withdrawal limitations. The good news about brokerage accounts is that this money is fairly liquid. If you were in a pinch, you could sell your investments and transfer that money back to your checking account in a matter of days. The less good news is that investments in a brokerage aren't as tax-leveraged as retirement accounts. If you invest in a stock or fund, and the stock makes money, you'll be taxed on those earnings when you sell the stock.

We put brokerage accounts in level 3 because they're a little less tax-leveraged than other priorities. If you've made it this far, though, and you're kicking ass on all of the items in level 1 and level 2, feel free to throw some extra money into a brokerage account and buy some stocks, bonds, and funds along the way.

VOLATILE INVESTMENTS

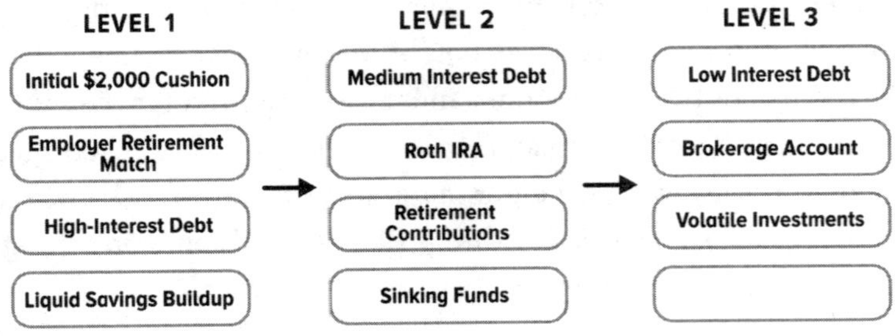

Volatile investments have the potential for high reward, but also the potential to fluctuate wildly in value. Real talk: You could lose your shirt out there (and not in the fun, warehouse rave-kinda way). This category includes things like collectibles, cryptocurrency, penny stocks, precious metals, foreign currency, and venture capital.

I know these investments look very sexy. And with sufficient research, you might find something that interests and excites you. Avoid putting all your money in something that can fluctuate in value or perception quickly. (Remember NFTs? Me neither.) Keep your exposure to these investments limited until you feel confident about the progress you're making on the priorities listed in levels 1 and 2.

There's one more reveal to the MSR roadmap, but it involves a little more context about taxes, so we'll unsnap that final button in chapter 7.

∘ ∘ ∘

When you put the 7-word plan to work, you start to live a more financially independent life. You become savvy and aware with your expenses, thanks to your Bedazzled Budget, and now have a clear action plan for increasing your income as well. Together, these actions, along with your newfound investing smarts, help you pour money into your Saving Rate Roadmap and secure your financial future.

From here, we'll move into Part III, a collection of power moves in which you'll wield your newfound money confidence to create a life you love.

PART III

MONEY PROUD POWER MOVES

7

TAXES

They Exist, Okay? Stop Crying About It, Know What You Owe, and Keep More of What You Earn

It was, by far, the most beautifully embroidered pillow in the classroom.

And it was made by 11-year-old me, Nicholas "definitely not a homosexual" Wolny from rural Illinois, desperately angling for praise from the home ec teacher, per usual. This time, the lure was to embroider *Starry Night* in painstaking detail onto a 9 x 9-inch square of linen from Jo-Ann Fabrics. ("It's Van Gogh's view from his asylum window after cutting off his own ear!" I exclaimed to a grimacing Miss Johnson as I watched her grade my assignment.)

Interestingly, the original intent of home economics class in America wasn't just so you and I could embroider a gay-ass pillow in seventh grade. It was about learning the homemaking and frugality skills that help you keep your shit together, and for a long time it included money management skills, like budgeting and taxes. Home ec in the twentieth century was mainly for women, whom we asked to manage the household's money, but dared not trust them to have it for themselves. Women couldn't open a bank account on their own until 1974, and couldn't get a business loan on their own without a man's signature until 1988, but were expected to balance the checkbook and figure out the taxes on the man's behalf.[1]

As gender roles (rightfully) softened, personal finance literacy drifted out from under the home ec umbrella, and somewhere along the way we all lost our awareness about how taxes work. If your parents didn't teach you about money, they *definitely* didn't teach you anything about taxes, so many queer Americans navigate a once-a-year ritual of stress and confusion as they try to figure out what they owe Uncle Sam (or just don't pay, which typically ends in even more taxes and penalties later). We sometimes accidentally set aside the wrong amount of money throughout the year, then are either devastated by a big tax bill or elated by a refund, and we act as though this uncertainty is the best we can do. But taxes aren't a game of chance; they're just arithmetic and some ugly printouts we get in the mail each year. Taxes suck, they know they suck, and they don't give a shit what you think of them.

They've also gotten a lot of work done over the years. The United States tax code is basically 6,800 pages of Swiss cheese, with holes and tunnels all over the place that rich people regularly leverage to avoid paying taxes. Many of them are completely legal. This is why you should go dig up your grandpa's old headlamp, glue a few rhinestones to it, and cave-dive into a few of these tax tunnels yourself.

One common way rich people avoid paying taxes is by storing their money in things like investments, companies, and other assets. The average American paid 14.5 percent of their earnings to federal taxes in 2022, but many billionaires paid far less than this, despite huge earnings, because they knew how to legally exploit the tax system to their advantage.[2] From the world's richest assholes to your friendly local postmaster, anyone with a good understanding of taxes will keep more of the money they earn throughout life.

Part of financial freedom means feeling unbothered by any money-related adulting that gets thrown your way. Taxes are a perennial money to-do, so understanding how they're filed will give you peace of mind. More importantly, there are tax-related actions you can be taking all throughout the year to owe less in taxes and grow your investments faster. Knowing your options might shape how you want to save and spend your money in the future.

To take our tax game from zero to hero, let's first unlearn some of the most common gripes about taxes, then go through how your tax bill gets calculated each year, along with where you're most likely to find those money-saving pockets of opportunity.

Tax Zingers to Know

1. They'll be here forever, just get over it
2. Tax mistakes often lead to debt
3. Taxes are one of life's largest expenses
4. Cheating on your taxes robs your peace
5. There are more tax forms than *90-Day Fiancé* spinoffs

ZINGER NO. 1: THEY'LL BE HERE FOREVER, JUST GET OVER IT

Tax revenue is what funds a lot of the amenities we have in our day-to-day lives. This is how it works for most organized countries across the world. Without taxes, there would be no money for public transportation or government-sponsored benefit programs. Tax money pays for government employees' salaries, veterans' benefits, and Social Security, which helps financially support millions of retired workers and people with disabilities so they can live their lives with dignity. Taxes fund education initiatives, defense initiatives, parks, scientific research, and more.[3] (America has a debt problem, too, with 10 percent of all our tax payments going toward debt interest. Maybe America should read this book.)

Where taxes encounter endless mudslinging and government lobbying is in the details: Who should fund the tax coffers, how much more some citizens should pay than others, and what the funds should and should not be used for. Turn on the evening news right now and it probably won't be long before there's a story about elected officials or lobbyists arguing about something related to taxes.

We can have strong opinions about tax corruption, sure, and it's important to channel that energy into learning and organizing. But you're still going to have to file taxes each year. Skipping out on paying your taxes is not the social flex you think it is. Allocate a bit of your protest zest toward how taxes work so you can check the box each year and get back to what matters.

ZINGER NO. 2: TAX MISTAKES OFTEN LEAD TO DEBT

Surprises are for birthday parties and burlesque shows, not taxes.

What's tricky about taxes is that you often don't realize you're undersaving until the spring, when you go to file your tax return and are suddenly slapped with a bill for hundreds or thousands of dollars. This can be devastating for adults who don't have much saved up, and is another reason people take on debt.

Side hustle culture has made these tax bombs increasingly common. When you have an employer, your company is withdrawing taxes from your paycheck on your behalf, but this isn't the case for other forms of income. You need to make sure you're setting money aside for taxes from any side hustles, gigs, independent contractor work, or sole proprietorship. The same goes for capital gains; if you sell an investment for more than you paid for it, you might owe tax on this difference, so remember not to spend every dollar.

How much should you set aside? It's hard to give a blanket estimate, because there are many different factors that affect taxes, including what state you live in. If you're making under $150,000 a year, though, and have self-employment income in the picture, setting 20 percent of that self-employment money aside for taxes should be sufficient. Later in this chapter, I'll show you how to calculate your own tax bill so you can make a plan.

ZINGER NO. 3: TAXES ARE ONE OF LIFE'S LARGEST EXPENSES

Taxes are one of the largest expenses you'll have throughout your lifetime, but there are small decisions you can make (really small, we're talkin' cream-in-your-coffee-level decisions) to whittle down the bill and keep more of the money you earn and invest. As we've seen throughout this book, a few more percentage points of savings can mean the difference between building wealth and coming up short.

Recall chapter 1, when we talked about thought patterns. The big idea in that chapter was that we must spot and overcome avoidance, numbing, and money malaise to build confidence with our money. For many people, taxes are perceived as a chore, something our parents hated or were stressed out by in the past, and something that takes a big bite out of our paycheck in the present. So our solution is to ignore them as much as we can.

The problem with this strategy is that we can't escape taxes unless we leave the country. (And lol, the United States *still makes citizens who live abroad file a tax return.* SO nosey!) Also, there are lots of tax loopholes, so when you're putting in effort to make and save more money, the Swiss cheese of it all becomes much more interesting. The path to wealth isn't to numb out or avoid, it's to learn and grow so you can keep more of the money you've worked hard to earn.

Try this: When you read or hear the word "taxes," what feelings come to mind first? Stress? Anger? Track your emotions about this stuff and perhaps jot a few notes down about it. Where did those feelings come from? Are they true? Can you leave them in the past? Tax wisdom is powerful money-saving stuff, so I want to ensure you're not cluttered up with past thought patterns or habits and have no space left to absorb.

ZINGER NO. 4: CHEATING ON YOUR TAXES ROBS YOUR PEACE

People cheat on their taxes because they're often able to get away with it. The reason cheaters slip through the cracks is that IRS resources have been limited for a long time. About 160 million returns get filed each year, and there are only so many people working at the agency to enforce everything.

The Inflation Reduction Act of 2022 included $87 billion for the IRS to modernize systems (their computers were still *from the 1960s,* y'all) and hire more personnel over a ten-year period. This investment may or may not see its way through because political power shifted in 2024, and rich people who cheat on their taxes really, *really* don't want the IRS modernized. One paper from Harvard found that every dollar spent auditing the wealthiest 1 percent returned $4.25 in tax revenue, and could return up to $12 in tax revenue.[4] Turns out when you try to eat the rich and start chomping on their arm, it really pisses them off.

Integrity aside, cheating on your taxes will just leave you feeling anxious and paranoid. There are cooler, sexier, and more legal ways to save money than to avoid taxes, and when you understand what you'll owe, you can be solutions-focused rather than let the confusion get you down.

ZINGER NO. 5: THERE ARE MORE TAX FORMS THAN *90-DAY FIANCÉ* SPINOFFS

It's all fun and games until these forms with weird numbers and letters on them start arriving in the mail every January. Ten-ninety-what? W-2 who? And what's up with these paper sizes?

Employers and companies are required to send you income documentation forms by January 31 of each year for the year prior. The most common types of forms to look out for are:

- **W-2.** This is a wages statement from an employer. It documents your employment income, taxes withheld, and any other relevant information.
- **W-2G.** You're a lucky duck, literally. Or you killed it on *The Price Is Right* playing Plinko. This W-2 is specifically for gambling or prize winnings.
- **1099.** A statement for non-wage income, such as self-employment income, interest income, or investment income.
- **1098.** These are not income forms, but rather documents that show interest paid on either a mortgage or student loan, or money you spent on tuition. You'll use these for adjustments and deductions to your income when filing your taxes, so keep them in a safe place.

If an organization or employer sent you one of these forms, they also sent a copy of the same form to the IRS to cover their own ass. So if you try to pull an "Oops, I forgot to include it," the IRS will know, and you're more likely to be audited. If the audit finds that some of your income wasn't initially reported, you'll be asked to pay taxes on that income, plus penalties and interest. Honest mistake, but it happens more often than you might think.

"What if I lost a form I was expecting, or never received it?" You can ask the IRS for a replacement form after February 15 if your forms went to the wrong address, or your company or employer never sent them to you. If you still have trouble tracking down the form, the IRS can send you a substitute form to use as a placeholder.

Focus on collecting and keeping track of these forms to make tax time easy.

A DIFFERENT KIND OF K

What Queer Artists and Creators Should Know

Queer performers and creatives have long operated in cash, and these days we often accept cash through Venmo and other payment processing platforms. The IRS is making a more concerted effort to document income received through these platforms so they can tax it, because again, she wants her coins. Income received on third-party apps is documented on a form called the **1099-K**.

Previously, the 1099-K wasn't sent to you unless you had over $20,000 in income received via a payment processor (apps like PayPal, Square, and Cash App) and over two hundred transactions in a given year. As the IRS ramps up, one of its efforts is to gradually lower this threshold to $600, a huge change that will impact many creatives.

Most apps now let you separate personal transfers from business transfers. If you use these platforms often, you'll want to categorize your transfers throughout the year so that personal transfers don't get interpreted by the app as business transfers or self-employment income when tax season rolls around.

"Can I just make everything a friends and family payment?" Look, I'm trying to not get thrown in prison here. So what I'll say is this: If it's income, it's taxable. If it's a transfer from a friend or family, it's considered a gift. Alaska's hypothetical $10,000 transfer to Detox via PayPal would have been a gift. But if Alaska LLC had transferred $10,000 via PayPal to Detox Incorporated for "services rendered" (a switch in lipstick vote), that would be considered business income for Detox, and would have been taxed. (I'm three layers deep in *RuPaul's Drag Race* lore here, so if you're lost, don't worry about it.)

TL;DR: If you accept payments via PayPal, Square, Venmo, or something similar, categorize the personal and business transactions separately, and know that you'll be getting a 1099-K tax form from these apps in the near future if your business transactions are more than $600 a year.

MAKING TAXES SIMPLE

Financially secure people know their way around taxes, and as the kiddos say these days, that's on periodt (*pouts lip and gesticulates pointer finger*). They know what income gets taxed, how it gets taxed, and how moving money around increases or decreases its tax burden.

I guarantee bits and pieces of the tax code will change every year. They've probably changed in the time it took me to type this sentence. But the gist of *how* we file our taxes will not change, so let's develop fluency around this now. The big idea here is to be able to estimate your **effective tax rate**, the average percentage of your income that goes to taxes in a given year.

TEA

Effective tax rate: The percentage of your income that ends up actually going to tax after we've gone to Mordor, thrown the ring into the volcano, and returned back home for pints. Some of your income gets taxed at a lower rate, while other income gets a higher rate. Effective tax rate is the overall average.

A working knowledge of tax breaks and other tax-advantaged or tax-exempt accounts can help you save money. Get out a piece of paper or a new spreadsheet tab as we review how taxes get calculated, where your potential tax breaks are, and how to leverage them in the Saving Rate Roadmap.

STEP 1: KNOW HOW YOUR INCOME GETS TAXED

Over the last couple chapters, we've developed a strong foundation about the different types of income that are available to us, thanks to the income stream rainbow. Different categories of income are taxed in different ways, so this knowledge will come in handy as we figure out what we owe and how we can save money along the way.

Here's how it goes down for each stripe of the income stream rainbow.

Stripe nos. 1 and 2: Wages and self-employment income. These two stripes of income, together known as earned income, are subject to up to three categories of taxes, all of which are shown on your pay stub if you earn money as an employee.

1. **Federal income tax.** This is tax you pay to the federal government based on how much money you made. The United States has a **marginal tax system**, which means that different portions of your income are taxed at different rates. As you make more income and cross various benchmarks, the tax rate goes up, but only for the portion of your income that's above each benchmark.

TEA

Marginal tax rates: Much like how I compartmentalize my feelings, the IRS compartmentalizes your income into different bands. It then assesses different levels of tax to different parts of your income. People who earn more theoretically pay more in taxes with this approach, but in practice there are lots of workarounds and loopholes.

These benchmarks vary slightly from year to year to account for inflation and any new tax laws passed. Marginal tax rates also vary whether you file your taxes as single, married, or head of household, a term for people who take care of dependents (not to be confused with HOH on *Big Brother*, which is far removed from both taxes and reality in general). The IRS defines a dependent as a child or relative who relies on you for financial support.

Here's a marginal tax rate chart from 2024 that has all that information in one place. Hold my hand as we look at the scary numbers together and I'll explain what everything means.

Tax rate	Single	Married, filing jointly	Married, filing separately	Head of household
10%	$0 to $11,600	$0 to $23,200	$0 to $11,600	$0 to $16,550
12%	$11,601 to $47,150	$23,201 to $94,300	$11,601 to $47,150	$16,551 to $63,100
22%	$47,151 to $100,525	$94,301 to $201,050	$47,151 to $100,525	$63,101 to $100,500
24%	$100,526 to $191,950	$201,051 to $383,900	$100,526 to $191,950	$100,501 to $191,950
32%	$191,951 to $243,725	$383,901 to $487,450	$191,951 to $243,725	$191,951 to $243,700
35%	$243,726 to $609,350	$487,451 to $731,200	$243,726 to $365,600	$243,701 to $609,350
37%	$609,351+	$731,201+	$365,601+	$609,351

This one chart applied to every taxpayer in America in 2024. Whether you made $11,600 in income, $116,000, or $1.16 million, the first $11,600 of income would have been taxed at a 10 percent tax rate (assume you're filing as single, so we're looking at column two). For the two higher earners, their income from $11,601 to $47,150 was taxed at 12 percent, the income from $47,151 to $100,525 at 22 percent, and so on. Our millionaire earner would theoretically see almost half their annual income taxed at 37 percent, but as mentioned, many of the ultra-rich use tax loopholes to reduce what they owe.

For wages, which include any income you make working as an employee, money is likely being set aside throughout the year for taxes. You might remember filling out a W-4 when you were first hired; it was the piece of paper that asked questions like whether you have dependents, if you work more than one job, and so on. Companies use the information on your W-4 to know how much tax they should withhold on your behalf. Maybe what you filled out was correct, or maybe it wasn't (because you weren't sure what a dependent was, so you just guessed). You won't get in legal trouble if there are mistakes, but since this information determines how much tax gets withheld, you want it to be accurate so you don't withhold too little tax and end up with a bill in April. You can always update your W-4 with your employer if your situation changes.

TEA

W-4: The form you rushed through on day one of orientation at your new job because the icebreaker was about to start and whoever paid the most attention got a $25 Starbucks gift card. Employers use this form to determine how much tax you want withheld from your paycheck. If you work as an employee, go track down this form so you can see what it looks like (and get a few extra brownie points from me).

For self-employment income, you're responsible for setting aside this money yourself so you can cover your tax bill at the end of the year. Yes, I know I've said this multiple times now. I just wanna make sure it's crystal clear, because it is by far the biggest tax mistake I see young queer people making these days.

2. **FICA taxes.** Next, you have Social Security taxes and Medicare taxes, which together are known as FICA taxes. These are taxes everyone pays to help fund two of the largest government benefit programs we have. For Social Security, 12.4 percent of the first $160,200 of your income gets taxed (these are 2024 income numbers). For Medicare, 2.9 percent of your income gets taxed on the first $200,000; it then goes up to 3.8 percent for any earnings after that.

TEA

FICA tax: One of the only times America has ever given a shit about old people. Created by the Federal Insurance Contributions Act, this tax is assessed separately from federal income taxes and is used to fund Social Security (income) and Medicare (health care). On pay stubs, the withheld Social Security and Medicare taxes typically each get their own line.

If you work as a W-2 employee, your company pays half of your Social Security and Medicare tax burden for you, and you pay the other half. For 1099 self-employment income, you're technically on the hook for both halves of the FICA tax (which is sometimes referred to as self-employment tax), but you can deduct the employer half, which we'll explain shortly.

3. **State income taxes.** Last, some states have a state income tax, while others don't. (This doesn't mean the states with no state income tax have no tax revenue, it means that revenue is collected from other sources, like higher property taxes or business taxes.) If the state you live in has state income taxes, they'll either be a flat rate or a marginal rate, similar to how federal income tax is calculated. In 2023, seven states had no state income tax, thirteen had a flat-rate state income tax, and thirty had a marginal-rate tax, so it really is all over the place, and you'll want to check your specific state requirements. (This is why Florida is so popular for retirees, by the way: There's no state income tax. No winter is just the cherry on top.)

To review: For earned income, you'll owe federal income tax, FICA taxes, and maybe a state income tax.

Stripe no. 3: Interest income. Way easier. Income from interest, such as money you earned in a savings account, is in most cases subject to federal and state income tax only.

Stripe no. 4: Capital gains and dividends. For capital gains, the tax rate varies based on how long you held your asset before selling it.

If you bought an asset and held it for less than a year, the money is taxed as ordinary earned income. If you bought an asset and held it for more than a year, then sold it for more than you paid for it, you'll instead owe a capital gains tax. Capital gains taxes are flat rates of zero percent, 15 percent, or 20 percent, based on how much capital gains income you had. (You'd need a lot of income to hit that 20 percent bracket—over $500,000 in a year as of this writing, so it doesn't apply to most.) Long-term capital gains taxes are lower than income taxes in most cases, so this incentivizes investors to hold onto their investments longer, which helps cultivate market stability.

Stripe no. 5: Other passive income. If you own a home and sell it for a profit, that money would be considered a capital gain. Some categories, like collectibles, have their own rules (of course they do). Otherwise, most of this income gets taxed like ordinary income.

For other categories of passive income, like royalties, tax rules vary. If you have these sources of income, take a moment to look up how they'll be taxed so you're in the know and can budget accordingly. Let's bring back the composites approach we took earlier in this book to help illustrate all this.

Marco

Marco is an assistant manager living in California who enjoys connecting with his gaymer community online and does the stylish "one dangly earring" thing when he goes out with his friends IRL. He makes $50,000 per year in gross income. California state income tax uses marginal tax rates.

Marco's federal income taxes, FICA taxes, and state income taxes would look like this to start:

Federal Income Tax

- First $11,600 taxed at 10% = $1,160

- Remaining $38,400 taxed at 12% = $4,608
- Federal tax due: $5,768

FICA Tax

- 7.65% of his gross income (employer pays the other 7.65%): $3,825

California State Income Tax

- First $10,412 taxed at 1% = $104
- Next $14,272 taxed at 2% = $285
- Next $14,275 taxed at 4% = $571
- Remaining $11,041 taxed at 6% = $662
- California state tax due: $1,622

Total: $11,215

Don't cry for Marco just yet. This total number looks high, but will come down later.

Action: Review your various sources of income. Identify how each of these categories of income will be taxed. Approximate the taxes you will owe on these income sources, based on marginal tax rules, the state you live in, and any capital gains you have. Use the bulleted structure shown in the example.

STEP 2: DEDUCT HER, CREDIT HER

The numbers in the Marco composite are based on gross income, which is the sum of all the income you received last year. But gross income is not the same as *taxable* income, which is what you'll actually be taxed on. And here's the good news: Taxable income is almost always lower than gross income (which means less tax owed!) thanks to adjustments, deductions, and credits.

1. **Adjustments.** As the name implies, adjustments adjust your gross income. Contribute to a 401(k)? You made the money this year, but aren't being taxed on it until you withdraw it later in life—adjustment. Had self-employment income, but there was no official employer paying the other half? You're off the hook for the employer part of the FICA tax—adjustment. Make student loan payments? Part of those payments probably went toward loan interest—adjustment. Get divorced? You might be receiving alimony payments—adjustment. Once you've applied these adjustments, you arrive at two numbers called your **adjusted gross income (AGI)** and **modified adjusted gross income (MAGI)**. (Straight people named all this stuff, btw.)

   AGI is what appears on your tax return, and it's what we'll charge forward with when calculating your taxable income. But MAGI, which adds a lot of the adjustments *back* in, is what's used to determine eligibility for various programs and investments that have income limits, such as poverty status, Roth IRA eligibility, and others. If you're near the income limit for one of these programs, the MAGI is the number used to define that income limit. Here's an example of someone who would be in that scenario.

Devon

Devon is a senior director of operations at an agriculture company. She made $150,000 in 2024, which was too high for full Roth IRA eligibility. But 401(k) contributions are an adjustment, and she put $10,000 of her money into her 401(k) that year, so her MAGI was $140,000, which *was* within the income limit. Devon can continue to contribute fully to a Roth IRA, even though her gross income is higher than the limit, as long as her MAGI stays *under* the annual income limit.

2. **Deductions.** Deductions are a series of tax breaks and write-offs that help you lower your taxable income. All adjustments are also deductions, but not all deductions are adjustments.

Common deductions include:

- Capital losses. If you sold stock or assets at a loss, you can deduct the loss, up to $3,000 per year, and the rest can carry over year to year. Losses also offset capital gains.
- Charitable contributions.
- Losses from a natural disaster or theft.
- Gambling losses.
- Large medical expenses. Medical expenses become deductible once they pass 7.5 percent of your AGI ("We won't give you universal health care, but we will give you a tax break if your medical bills were devastating this year!").

There are a lot of deductions, but they're kind of a pain in the ass to itemize and document for your taxes. They take up time and often lead to more filing mistakes. So to help with this, the government created the **standard deduction**.

The IRS hates going through your receipts just as much as you do, so this is kind of their way of offering you a buyout: "Look, boo, if you don't have much to deduct, I'll just offer you this flat deduction that's probably a better deal, and we can turn the page and all move on with our lives." The standard deduction was $14,600 in 2024, so if you don't think you'll have more than that in deductions, you should be like 87 percent of Americans and take it.[5]

Fortunately, many people file their taxes online now, and tax software will calculate both your standard and itemized deductions for you to see which one saves you more money.

3. **Credits.** Credits work like coupons. They're a one-time adjustment that is tacked on at the end to reduce your tax bill or increase your refund. And who doesn't love a good coupon?

For example, since kids are expensive, the Child Tax Credit gives you a $2,000 credit off your tax bill for each kid you're taking care of. There's also an adoption credit to help offset adoption expenses. This has become increasingly relevant for queer people: About 21 percent of same-sex couples' children are adopted, compared to just 3 percent for opposite-sex couples, and one in six LGBTQ+ people are parenting a child under 18, a 2024 Williams Institute report found.[6]

Let's revisit Marco's math with deductions added in.

Marco

Marco read chapter 3, so he's now contributing 3 percent of his paycheck to his 401(k) in order to get his employer match ($1,500 for the year from Marco, and then another $1,500 in free money from his employer as a result). He can claim this $1,500 as an adjustment. He also made student loan payments every month this year, and a total of $500 from those payments went toward interest. He can also claim that $500 as an adjustment. Marco's AGI is $48,000 ($50,000 – $2,000 in adjustments).

Marco then takes the standard deduction of $14,600, which brings his taxable income down to $33,400. His calculated taxes would now shake out as follows:

Federal Income Tax

- First $11,600 taxed at 10% = $1,160
- Remaining $21,800 taxed at 12% = $2,616
- Federal tax due: $3,776

FICA Tax

FICA tax is on gross income, not taxable income, so this remains the same.

- 7.65% of his gross income (employer pays the other 7.65%): $3,825

California State Income Tax

- First $10,412 taxed at 1% = $104
- Next $14,272 taxed at 2% = $285

- Remaining $8,716 taxed at 4% = $349
- California state income tax due: $738

Total: $8,339

Overall, Marco's tax bill for federal and state income taxes would be $8,339, nearly $3,000 lower than the figures we calculated in step 1 before taking adjustments and deductions.

Don't obsess over calculating this stuff down to the penny. The big takeaway here is to know how income and deductions work and what these terms mean (and maybe not wait until the absolute last second to file your taxes each year so you're not rushing and leaving money on the table as a result). Adjustments, deductions, and credits help you keep more of the money you've earned.

Action: Calculate any deductions and credits you anticipate receiving to estimate how much tax you'll owe for the year. For most people, the standard deduction leads to the biggest savings. Then, repeat the tax calculation exercise above. Look at a past year's tax return if you have it handy for reference.

HOMEOWNER TAX DEDUCTIONS

Homeownership has several tax breaks.

- **Retirement account withdrawal for a down payment.** You can withdraw up to $10,000 from an IRA for a first-time home purchase, penalty-free.
- **Mortgage interest deduction.** Money you put toward your mortgage payments that went toward interest can be deducted from your income.

- **Property taxes.** If you paid state or local taxes on your property, you can deduct up to $10,000 of them on your federal tax return.
- **Necessary home improvements.** Some categories of home improvements create a deduction if they increase the value of the home.
- **Capital gains tax deduction.** If you sell your primary home, owned it for at least two years, and lived in it for at least two of the last five years, you can deduct up to $250,000 of the capital gain on your taxes. (Uh . . . that's a lot.)

Much of the value of homeownership emerges in the form of tax deductions and credits. If you want to take advantage of them, you'll have to itemize deductions rather than take the standard deduction, so keep those records right and tight throughout the year.

STEP 3: ARRIVE AT YOUR EFFECTIVE TAX RATE

Much shorter than the first two steps! We're now ready to calculate your effective tax rate with a single flourish of arithmetic. Simply divide your tax bill by your gross income to land on your effective tax rate.

Marco's tax bill was $8,339, and he made $50,000 in gross income, so his effective tax rate was 16.7 percent ($8,339 / $50,000). If his income remains similar from year to year, he can expect a similar effective tax rate, which can help him avoid unexpected tax bills that could derail his financial goals. Marco didn't have any interest income, capital gains, dividends, or other income sources, so when you do these exercises for yourself, be sure to include those as well.

Action: Calculate your estimated taxes on earned income and investment income. Add these together, then divide by gross income to get your effective tax rate for the year. This is what you paid on average in taxes.

WHAT TO CARE ABOUT AND WHEN, THROUGHOUT THE YEAR

Most of us don't have much to manage throughout the year when it comes to taxes. If you're an employee, it would be good to know how to see and/or download your past pay stubs. And if you change addresses at any point, set up mail forwarding and update any employers to ensure you receive end-of-year forms at the correct address when filing season rolls around.

Also, if you're planning to itemize your deductions, you'll want to keep and track your expenses receipts throughout the year, too. For example, if you drive Uber for income as a side gig, and you wanted to deduct the costs of operating and maintaining your vehicle from this income, you would have to keep those receipts and include them in your tax filing to prove you actually had those expenses. (More on this in chapter 8 when we dip into entrepreneurship, which is another vehicle for being smart with taxes.)

Your year in taxes will go something like this.

January: January kicks off with everyone pooping their pants about their new year's resolutions, then giving up on them three weeks later. This is fine, because there isn't a whole lot for you to do at the top of the month. Near the end of January, you'll start receiving tax forms either electronically or through the mail.

Organizations distributing a tax form to you have until January 31 to send either electronically or by mail, so you may not have all the forms you need until the first week of February. It's not the end of the world if your tax forms got lost in the mail or you changed addresses;

the IRS website lets you log in and see what forms you should expect, and if you don't receive a form by mid-February, you can request a replacement copy of that form.

Also, if you're someone who hires an accountant to do your taxes, you should get that meeting on the books now, as their busy season is about to pick up.

February and March: Once you have all your forms, you can file your taxes whenever you want between now and April. It can be tempting to procrastinate and wait until the last second, but you might end up leaving out some deductions or forgetting some income forms, which leaves money on the table and can lead to an audit later on. It's cool to not be rushed and ensure you have plenty of time to get things done.

"Where do I file my taxes?" You could pay for an online tax filing service, or work with an accountant if your taxes are more complicated (or you just don't have the time). At the time of this writing, the IRS is also working on rolling out its Direct File program, which lets you file online for free.

April: Everywhere around you, the sky is falling as people stress and agonize over getting their taxes done in time. Meanwhile, you're relaxed and at ease because you took care of all this stuff weeks ago. Plus, if you received a refund this year, you're likely to get it sooner since you beat the crowd.

May to November: For most of us, nothing to do here regarding taxes. Peace out and live your best queer life.

December: Make any big money moves that you want to land in a particular tax year. This might include selling stocks or other investments to declare a capital gain or loss, making some deductible home improvements, or buying some deductible equipment for a side hustle that makes you self-employment income.

COMPLETING THE SAVING RATE ROADMAP

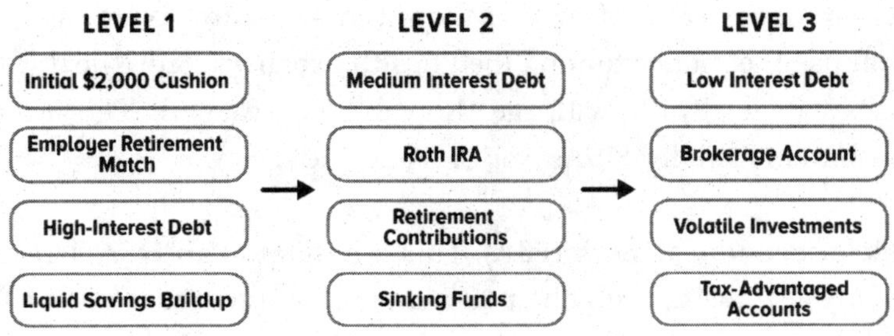

Now that you're all grown up with how taxes work and how to owe less of them, we can introduce another section of the modified Saving Rate Roadmap that might be beneficial to your goals: **tax-advantaged and tax-exempt accounts**.

Tax-advantaged accounts are special accounts in which you can save money (and even invest it) and won't owe any taxes on the earnings as long as you use the money for certain categories of expenses. A subset of tax-advantaged accounts, tax-exempt accounts, let you contribute pre-tax money, meaning you avoid taxes entirely. The government acknowledges there are some expenses in life that a lot of Americans deal with—health, education, and childcare, to name a few—so the IRS gives you a "get out of jail free" card on income used for some of these expenses (translation: no tax) as long as you put this money into said accounts. The accounts often have annual contribution limits, so a "save a little at a time" approach works best here.

Like retirement accounts, your money isn't locked up to only these use cases. If you need the cash for some other emergency, you can withdraw, but you'll owe taxes on the money and, in some cases, a penalty.

Common tax-advantaged and tax-exempt accounts include:

Health savings account (HSA). HSAs offer "triple tax savings": The money you contribute to an HSA is pre-tax, the earnings from the invested money are tax-free, and the withdrawals are tax-free as long as you use the money for qualified health expenses. Since health expenses statistically rise with age, this can be a great perk. The annual contribution limit for HSAs was $4,150 in 2024.

Flexible spending account (FSA). This is similar to an HSA, but you can only get one through an employer. FSAs are sometimes used for health-care expenses. There's also a dependent care flexible spending account, which can be used for expenses related to childcare (babysitter, preschool, and even summer camp) or elder care (if an elderly loved one lives with you for more than eight hours a day).

529 plan. (That's the name of the account, not me saying "529 separate plans" in weird Neanderthal speak.) 529 plans were first implemented in 1996 as a way to help parents save money for their children's college education, and they've gotten more useful over time. Nowadays, if you anticipate investing in a certification or continuing education for yourself at some point, you can use a 529 plan to help pay for it. This money can be invested, the earnings are tax-free, and the withdrawals are also tax-free if you use them for education-related expenses. More recently, if you keep a 529 plan open for fifteen years, you can convert it into a Roth IRA (which, remember, allows for tax-free earnings).

ABLE accounts. The Achieving a Better Life Experience (ABLE) account is designed to help people who have disability-related expenses cover them with tax-free dollars. One report from the National Disability Institute found that households in which someone has a disability require 28 percent more income to replicate the same standard of living as non-disability households.[7]

Action: Go to werk on the 7-word plan for building wealth (lower expenses, increase earnings, invest the difference) and use the tools in this book to set goals for your financial future.

- Use the Bedazzled Budget to monitor your money, aligning your spending with a life you love.
- Use the Increase My Income action plan to take meaningful steps toward making more money and bringing more resources into your life.
- Use the Saving Rate Roadmap to guide your saving, investing, and debt payoff decisions. Give most of your attention to Level 1 priorities until they've been maxed out or achieved, then move to Level 2 and Level 3 priorities and repeat.

∘ ∘ ∘

Knowing your way around taxes creates confidence. Knowing where to save your money and in what order creates confidence. With the Saving Rate Roadmap fully revealed, you have a game plan on what to do and in what order to make your money work for you. The higher your saving rate, and the more dollars you can pour into this roadmap each month, the further and faster you'll go on your financial independence journey.

We mentioned earlier that earned income is the fuel you need to navigate your roadmap successfully. In the next chapter, we'll dive deeper into the power moves you can make with self-employment income to bolster your saving efforts, speed things up even more, and live a great queer life along the way.

8

ENTREPRENEURSHIP

Channel Executive Realness (and Get Paid Like One, Too)

Working a job means being a cog in someone else's machine. *What if you built your own machine?*

This question dominated my mid-twenties while I worked in retail. My days were spent folding stacks of pants, showing coworkers how to stack the pants, dying a little inside every time a customer would mess up said pants, and wondering if I had squandered college and wasted my golden ticket to a financially secure future. Quarter after quarter, the earnings calls would trumpet the millions of dollars the company had made. Meanwhile, I was stuck in the land of the 3-percent annual raise, scraping by while others who had equity in the company got rich off my pants-tastic labor.

To make more money, I picked up various side hustles and odd jobs. I also fell into the online hustle culture k-hole, watching videos from creators who preached the benefits of personal development, entrepreneurship, and financial freedom, then sold you something that promised you similar results (this was 2014, our online grift radar wasn't as good back then). I bought every book and course I could get my hands on. Other people's retail kinks are things like clothes, electronics, or vacations; my retail kink is self-help. Eventually, I decided it was the right time to "trust the process" and make the leap into full-time self-employment. In 2016, I established Less Noise More Volume LLC, my consulting business (the name is a hat-tip to my music school days), and began telling my network I was available for hire.

Unbeknownst to me, this "jump in headfirst" approach to entrepreneurship is 100 percent USDA-certified ass-backwards. I could have had a lifeboat waiting for me when I abandoned ship by learning, oh, I don't know, *anything* about business, or sales, or time management. Instead, I was too focused on making a dramatic work departure that *symbolized* freedom, rather than laying a foundation that would actually *lead* to freedom. I had to pull money from my cash cushion every month to help cover my expenses, and in about a year burned down my entire life savings—about $30,000 at the time—which meant crawling back to a day job, defeated, tail between my legs.

Despite these early battle scars, entrepreneurship turned out to be one of the best lifestyle decisions I've made in adulthood. I learned a ton about my strengths and quirks, enjoyed incredible time freedom (I could go to a museum at 11 a.m. on a Tuesday if I wanted), and discovered that day job income and self-employment income can be mixed and matched as necessary to reach your money goals. Nine years of business ownership have given me confidence in how to lean into my LLC a little or a lot to shape my life, and now I want to share this measured, not-overhyped approach with you.

Entrepreneurship is how many people end up becoming financially independent or even rich-rich, because when you own a business, you don't just pay yourself in wages; you can also pay yourself in *profits*. Your business is an investment, like a stock or a bond or a piece of real estate, but in this investment you are very much in the driver's seat with regard to its value.

You also might already be running a business without even realizing it. Making side income as a creator? Entrepreneur. Doing photography at weddings and events on the weekends? Entrepreneur. Let me save you the $100,000 you would have sunk into an MBA: Most of the nuts and bolts of business can be learned on the fly, and you can ramp up or down your efforts as needed to align with your goals.

This flexibility is one reason entrepreneurship has become increasingly popular. Prior to 2021, the US had never seen 300,000 new businesses in a single quarter. That number has now been surpassed—for twelve quarters in a row.[1] The internet in particular has made entrepreneurship easier to leverage because there are fewer obstacles to marketing and fulfillment. You could truly create the most niche line of bright pink leather studded thongs in history and I guarantee there are people online already looking for that exact product.

Even if you have no interest in owning a business or becoming an entrepreneur, you should still read this chapter, because doing so will give you a deeper appreciation for what it *takes* to run a small business. You'll be inspired to seek out and support queer-owned businesses, and you'll gain a deeper appreciation for how doing so builds wealth in our community. You will understand how being a business owner might influence your financial goals and personal budget. And if you later have a change of heart and decide you do want to dip your toe in self-employment, you'll know how to test a business idea, file the paperwork, and build the bridge that lets you leave a work situation that's no longer serving you.

Entrepreneurship changed my life, and I know it has the power to change yours, too. To set money goals that truly excite and inspire you, we must go beyond the spreadsheet and really look at the lifestyle we want to live, then start making power moves on how to get there. This chapter goes over how to think about entrepreneurship and capital, as well as how to find a profitable business idea that gets you paid.

Reasons to Care about Entrepreneurship

- Entrepreneurship gets you into action
- Entrepreneurship can lead to investment income
- Entrepreneurship can influence other aspects of wealth

- Entrepreneurship reveals hidden opportunities to save money
- Entrepreneurship funnels economic power to our LGBTQ+ family

REASON NO. 1: ENTREPRENEURSHIP GETS YOU INTO ACTION

We previously touched on entrepreneurship in chapter 5 when we introduced the income stream rainbow. Whether you're producing self-employment income as a freelance MUA, a food influencer, or a handyman on the weekends, the IRS already categorizes you as an entrepreneur.

My favorite thing about entrepreneurship is that it helps you build confidence. You're in charge, it all comes down to you, and the challenges that are bound to come up from time to time make you tougher. You launch to the sound of crickets. You make a big mess with a customer and have to clean it up. You make decisions with conviction. All of this builds thick (but still supple) skin, and I like that for queer people.

Entrepreneurship means betting on yourself. If you're confident in what you do, it can be a way to get paid more (and more fairly) for your knowledge and skills.

Vee, 32, Colorado: *Entrepreneurship taught me how to speak up for myself and take up space. As a queer woman who grew up in the South and spent most of my life closeted, it was a new feeling. I was tired of applying to all these jobs when I knew I could run my own show. I knew all of the content creators in my industry. I knew they needed help with content creation. I was like, "You know what? I'm just going to start my own f***ing business."*

Your entrepreneurial pursuit could be something you do a few hours a week, or it could be all-out executive realness with you as the CEO of a company. There's a wide range. But if you're new to it, I think you should start small (the total opposite of what I did when I pancaked that first year).

There can be a strong temptation to quit your job and jump headfirst into entrepreneur life. And there's certainly no shortage of online personalities egging you on to do so. But business ideas often fail, or they require a lot of trial and error, so I want you to be aware of that risk. Despite our best intentions, 20 percent of businesses shut down in the first two years, 45 percent shut down within five years, and 65 percent have shut down after ten years, according to the Bureau of Labor Statistics.[2] Businesses have a higher fail rate than other types of investments (but not as high a fail rate as Susan Lucci had at the Daytime Emmy Awards), so you'll want to do your due diligence before deciding how much time, money, and energy you want to sink into starting one.

As we mentioned earlier, you can make self-employment income by trading hours for dollars (the gig economy). You can also make money by creating assets. In this setting, assets can be physical things, like products or real estate. They can also be content or information, which is known as **intellectual property**, a term we introduced in chapter 5 and are now ready to expand upon here.

TEA

Intellectual property (IP): Property that doesn't require a mechanic or an electrician to maintain, though you could have a buff burly man stand next to you while you create it if that motivates you. IP is content that gets used as an asset to make money—most commonly a piece of writing, an image, a song, or a video.

Let's say you put up a video on YouTube that begins to go viral, so you sign up to start running ads on that video. You'll get paid a fraction of a cent every time ads are shown to a user (hard to give a clear number here; some statistics for 2023 say it's as little as $2 for 1,000 views, others say it can be as much as $30 per 1,000 views). You've uploaded the video and done nothing else, but the video continues to hum along in the background, with the ads running, so YouTube continues to pay you each month.

In this case, the video is an asset. You're then letting a company host your asset on their platform so they can run ads against it, and in return they give you some of the ad revenue. YouTube retained you as an independent contractor when you signed up for its YouTube Partner Program to make money by showing ads. This would be considered self-employment income.

A TV show is intellectual property. A hit song is intellectual property. Your favorite modern cartoon characters are intellectual property. The advantage of intellectual property is that it can be monetized again and again without necessarily requiring more labor. Intellectual property can also attract an audience, which can become another asset (the creator economy), much to the delight of influencers. I don't make the rules, that's just how it is.

Entrepreneurship and side hustles are becoming increasingly common because people want to make more money, and they don't want to wait for a promotion to do so. You could make this money by trading hours for dollars, but you could also use those hours to create intellectual property that can then make you money in the background. And if things change down the road, like they did for me, know that entrepreneurship doesn't have to be a permanent decision.

Kellye, 34, Virginia: *I think my desire to pursue entrepreneurship came from a place of wanting to build something of my own. But I ended up going back to work full-time because it was hard for me to be earning so much less than my wife was. The most challenging part of business ownership is the experimentation phase and the vulnerability that comes with not seeing the fruits of your labor right away.*

I'm blessed to have a very supportive partner who gave me space to explore this. But I struggled with feeling like I wasn't equitable in my contribution to our family. Entrepreneurship changed the type of work I sought out; I used to be very motivated by external validation, getting pats on the back, and now that doesn't do anything for me. My job matters to me less than it did before, and I like that.

REASON NO. 2: ENTREPRENEURSHIP CAN LEAD TO INVESTMENT INCOME

Everything we talked about above was self-employment income. But there's also a world in which your business becomes a source of investment income, because it can hum along even if you are mostly or completely out of the picture. This is the passive income stuff everyone likes to lose their shit over.

Let's say you're a software developer who creates an app that becomes successful. You set up the app as a business and eventually hire people to run the business for you. There might come a point where you don't have to work in the business anymore, in which case you step out. But you still own the place. The business is now considered an investment, so this passive income is considered investment income.

Every day you go to work, whether you enjoy it or not, you're a cog in someone else's machine. They get the profits, not you; your backbreaking labor is someone else's investment income stream. What makes entrepreneurship compelling for many people is that they get to reap the full value of their labor and not give away all the profits to some corporation.

Some investors are business nerds, but don't have time to start a business themselves, so they choose to invest in other emerging small businesses instead. These investors are often known as **venture capitalists**. Other investors don't want all that risk—they want a paint-by-numbers business idea that's already been sussed out—so they buy a franchise. A **franchise** is a "business in a box," in which the investor gets to be the business owner but doesn't have to waste time or money figuring out the business model, because all that trial and error is done. That new UPS Store or Smoothie King that opened down the street from you is probably a franchise in someone's investment portfolio.

We won't touch on venture capital or franchising any further in this book, but if you're far along in your investing journey and want to spice things up, investing in businesses lets you pursue monetary wealth in a creatively fulfilling way.

REASON NO. 3: ENTREPRENEURSHIP CAN INFLUENCE OTHER ASPECTS OF WEALTH

Who decided that 9-to-5 five days a week should be the norm, anyway? Corporations, probably.

Many people get started with entrepreneurship because they want an arrangement in which they can work on their own time and terms. Or they want to be location-independent, traveling as they please and seeing the world. There's a buzzword for this stuff: "lifestyle design." You're intentional about how your furniture is arranged, and what order the songs are in the playlist, so why not bring that design mentality to how you live your life as well?

Michael, 28, Oaxaca, Mexico: *I grew up in Canada in a very Catholic immigrant household. I was afraid my parents would abandon me because I was gay. Everything was about survival. So, I became an accountant. I never wanted to be an entrepreneur; it seemed too unstable for me. Later, I spent some time backpacking around Europe and really fell in love with traveling. I realized I wanted a career where I could be a digital nomad and work from* *anywhere in the world. And I knew staying in a corporate career would never allow me to do that. So I started my coaching business in 2020, did it on the side for three years to build it up and get my personal finances really strong, then quit my job to go full-time, and here I am.*

Over the last few decades, moms have very much shaped the direction of lifestyle-driven entrepreneurship. Many are intelligent, career-driven women across America who wanted to start families, but had to stare down the very real motherhood penalty. There's been a huge influx of women creating lifestyle-first businesses that allow career and family to coexist in a fulfilling way. Some are corporate consultants. Others run tiny media empires in the form of cooking blogs. Many are not trying to build businesses that produce billions; they're building businesses that enable time freedom, which is often the bigger wealth flex.

If work life gives you the ick, start learning about entrepreneurship now so you can pursue something that both lights you up and helps you reach your money goals.

REASON NO. 4: ENTREPRENEURSHIP REVEALS HIDDEN OPPORTUNITIES TO SAVE MONEY

Back when I worked at the yoga studio, I remember the housewives (and househusbands) who taught their midday classes in a new outfit every week. "It's a tax write-off!" they would exclaim, and I didn't grasp what that really meant for years.

Entrepreneurship helps you not only make more money, but keep more of it, too. Remember from chapter 5 that if you have any independent contractor or sole proprietor income, but don't have a formal business setup, the IRS will classify you as a business, a sole proprietorship, for tax purposes.

Raked your elderly neighbor's leaves for twenty dollars? Sole proprietorship. Did some college meathead's homework for him for a hundred bucks? Shame on you for robbing that man of the gift of education (but also good job getting those coins)—sole proprietorship. If you have income from sole proprietor activity and had expenses from "the cost of doing business," you may be able to deduct some of your expenses from this work on your taxes.

COMMON BUSINESS WRITE-OFFS

Don't make a write-off boo-boo like David Rose did in *Schitt's Creek*. "Within reason" (the IRS's words, not mine), you can deduct:

- **Cost of advertising and promotion.** If you paid money to set up a website, or had a banner printed for your farmer's market booth, you can write off that expense.
- **Clothing for work.** If you need a uniform to do the job, or need a new wig for the gig, you can write off that expense. (Deducting new apparel to teach a yoga class would be, ahem, a *stretch*, but possible. The IRS says the clothes must be "necessary" to do the job, and "not suitable" for everyday wear.)
- **Meals.** If you went out for a meal with someone and talked about your business, that's considered a business meal, and you can write off part of that expense.
- **Vehicle.** If you use your car to get to/from business-related activities, you can write off gas (by tracking your mileage) and potentially also some of the maintenance expenses.
- **Contractors.** If you hired people to help you do a job, that labor is an expense.
- **Education.** If you make an investment in your training or development for work-related skills, you can write off that expense.
- **Home office.** If you have a business, and work from home, you can write off home office setup expenditures and even a portion

of your rent or mortgage. (You *cannot* write off home office expenses if working from home as an employee—cue the sad trombone sound for employees who work from home.)

- **Travel expenses.** If you're traveling for business, the cost of your flight, train, and hotel are likely deductible expenses.

The IRS wants you to be entrepreneurial and productive. Know and use these tax perks to your advantage.

REASON NO. 5: ENTREPRENEURSHIP FUNNELS ECONOMIC POWER TO OUR LGBTQ+ FAMILY

As you learn about what goes into running a business, you might become more intentional about where (and with whom) you spend your money.

When you buy from a queer person or queer-owned business, you are directly contributing to that person's wealth and well-being, rather than your money being sucked up into some corporate conglomerate (that might be actively working against you in the form of lobbying or political donations). The same holds true for women-owned businesses and minority-owned businesses. With Gen Z identifying as queer in record-high numbers, there will likely be more opportunities to buy from and financially empower other queer people in the future, which is very exciting.

Try this: Go back through your expenses over the past month. Was there an option from a queer-owned business you could check out instead? For more essential expenses like rent and groceries, there often aren't LGBTQ-owned options. But for things like clothes, jewelry, hospitality, and local service providers, a little due diligence can help you find queer-owned and minority-owned companies to support.

BE ENTREPRENEURSHIP-FLUID

You don't need to go back to school for years or write a fifty-page business plan before making your first dollar in self-employment income. You also likely don't need to file any of your business paperwork yet (and the IRS won't care: They already know there's a lot of unstructured, scrappy entrepreneurial activity in America, so they just classify this income as sole proprietorship unless you say otherwise on your taxes).

What you *do* need to figure out is whether your idea will fly so that you don't end up plunging thousands of dollars into something that ends up being little more than an expensive hobby. Hobbies are great, but if the goal of your hobby is to bring in some extra income, let's be rigorous in pursuing that goal so you don't waste time or ruin a pastime you love through mounting frustration.

I want to equip you to be entrepreneurship-fluid in life, so in this chapter we'll be doing a series of writing exercises to help you unlock more self-employment income. Grab a pen and have some extra paper or an online document ready if you want extra writing space.

STEP 1: FIND A PROFITABLE IDEA

At the root of self-employment income is a value proposition: You give me this, I give you that. And as we've seen from people eating Tide pods for social clout or pouring Pop Rocks in their mouths and then washing them down with a can of Sprite, some ideas are better than others.

Step away from the binary, oversimplified world of "good" and "bad" ideas. What matters more is that your idea is *profitable*, meaning you have money left over after completing the job and covering the expenses necessary to get it done. If you don't eventually make a profit, your business or side hustle is just more work.

Do the following five tests when thinking about a business idea to determine if it is profitable.

1. **There's a problem, pain point, or desire.** Your customer is thirsty (in this case, for beverages, not photos in their DMs). Or their toilet is clogged. Or they need to buy a helicopter. Or a massage. Or some tutoring so they can pass the bar exam. Or they need a new pair of steel-toed boots for work. So you sell them a solution that is, in the moment, valuable.

   The more annoying or compelling the problem is, the more urgent the solution becomes. A butt pimple is inconvenient, sure, but it's nothing compared to a migraine. There are urgent solutions, and then there are nice-to-have solutions. Consumers buy both. And often, consumers don't care too much about what goes into the product or service. They care more about the end result, the feeling or transformation that comes from their purchase.

Prompt: *What is the problem, pain point, or desire that your idea solves? Who is it for?*

___

___

___

2. **Your customer is aware of the pain or desire.** Your business idea solves a problem—great. Now, do your target customers realize there's a problem? It sounds silly to ask that question at first, but doing so can be very clarifying.

   In some scenarios, both the problem and solution are clear. "I have a headache // taking a painkiller will help my headache go away." Gays in marketing would label these consumers as **solution-aware.** The consumer knows what the problem is, and they know what the solution is. Your work is in making sure these consumers know who you are, why they should buy from you, how to buy from you, and why they should do it now.

   Then you have a larger category of people who know what the

problem is, but don't know what the solution is. "We need more patrons at the bar // we've tried different strategies, some have worked and some haven't // let's try something new." These people are **problem-aware**. They know that there's a problem, but either can't figure out how to solve it or haven't had success solving it with anything they've tried so far. When your audience is problem-aware, your work is to introduce them to your solution and help them understand why your solution is right for them.

Finally, you have the giant swath of people who either don't have a problem or don't know there's a problem. These people are **unaware**, and they're the toughest to win over because they're not experiencing a burning pain or desire. Ignorance is bliss; it's hard to sell a solution to a problem if people don't realize the problem exists.

TEA

TARGET MARKET 101:

- **Solution-aware:** Aware of the problem or desire, aware of the solution.
- **Problem-aware:** Aware of the problem or desire, unaware of the solution.
- **Unaware:** Unaware of the problem or desire (e.g., my ex).

Focus on solution-aware or problem-aware customers. These people are more likely to pay you more and pay sooner, because you don't have to spend time and resources convincing them there's a problem in the first place.

Prompt: *Is the target customer aware that there's a problem? Are they aware that there is a solution? Have they tried* your *solution? What makes you different?*

3. **The customer is able and willing to pay.** Creators, this one's for you.

   People will tell you they love your business idea ("Love that for you!"), and they are kind and thoughtful for saying so. But compliments, likes, and followers are not the same as cash in the bank. We want to ensure our customers are able and willing to pay.

   "Able to pay" means the customer has the disposable income or budget to buy, and that they can access this money. "Willing to pay" means the customer is solution-aware and ready to pay now because they see value in doing so. Encouraging people to pay now and not later is an ongoing challenge for nearly all businesses, so think about how you might encourage customers to buy today rather than tomorrow. Also reflect on how businesses of all shapes and sizes encourage you to buy sooner using scarcity techniques like countdown clocks, early-bird prices, and low-inventory or low-availability notifications.

Prompt: *Does the customer have the money? Why should they spend this money now and not later?*

4. **The solution is lucrative.** Now—*how much* are people willing to pay for the solution? If you were thinking you were going to sell these bracelets for $100 each and customers won't pay more than $20 (when they each took $35 in supplies to make), that's going to be an issue.

   Do a little research on what other businesses or self-employed individuals typically charge for their solution. Is this similar to what you would charge? Is there something that would make you stand out—more experience, a different approach, better ingredients, more credibility—that would merit charging more? Map out what you'd like to be taking home per month from this stream of self-employment income, along with how many hours it will take to do so, and use this to calculate your effective hourly rate (a number we also referenced in chapter 5 when referring to work). Decide if this number is worth the extra work to you.

Prompt: *Is it lucrative? What price will you need to charge for this effort to be worth your time? What are the current prices in market?*

____

____

____

5. **The target customer base can be reached, thoughtfully.** Imagine you have a lemonade stand, and your job is to sell lemonade (pink, boozy, whatever you want—founder's choice). You wouldn't set up your lemonade stand in the middle of the desert, would you? No one would ever drive by.

   But you also wouldn't set up your lemonade stand on the side of the highway. That's absurd, right? People aren't going to pull over for some lemonade, and even if they wanted to, they're going too fast to be able to safely slow down and pull over. There is traffic, but it's not the *right* traffic. You need something in between, like a table at a farmer's market, or a busy neighborhood sidewalk.

   A profitable idea includes a plan for how to reach potential customers and create traffic or buzz. Are the customers already looking for your solution, or will you need to go to them first and pitch yourself? Take a moment to think about how you would market your idea in a way that is productive and profitable.

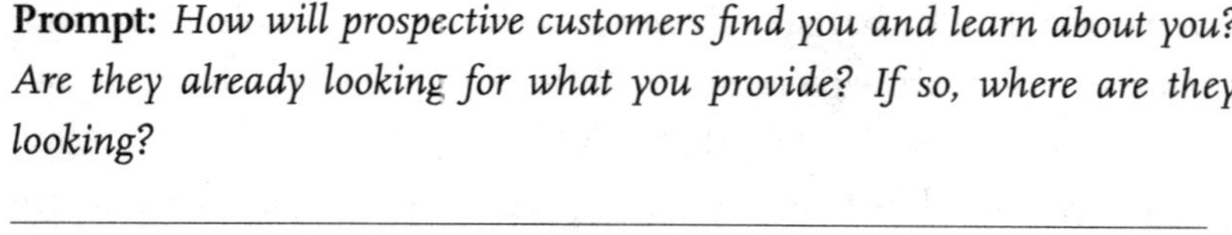

Prompt: *How will prospective customers find you and learn about you? Are they already looking for what you provide? If so, where are they looking?*

____

____

____

Action: Do five tests on your business idea to determine whether it's profitable and worth your time. These tests are:

- There's a problem, pain point, or desire.
- Your customer is aware of the pain or desire.
- The customer is able and willing to pay.
- The solution is lucrative.
- The target customer base can be reached, thoughtfully.

STEP 2: VALIDATE YOUR IDEA

We *theoretically* have a profitable idea. Now . . . will it work? And *do we like doing it?* Let's find out.

The quickest way to validate an idea is to go sell it. This can freak you out at first, because it means putting yourself out there and potentially failing *a lot.* We'd much rather hide behind a screen, or update our title to "Founder and CEO" on LinkedIn and get a bunch of oohs and aahs, or tell our mom (who of course will say it's amazing) about our business idea. These things are great, but they are not the same as sales, which are the kind of validation we're looking for.

Also figure out whether you actually like your idea in practice. At one point in my self-employment journey, I tried my hand at ghostwriting personal essays for executives. The money was great, but it was soul-sucking to cosplay as someone else for a living (and I'd get jealous when these articles with their names on them got huge praise and led to new opportunities). Had I not tried, however, I never would have figured that out.

Entrepreneurship can be uncomfortable at times; make sure you enjoy what you're doing.

TEA

Uncertainty holding you back? To build confidence in your new venture, consider offering a "beta test" price at the start. This can be a lower rate, or you can throw in some other bells and whistles for free, in exchange for feedback from clients. Do this to work out the kinks in your offering and delivery, and be sure to get positive reviews from happy customers. Once you've found your groove, raise your prices.

Many people skip this step. A few friends tell them their idea is amazing during happy hour, so then they skip all these other steps and go build the side hustle or the business, then wonder why it tanks. Validate your idea first to save yourself from heartbreak down the road.

STEP 3: TRACK INCOME AND EXPENSES

Now for the fun part—getting paid. Here is what you'll need to start earning self-employment income smoothly.

A point of sale (POS). This is how you accept payment. It can be the credit card reader you plug into your phone, a website like Stripe, or a third-party app like Venmo, Cash App, or PayPal. When using these tools for business, there's typically a small payment processing fee. (Again, don't mark the payments as "Friends and Family" to try to save a few bucks. In addition to it being tax evasion, you're also sidestepping the app's business model when you do this, which is grounds for your account getting terminated.)

A way to provide an invoice. Most POS systems give customers the option to get a receipt by text or email. If your customers are businesses, they may want an invoice prior to the transaction, or a copy of an invoice post-transaction for their records. An invoice is an itemized list of what has been purchased, along with the total to be charged. You can find free invoice templates online and fill them in yourself as needed.

A way to store your expense receipts. You can't deduct expenses on your taxes unless you have the receipts to prove they actually happened. Photos or scans of receipts are fine, as long as the method of payment is showing. Find a way to save your receipts diligently, and consider organizing them by category and month. If your business involves a lot of expenses, and you don't want to spend time or energy sorting through receipts, consider using bookkeeping software or getting a professional bookkeeper to help you. Do some online research, or see my recommendations at https://nickwolny.com/book-resources.

After covering your expenses (and setting aside money for taxes), you're free to do as you please with whatever's left. This money is self-employment income that you can incorporate into your monthly budget and saving goals however you like.

Action: Prepare yourself to receive payments from customers. This includes having a point of sale, a way to save receipts, and a place to set aside money for taxes.

FROM "ON THE DL" TO OUT AND PROUD

Many, many people leverage entrepreneurship without ever registering a business in their state, and it's fine. You're not in trouble for doing so. But there might be circumstances in which you *do* want to make your business official and register as a partnership, LLC, or corporation.

A few perks to business formation are:

You look more official to customers. "Sassypants892x@gmail.com" is fine for personal use, but might not be the most compelling email address when doing business outreach (unless the name of your company is Sassy Pants, in which case, go off, sis). For customers to give you money, they have to feel like they can trust you; officially registering your business gives you credibility. It'll keep your personal contact information private, too.

Pushes you to separate the finances. Most banks will let you open a separate business checking account at the same bank. This can also help you keep things organized and see at a glance how much money you're actually gaining or losing in your entrepreneurial efforts each month.

You'll have liability and bankruptcy protection. No one running a business or working a side hustle expects to get sued, but the reality is that it sometimes happens. Maybe someone comes to your apartment because you offer chair massage, and on the way out they trip and fall down the stairs, then try to blame it on you. Or perhaps things go sideways because of something unexpected—like, oh, I don't know, a global pandemic—and the money stops coming in. If for no other reason, consider officially forming a business so that you have liability protection.

Liability protection means that, in the event someone tried to sue you and the lawsuit ended in a settlement or judgment, or your business goes bankrupt for other reasons, your personal assets won't be up for grabs. Your business will go under, but you won't lose your house, your car, or your precious collection of vintage gay pin-up magazines (I have nightmares about this outcome sometimes) in the business bankruptcy process.

A sole proprietorship does *not* provide liability protection, so if you want this level of separation, you'll need to formally register your business.

It's a must if you ever want to sell your business or have investors. I once had a client who co-owned a small business acquisitions firm and had written a book about the subject. I learned a lot about how businesses are bought and sold from working with him, and got to learn about a few of his clients, too (one was a woman who had invented a board game).

Did you know that half of *all the money* an entrepreneur will ever make from their business comes in the day they sell it? A typical rule of thumb is that a successful business price tag (aka its **valuation**) will be one to three times its annual revenue, often paid up front in cash when the deal goes through. Cha-ching! (With my client's help, board game lady sold her business for $5 million. Excuse me while I go scream into the abyss.)

This is an incredible payout, and I don't want to understate how much work board game lady did to get to that point. It usually takes several years to get a business ready to sell. But it is possible. And no one's gonna buy your raggedy-ass business until you get all your paperwork in order. The same goes for getting investors, too.

All these reasons aside, officially forming your business will make you take it more seriously and give it your quality attention.

"ALEXA, PLAY 'FORMATION' BY BEYONCÉ"

When forming a business, you have four options: **sole proprietorship**, **partnership**, **LLC**, or **corporation**. If you want liability protection, the sole prop is out, and many types of partnerships are out, too. Of the remaining options, corporations are more complicated because there's more paperwork, and you have to do your business taxes separately.

That leaves the LLC—convenient, because that's what I have (#biased). Other entrepreneurs seem to agree, though; LLCs have been on a rager these past twenty years because they're easy to manage while also providing liability protection, tax benefits, and flexibility. If you're the only owner of your LLC like I am, it's called a **single-member LLC**, which is nice because you can just paper-clip your business activity to your personal tax return at the end of the year.

TEA

Single-member LLC: Official, professional, and all you, baby. In a single-member LLC, you are the only owner (member) of the company. When you do your taxes, you can just attach your business numbers to your personal tax return.

Like sole proprietorships, your LLC's profits are what get taxed. Whatever profit you had at the end of the year is considered taxable income, and deducting your expenses will help lower this number (and your overall tax bill). If your LLC made you $20,000 last year, and you had $8,000 in expenses, the remaining $12,000 gets added to your taxable income. If you didn't document the expenses, the full $20,000 would get added. Assuming a 20 percent effective tax rate, that'd be an extra $1,600 you'd owe at tax time.

Be pleasantly persistent about getting those expense receipts, and if doing so hurts someone's feelings, blame it on me.

Adrian, 28, Illinois: *My brother and I always had a passion for creating videos and films. We would sometimes do freelance projects—advertisements for companies, music videos, and so on. We wanted* *to put all those offerings under one roof, so we formed an LLC outside of our day jobs, which has really helped us establish ourselves as creatives here in Chicago. Part of my definition of wealth is getting to do what I love with people I love, and this LLC really supports that.*

CHECKLIST: HOW TO SET UP AN LLC

Setting up an LLC can feel scary at first, but the steps are straightforward and similar from state to state. From start to finish, the process can take anywhere from a few days to a few weeks. Here's an overview of what the overall effort and cost will look like.

1. **Decide what state you're incorporating the LLC in.** LLCs are governed at the state level, so you'll set your LLC up with the Secretary of State's office. Every state has step-by-step instructions that are easy to find on the internet.
2. **Pick a name for your LLC.** Your LLC name must be available in the state of registration. I can't call my business "Nick's Consulting Shack" if someone else already registered it.
3. **Name a registered agent.** A registered agent is a person or entity who can receive important information and legal correspondence on behalf of an LLC. States require this. You can appoint yourself as the registered agent, or, more commonly, can pay an organization to be your registered agent on your behalf.
4. **File Articles of Organization and other paperwork.** Articles of Organization are the official documents that declare your company is ~~a real boy~~ legit. In some states, they're known as a Certificate of Formation. These and other documents will have upfront filing fees, which vary from state to state.
5. **Get an employer identification number.** An employer identification number (EIN) is like a Social Security number for your business. Don't let online ads make you think you have to pay for one; you can get an EIN from the IRS website for free.

6. **Open a business bank account.** With your EIN in tow, you can open a business bank account, either at your existing bank or a new bank.
7. **Maintain good standing.** After your LLC is set up, you'll file an annual report each year to maintain good standing. In most states, you'll also pay an annual fee to keep the LLC open, typically between $50 and $300 (except California, where it's $800). If you're making at least a thousand dollars per year from your business formation, the pros outweigh the cons of annual fees in most cases.

° ° °

Entrepreneurship helps you use your time and skills to bring in more money. More money means a wider gap between income and expenses, which you can then use to both increase your saving rate (building wealth for the future) and utilize for day-to-day expenditures (having queer joy in the present). For queer people, knowing our way around self-employment income and how to go get it on command is an incredibly useful skill.

The lifestyle design potential from entrepreneurship is hard to beat. And when we really get moving and grooving on the Saving Rate Roadmap, the potential for a new future emerges, one in which you can eventually work less or stop working altogether, on a timeline you choose.

That's the big idea behind financial independence, and we're now ready to reveal where the Saving Rate Roadmap is taking us.

9

FINANCIAL INDEPENDENCE

Reject Retirement Culture and Become Work-Optional at Gay Walking Speed (i.e., Faster)

Oh, what's that? You need help sedating an elephant? I have the perfect tranquilizer dart to get the job done—it's called "talking about retirement."

Nothing puts readers to sleep faster than talking about retirement. It's simply too far off as a financial goal. It's intangible, an ultramarathon in length, without much clarity on how far along the journey you are or whether you're on track. (The exception is when people are close to retirement and realize they're nowhere close to having enough money, in which case they quickly start caring *a lot* about retirement.)

Throughout the 2000s and 2010s, you would have found few people on Tom from Myspace's internet less interested in learning about retirement than I was. My parents were lower-middle class, and estranged from their respective families, so there wasn't much family chatter about retirement or inheriting generational wealth. Being gay, I avoided societal pressures to settle down, start a family, and buy a craftsman house with a white picket fence (goals that typically jumpstart long-term financial planning). I was just trying to survive my twenties on my own, which meant I needed every dollar to make ends meet. I was focused on getting through the month, not some finish line forty years away.

And can I be dark for a moment? My first years of exposure to queer culture were so mortality-drenched that it took me a long time to believe queer people actually can grow old and live long, happy lives. From the Lavender Scare, to Don't Ask, Don't Tell, to violence against trans people, to religious oppression around the world, it feels like a lot sometimes. And I'm still pissed off about the AIDS outbreak, how we're supposed to have all these brilliant queer mentors and friends who would have been in their sixties and seventies now, but don't, because Reagan laughed it off for years.[1] I think we're all still recovering from the shock of that time, and all the other ways queer people's lives have been diminished throughout our history. We *can* and *should* expect to live long, healthy lives. Retirement is something our culture is only just beginning to know.

And so, for all the reasons explained above, I was not cast on Season 19 or any other season of *America's Next Top Retirement Planning Spokesperson*. But then I got this editor job with a personal finance publication, with a directive to make topics like financial freedom fresh and readable. As I poked around on the internet for sources, I soon came across countless blogs and social media accounts of people who had retired early—like, really early. We're talkin' people who stopped working in their fifties, forties, and thirties, even. These mega-savers didn't consider themselves retired, or even use the word "retirement." They called it something else: *financial independence*.

Financial independence is sexy. Financial independence is fresh. It's what retirement would be if it got a publicist, an image consultant, a stylist, and maybe a good MUA on speed-dial. Trailblazed by boomers and Gen X, then popularized by self-improvement-obsessed millennials ("if I watch enough tutorials on YouTube, I CAN DO ANYTHING"), financial independence is where our Saving Rate Roadmap is ultimately headed. How fast we get to the destination is up to us.

Often abbreviated as FI, financial independence means not having to work for money. Using our terminology from the income stream rainbow, it means being able to cover most or all of your monthly expenses through investment income, the income you produce from assets, rather than earned income, the income you produce from labor (which is probably the opposite of what your income sources are now). Financially independent people can retire years or decades ahead of typical retirement age and not have to wait for things like Social Security benefits (which aren't available until age 62 at the earliest) before making big career or lifestyle changes. As such, an alternative retirement mentality among personal finance enthusiasts was born: **Financial Independence, Retire Early**, better known as **FIRE.**

As I interviewed FIRE enthusiasts and wrote profiles about their approaches to money, I realized that FI wasn't about discovering the next get-rich-quick idea. It was simply a bolder, heightened, drag-queen version of the healthy money habits you and I have been talking about throughout this whole book. It also gives you goals, and goals provide structure. Saving an extra $300 a month "because I'm supposed to" doesn't inspire me. Saving an extra $300 a month because it will let me stop working five years sooner? Okay, I'm interested, tell me more.

FIRE gives you tangible goals for your future, which in turn will give you confidence about your money. When you know your goals and whether you're on track, you can fly your present-day queer joy airplane wherever you want without wondering if you'll run out of gas in the middle of the trip. And if you don't like what your financial forecast shows you, you can change your flight trajectory by taking action today. Even better, we've been quietly breadcrumbing the principles of FIRE all throughout this book; you already have a running start.

Financial independence is a more proactive and flexible approach to retirement and money in general. Before we get into the nuts and bolts of how it works, though, let's clarify some of the current flaws in retirement thinking and why a more FI-minded approach can breathe new life into a goal that often feels stale. From there, we'll use principles lifted from FIRE to help you plot your path to an awesome queer existence.

Reframing Retirement

1. Retirement is determined by assets, not age
2. A lot of people depend on the government to save the day
3. Waiting until retirement to pursue your passions is a bad idea
4. States that are "good for retirement" may not be good for LGBTQ+ people
5. FIRE people are a lot like us, they just go harder

REFRAME NO. 1: RETIREMENT IS DETERMINED BY ASSETS, NOT AGE

Retirement is typically associated with being in your sixties at the earliest. Part of the reason for this is that various government programs and tax benefits don't kick in until then: Withdrawals from retirement accounts like 401(k)s and IRAs don't become penalty-free until age 59.5, Social Security becomes available (for most) at 62, and Medicare at 65. Other than eligibility for these benefits, age has nothing to do with retirement. As long as your assets generate enough investment income to live off of, and can keep pace with inflation, you can theoretically stop working whenever you want.

Recall the exercise in chapter 6 where we introduced the 4 percent rule. If you withdraw 4 percent of your investments every year, and keep the rest invested, the odds are very good that your investments will last you at least thirty years. Financial independence isn't about being old enough to retire, but rather having enough in assets that you can live on investment income alone, whether you're 35, 65, or 95 years old.

How much in assets will be enough? This number is known as the **FIRE number**, and it uses the 4 percent rule to help you establish a finish line. That finish line will be unique to you based on what you think your expenses will be later in life.

TEA

FIRE number: Your financial independence finish line. The FIRE number is the amount of money you need in income-producing assets to be able to live on investment income alone.

Later in this chapter, you'll calculate a ballpark FIRE number for yourself that can serve as the "destination" of your Saving Rate Roadmap.

The planning technology of the FIRE number isn't only for people who aspire to retire early. It can also help you decide whether and when you want to start making and saving *less* money. The FIRE number can show you when it'd be a good time to shift out of an intense career, grow your family, buy a condo, or increase travel to different countries to experience new cultures. With a few flourishes of the calculator app, you can figure out how long you'll need to keep working, and whether you like the timeline you see or want to change it.

The money malaise of "I am going to have to work forever" begins to dissolve. In FIRE, you can create a forecast for how your life will unfold.

REFRAME NO. 2: A LOT OF PEOPLE DEPEND ON THE GOVERNMENT TO SAVE THE DAY

We've thrown around the term "Social Security" a few times now, and perhaps you've previously heard of it only because your grandpa would loudly complain that his monthly check hadn't yet arrived in the mail back when you were a kid. You don't really get what it is; you wouldn't be able to explain it to a friend. Let's fix that.

Established in the 1930s, Social Security is a government-funded benefits program that people typically opt into between the ages of 62 and 67. The program is funded by tax dollars, and is designed mainly to pay retirees and people with disabilities a monthly income each month. It also pays benefits to spouses or children of recipients, as well as spouses or children of workers who have died.

Since a lot of people in their sixties couldn't or didn't save for retirement as much as they would have liked, they lean heavily on Social Security when they stop working. But the benefits rarely replace one's entire working income; on average, Social Security only provides about 39 percent of what someone was making when they were still employed. Many older people (by many, I mean millions) had nothing saved for retirement at all, so they must survive on Social Security benefits alone, which isn't really how the program was intended to work, but alas, here we are.

You can see what your expected Social Security benefit will be at any time by making a profile on SSA.gov. You'll see every year that you've filed your taxes, which is how the administration determines what your Social Security benefit will be (ahem, another win for filing your taxes, I see).

Perhaps this is me projecting my disdain for the US government's track record toward LGBTQ+ people, but I really don't like the idea of the government being your financial plan. Governments change laws. Governments open and close public service programs depending on who's in power at the time (Social Security is a frequent political talking point), and they can add or remove conditions for eligibility to these programs to please their constituents. These are real problems, with real financial impacts, and we must not tolerate elected officials toying with our financial well-being for the sake of identity politics.

LGBTQ+ people should be aware of Social Security because it's a potential income stream later in life, but should also prioritize having their own financial affairs in order to help ensure self-sufficiency.

REFRAME NO. 3: WAITING UNTIL RETIREMENT TO PURSUE YOUR PASSIONS IS A BAD IDEA

Don't forget to live that queer life, babes! Rather than wait until retirement to discover your passions and purpose in life, set out to find them now. Do a retirement psyop on yourself by finding what gives your life purpose sooner so you can look forward to doing more of it later.

What parts of the country or world might you want to visit on a regular basis, or even move to permanently? What hobbies might you take up in your non-work time, activities that will likely increase when you no longer have to work for money? This is one reason I lean pro-hustle, and IDGAF who has beef with it. I want you to go out there and get those extra coins so you can go on adventures, try new things, taste new flavors, and get clear about how you want to spend your time on this Earth before it's too late.

FIRE unlocks an enormous amount of time freedom. Without the burden of having to work for money—an agreement we all involuntarily accept that consumes tens of thousands of hours of our lives—you are free to do as you please, travel where you want, and stand on your own financial footing.

Cosplay as a full-time relaxer on your off time so that, as you age, you know how to use your leisure time to the fullest. This work will also help you forecast how much money you want to have in your later years so you can spend on these passions generously and really enjoy them.

REFRAME NO. 4: STATES THAT ARE "GOOD FOR RETIREMENT" MAY NOT BE GOOD FOR LGBTQ+ PEOPLE

Florida is great for retirement on paper. But as of this writing, it's also one of the most hostile states in the country for queer rights, particularly for transgender and non-binary people. I'm not saying Floridians are bad (the Eagle in Fort Lauderdale is great, I love y'all!), but the recent state legislative track record is well-documented. Queer people should do adequate research and weigh their options.

"Best states for retirement" lists are usually ranked through data points like state taxes, cost of living, and weather, and these factors indeed influence millions of Americans to relocate in their later years. As a queer person, you should take an area's LGBTQ+ rights track record into consideration, too. When it comes to setting personal finance goals, we sometimes need to look up from our spreadsheet and take other factors into consideration. Remember that money is just one category of wealth.

REFRAME NO. 5: FIRE PEOPLE ARE A LOT LIKE US, THEY JUST GO HARDER

You've already learned most of what you need to start pursuing FIRE. Approximately 99 percent of your energy and attention should be spent on the 7-word plan we went over throughout Part II. Say it with me: (*cues with hands*) "Lower expenses, increase earnings, invest the difference."

FIRE enthusiasts are just people who go harder on the 7-word plan. These are the "extra extra credit" people that queer folks already know well (you might even be one). Ask them to make a diorama, and they'll install functional lighting and flying buttresses over the doorways for their miniatures. Ask them who won Best Actress at the 1982

Tonys, and the instant recall will put any AI chatbot to shame (*yells* IT WAS JENNIFER HOLLIDAY IN *DREAMGIRLS* AND SHE WAS 21 AT THE TIME). Ask them to lower expenses and they'll push their budget down to the floor. Ask them to increase earnings and they'll monetize every hour of their life they possibly can—sometimes to the detriment of other priorities. The result of these efforts is a very high saving rate, often 50 percent or more, which is how FIRE proponents accelerate toward the financial freedom finish line.

Jeff, 45, California: *I got out of the military after six years of service and expected to get a regular ol' job. But 2008 was the start of the Great Recession, and there weren't many opportunities. I was taking out cash advances on my credit card, and eventually had to short sell my condo. I considered living in my car to save money. Hard work had always worked out for me in life, so it was a real smack in the face. I eventually found work, but kept that frugality muscle wound tight. Over the next thirteen years, I went from negative $10,000 to $1 million in assets. I tried sharing about my money journey online, but found there are some real haters out there. So I just keep this win to myself and focus on my own life and relationships. I now put $1,000 a month into a sinking fund for vacations because I love to travel. But in other ways, I'm still frugal. The car I recently bought was a Honda Civic.*

Not everyone interested in FIRE wants to retire early, though, so you'll sometimes see the acronym abbreviated to FI, with the "early retirement" part of the acronym dropped. FI people are money nerds, but they aren't going to eat rice and beans every day for twenty years to hoard every penny they can. What they *will* do is practice the principles of FIRE to create more intentionality in their lives, because maybe they want to set a timeline for when they can afford to leave that high-paying-but-also-exhausting job. Or maybe they want to prepare themselves to take care of an elderly loved one in the near future. If you like the money vibe we've been cultivating throughout this book, FI might be a healthy approach for you.

THE FLAVORS OF FI

Great news, everyone: We got some marketing gays to join us in the conference room; the vocabulary will be much livelier now.

As you might have noticed, FIRE is just retirement planning with good marketing slathered on top. Because FIRE enthusiasts have a kink for self-reflection, they began gathering in forums and finding one another online, organizing themselves into their own little sets of genus and species based on their varying circumstances and life goals.

Here are a few of those subsets and how their communities have adapted the idea of FIRE for themselves. One or more of them might resonate with you.

CoastFI: An approach that doesn't involve retiring early. Instead, you save aggressively in your earlier years to frontload your retirement savings, then slow down or stop contributing and "coast," letting the compounding carry you the rest of the way to your goals. You work harder upfront, but then have the freedom of more spending money in midlife, and still reach your target retirement number on time.

BaristaFI: Also an approach that doesn't involve retiring early, but instead prioritizes reaching the point at which you can downshift to part-time work or a less stressful job, upon which your investments provide a stream of passive income. One of the biggest reasons these mostly financially independent people keep a job is to have health insurance, because health insurance is expensive in this country. The name "BaristaFI" is a reference to Starbucks, which offers part-time employees health insurance coverage.

Lean FIRE: In lean FIRE, you aspire to retire early by keeping a *really* tight budget. Since you'll need less income to live, you don't need as much in assets, which means you could leave the workforce sooner.

Fat FIRE: The opposite of lean FIRE. You don't want a bare-bones lifestyle when you stop working, so you'd rather work longer and stack more cash in order to have a better quality of life when you leave the workforce.

THE FIRE NUMBER

FIRE enthusiasts took the 4 percent rule and used it to reverse-engineer a finish line of their own, which is so on-brand for "extra extra credit" people. They take the amount of money they expect to need each year in expenses when retired, then divide it by 4 percent (or, put another way, multiply by 25) to see how much they need in investments to live off of investment income alone. In FIRE culture, this calculation is known as the **FIRE number**.

Annual Expenses x 25 = FIRE Number

Your FIRE number is the finish line of your Saving Rate Roadmap. It's also typically a big number, which is why I've held back on blabbing it to you for nearly 250 pages now. I didn't want to scare you off. I have an exercise for you shortly that will help take the fear and skepticism away, but I need you to trust me on this one, see the exercise through, and not let money malaise short-circuit our efforts.

As a general approach to money, the pursuit of FI is healthier. Some people eat protein and vegetables because they're professional athletes or passionate about bodybuilding, so they need top-notch nutrition. The rest of us aren't that intense, but we still eat protein and vegetables occasionally (or know we should) because doing so gives us more energy and makes us feel better. (Keepin' it going with the nutrition metaphor: If you get too obsessive about your food, it can lead to dysregulated behaviors. Know that that can happen with money, too.)

Think of the FI approach as eating financial protein and vegetables. It's healthy, it gives you confidence, it makes you poop, and turning it into a habit will improve your quality of life. Let's follow our composite Marek, who's come a long way from being overspent and undersaved, as he gives the FIRE number a try.

Marek

It's been a transformative few years for Marek. He's gotten both a better-paying job and a side hustle, and has also kept his expenses low. As a result, he's now saving 35 percent of his income. Marek calculates that he would need about $4,600 a month for expenses when he stops working. $4,600/month x 12 months/year x 25 = a FIRE number of $1.38 million in investments.

I know $1.38 million looks like a lot. I'ma do some warlock-craft in a moment that will make $1.38 million *not* feel like a lot, but you have to stick with me on this one.

The FIRE number is a tool that challenges us to build up our income-generating assets by following the 7-word plan. Let's now see what this would look like in your own life.

HOW TO REACH FINANCIAL INDEPENDENCE

Get out a pen and paper, or open up another tab in your spreadsheet. Create two columns and a total of six rows. Also leave lots of room in the margins; you might want to model out different scenarios.

Label the boxes as follows:

Future monthly expenses	
Future earned income	
Monthly investment income need	
FIRE number	
Monthly investing goal	
Over/under	

STEP 1: ESTIMATE YOUR EXPECTED FUTURE EXPENSES

First, we need to approximate what our future expenses will be.

Consult your budget from chapter 4 and its categories. Go through each of your expenses and determine whether or not that expense will be the same, go up, or go down in the future (create an additional column off to the right if that helps). Also, don't worry about inflation for the purposes of these projections for now.

Expenses that may go up:

- **Health care and health insurance.** Health care costs statistically rise with age. Also, if no longer working, you'll need to have your own health insurance.
- **Travel and leisure.** So much more free time, what will you do with it? If travel and adventure are on the agenda, budget for this accordingly.

Expenses that may go down or disappear:

- **Housing.** One advantage of owning a home is that, once the mortgage is paid off, you'll reduce your housing expenses considerably. You may also want to downsize to a smaller home or move to an area with a lower cost of living.
- **Loans and debt.** At some point, your credit card debt, student loans,

personal loans, and auto debt will be paid off. The money you have allocated for "additional debt paydown" won't be needed in your budget anymore.

- **Savings and investments.** If you've reached financial independence, you're at the finish line, so you technically don't need to keep putting money toward saving and/or investments unless you want to. You can exclude some, most, or all of these monthly expenses from your projections.
- **Work-related expenses.** No more business professional attire, no more commuting, no more getting lunch at the office. Also no more pet daycare or dogwalkers, because now you'll be home more often, so if Fido needs to go outside four times a day to shake out his zoomies, you'll be there to open the door. Think about what expenses will no longer be necessary once you stop working.

Remember to include annual expenses. Divide any annual expenses by 12 so that you can include them in your monthly expense calculations.

Action: Calculate your expected future monthly expenses, then put this number in row 1.

STEP 2: FACTOR IN ANY FUTURE EARNED INCOME

Technically, "financially independent" means going full-doomsday prepper in that you don't plan to rely on work or government programs like Social Security to meet your needs. But maybe you do want to still work part-time, or focus on doing work you love, like what proponents of BaristaFI aspire to do. Knowing you'll have other income sources or benefits like health insurance can help cover some of your expenses, which means you won't need as much in investments, which means a lower FIRE number.

If you have a job that offers a pension, such as working for a police or fire department, you can factor that in here as well. We won't factor in Social Security or Medicare here, but you can always make a profile at SSA.org and see your projected benefits if you'd like that information in your periphery.

Action: Calculate any expected future earned income, then put this number in row 2.

STEP 3: CALCULATE YOUR FIRE NUMBER

Subtract row 2 from row 1. This gives you the amount of money your investments need to generate each month, which is the number you will use to calculate your FIRE number. Write this number down in row 3. Multiply row 3 by 12 to arrive at future expected annual expenses. Then, multiply this number by 25 to arrive at your FIRE number, and write it down in row 4.

For reference, here's where Marek would be in the exercise:

Future monthly expenses	$4,600
Future earned income	$0
Monthly investment income need	$4,600
FIRE number	$1,380,000

Know that you don't have to hit your FIRE number in order to retire. Many people retire with less money than this and have great lives in their later years. They're just not *technically* financially independent; they're slowly eating away at the nest egg, with the hope that it doesn't run out.

In contrast, financial independence means your assets are renewable resources, like solar panels; they self-generate the money you need, without losing any of their original value. We're taking a "shoot the moon" mentality here and forecasting what you'd need to become fully financially independent to create a reference point.

Action: Subtract row 2 from row 1 to determine your investment income needs, then write this number down in row 3. Then, calculate your FIRE number, which will be the amount of invested assets you need to generate row 3 through investment income alone. Put your FIRE number in row 4.

STEP 4: REVERSE-ENGINEER WHAT YOU'LL NEED IN INVESTMENTS TO GET THERE

Now for the fun part: We want to figure out how much money we'll need to put into investments each month to get us to our FIRE number in a given timeframe. Investor.gov has a free calculator that will help model this for you, or just type "savings goal calculator" into a search engine.[2]

You will enter the following information:

- Your FIRE number (aka your end goal).
- How much you currently have in investments.
- Your timeframe—the age at which you'd like to stop working.
- Expected rate of compounding—we'll use 6 percent here. 5 to 6 percent is considered more conservative; 8 to 9 percent is considered more optimistic. You can forecast more than one compounding scenario if you want.
- Compounding frequency—almost everyone should do "annual compounding" for this. The planning is way easier.

You can tinker with different scenarios to see your options, and in fact you should, so that you can weigh the pros and cons of pursuing financial independence sooner rather than later. Here's Marek again:

Marek

Marek, now 29, determined that his FIRE number is $1.38 million. He currently has $20,000 in investments. He models two scenarios: leaving the workforce at 54 and leaving the workforce at 44. At a 6 percent rate of return, compounding annually, Marek will need to invest a total of $1,966 per month to hit his FIRE number at 54 (this is everything altogether: retirement contributions, brokerage, and other tax-advantaged or tax-exempt accounts). To hit it by 44, he'll need far more oomph: $4,769 per month. Achievable, but only if he dramatically ramps up his earnings somehow while also keeping his expenses low.

Action: Use free online calculators to model one or more timeframes for reaching your FIRE number. Determine how much money you'll need to invest each month to reach your goal for each scenario. Write down this monthly goal in row 5.

STEP 5: MODIFY YOUR SAVING AND SPENDING GOALS ACCORDINGLY

The previous step showed you what you'll need to be saving and investing each month to reach your goals. Compare this with your budget and what you're currently contributing each month.

You'll want to include:

- Retirement account contributions, such as 401(k)s and IRAs
- Brokerage account contributions
- Any other interest-generating investments

Subtract the monthly goal you wrote down in row 5 from your current monthly investing contributions, and put this number in row 6.

Marek

Marek is currently putting $1,200 a month toward investments. He does the FIRE planning exercise, as shown below, and finds that, if he wants to be financially independent by 54, he needs to find a way to contribute an extra $766 a month to investments (row 6).

Future expenses	$4,600
Future earned income	$0
Monthly investment income need	$4,600
FIRE number	$1.38 million
Monthly investing goal	$1,966
Over/under	-$766

IMPORTANT: Row 6 is your magic number. This is the one we're focusing on. I told you I would make $1.38 million feel smaller—this is how. If you're Marek, it's useless to focus on the $1.38 million number. He should instead focus on working his 7-word plan so that he can bring in an extra $766 per month if he wants to retire at 54. Or he can bring in more than that and have some fun money on the side. Or he can adjust his timeline. His future is in his hands.

The reason people tune out retirement planning is that the timelines are so long (and the numbers so big) it feels impossible to reach, a perfect formula for destructive money malaise. But then, later in life, many people regret not being more diligent with their personal finances in their early years, when their money would have had more time to grow and compound. Instead of focusing on that million-dollar number that feels impossible, focus on what you can do to tackle the number in row 6.

This number will likely change a bit over time, and that's okay. When you know you're on track with your financial future, and can see how the future might potentially play out, this money knowledge gives you confidence about both your current spending and future well-being. Like investing, and many other strategies presented throughout this book, we want to set it and forget it as much as possible so we can spend our time enjoying life.

Think of retirement planning as a way to reduce anxiety, inspire confidence in the present, and secure your future.

Action: Subtract row 5 from your current monthly investment contributions. Plot this over/under in row 6.

YOUR SAVING RATE ROADMAP FOR FINANCIAL INDEPENDENCE

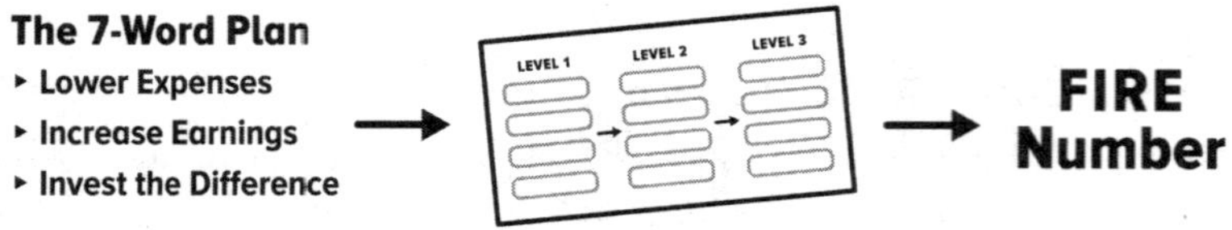

The promise of this book is that you will walk away with a roadmap to financial independence. Let's now put it all together so your next action steps are clear.

The way you handle your money is driven by your thought patterns and habits. When left unattended, mindless spending can push you into debt through avoidance and numbing behaviors, as well as **money malaise**, a specific flavor of avoidance in which you throw your hands up in frustration and give up before you've even started. You may also have been mindful with your money, yet still don't have much to show for it because of a mix of blind spots and learning things about money that weren't true. Many of us find ourselves in debt not through frivolous spending, but through the pursuit of education, trying to get our adult lives off the ground, or an unexpected setback.

As long as you have debt, you also have **debt drag**, which erodes your purchasing power. The higher the interest rate on your debt, the stronger this drag is. Debt drag is like running with a parachute tied to your back. But many of us stumble into unintentional debt anyway because (1) we don't have much in savings, (2) our cash flow isn't great so we put things on a credit card "just to be safe," or (3) we use the credit card when shit hits the fan. This other investing stuff is certainly sexy, but your money will be better used initially to pay down high-interest debt (debt with an interest rate above 10 percent), build up savings, and swear off debt drag for good.

A good money metric that can apply to queer people of all ages and income levels is **modified saving rate**. This is the percentage of your monthly income that goes to savings, investments, and debt payments (beyond the minimum required monthly payment). It's not uncommon for people to have a saving rate of zero or close to zero. Focus on increasing your saving rate to a goal of 15 percent. By working up to this, you build a money muscle that will serve you well in the future and ensure you don't succumb to **lifestyle creep**, in which expenses rise with income. Put your saving rate money toward "level 1 priorities" first, building up savings (preferably in a **high-yield savings account**), paying off high-interest debt, and participating in your employer's 401(k) match if they offer one.

To increase saving rate and work toward financial independence, follow the **7-word plan for building wealth:** lower expenses, increase earnings, invest the difference. The first part of the plan is to **lower expenses**, because expenses are usually what is most within your control. Take a more holistic approach to expenses; look at what you spend money on and why, and whether that supports your best queer life. Be honest with yourself about what really matters. We do want frugality, because that saves you money, but not if it means unsustainable discomfort. The best budget is a sustainable budget. Also think about fun things you want to save up for, then create one or more **sinking funds** to save up for these items or experiences and pay for them in cash.

Next, figure out how you can **increase earnings**. For many, this is the most transformational piece of the puzzle; it's the set of actions that collectively bring more money into your bank account every month. There are different types of income: **earned income**, which comes from labor, and **investment income**, which comes from assets. Most people make their money from earned income during their working lives. To increase earned income, you can focus on increasing **wages** by getting a promotion or better-paying job; increasing **self-employment income**, which is income you are paid without being an official employee; or a combination of the two. "Job-getting skills" are often different than the work skills themselves. These skills include job hunting, interviewing, and negotiating a compensation package.

When you lower expenses and increase earnings, the gap between the two will widen. We can then **invest the difference**, putting this money toward savings and investments that will turn into an asset and generate investment income in the future. In this book, we mainly focused on **stocks, bonds, and funds** (which are collectively known as **securities**) because they have both a low barrier of entry and a strong track record. Real estate, cryptocurrency, a business, and other types of property can also be assets.

We suggest investing in securities through **tax-advantaged accounts** first, such as retirement accounts, because they have tax perks that will help you keep more of the money you earn. In your Saving Rate Roadmap, these are level 2 priorities, only to be addressed after the level 1 priorities are in motion. They include the **Roth IRA** (which gets its own callout because it's very tax-advantaged), other retirement accounts, and paying down medium-interest debt (debt with an interest rate between 4 and 10 percent). Sinking funds are also a level

2 priority, because they help ensure you're making memories and improving your quality of life now. If you still have coins left over, you can move on to level 3 priorities, which include a brokerage account, other tax-advantaged or tax-exempt accounts, low-interest debt, and volatile investments.

Speaking of taxes, it would be good for you to learn the basics, because taxes are one of the largest expenses we encounter throughout our lifetimes. They're inescapable (boo), but help us function as a society (yay). People who know their way around taxes continue to build wealth as they age. People who don't know their way around taxes make mistakes along the way that result in missed savings opportunities or even penalties. The big opportunities in tax planning come in the form of **adjustments, deductions, and credits**, which together lower your annual income on paper, therefore lowering your tax bill. Knowing about taxes might change your financial goals for later in life, such as where you want to live and whether you want to one day buy a home.

Tax knowledge is also helpful if you're dabbling in **entrepreneurship** as a form of self-employment income. Self-employment income is any earned income you made without being an employee, and encompasses independent contractor work, consulting, gigs, the creator economy, and more. It can be a lot of work, but it's also great because you are in the driver's seat of your earning potential. You can exercise entrepreneurship without forming a business—the IRS will just categorize this income as **sole proprietorship** on your taxes—but if you expect to rely on this self-employment income regularly, it might be worth the cost to set one up. A **single-member LLC** is common for a one-person business. Partnerships, multi-member LLCs, and corporations are also options. Meaningfully, businesses present many opportunities for tax deductions, which lower your taxable income and therefore your overall tax bill.

With all this money knowledge, we can redefine retirement as the pursuit of financial independence, in which some, most, or all of our money comes from our assets in the form of investment income. In **Financial Independence, Retire Early (FIRE)** culture, enthusiasts use the **FIRE number** as an aspirational finish line, which gives them timeframes that then let them make decisions about how they want to live their present-day life. Some FIRE enthusiasts save very aggressively to achieve their FIRE number sooner, often reaching a saving rate of 50 percent or more. Others go slower, following FI principles, but not living so frugally that they end up miserable.

∘ ∘ ∘

By following your 7-word plan, Saving Rate Roadmap, and FIRE number calculations, you have everything you need to pursue a financially independent life. Our goal is that this work doesn't become your whole life or take over your identity. Instead, we want this work to be relegated to the background as much as possible so that you can enjoy your queer life to the fullest.

We can't predict the future, so there's one more money task we must address to live a truly fabulous financial life.

10

LEGACY PLANNING

Embrace Iconic Behavior and Lead a Legendary Life

All this work, all these miles traveled, fording a damn RIVER, and then out of nowhere we all die of dysentery? Really, *Oregon Trail*—really?!

And who's going to come and get all these damn LIVESTOCK I just bought? Well, that'll depend on how much I had my shit together back when I was still alive. If I had a will and trust, everything will be taken care of, and my loved ones can just lie around while Greek-God go-go boys rub their feet and feed them grapes (which I will have funded for them as part of my final wishes . . . for one brunch only). If I didn't have a will or trust, my loved ones might have had a much harder time receiving both the literal and figurative fruits of my labor.

Here's the bad news: You're gonna die one day. Everyone else around you will, too (sad face emoji), and there ain't much we can do about it in this game we call life. Although life after your death won't be time-consuming for you per se, a lack of planning for it can be both stressful and financially destructive for your chosen family.

Talk to someone who's had to navigate a loved one's end-of-life paperwork (or lack thereof), and you'll quickly see the grief and fatigue wash over their face. When people suddenly become incapacitated or pass away, and there was no estate planning or power of attorney, family and friends must navigate a labyrinth of courts, forms, and cold calls to get things sorted out. For families who are estranged, a civil war can break out when inheritance money is suddenly up for grabs. One of the greatest gifts you can give your loved ones is to take care of everything upfront so they don't have to.

When we avoid the topic of our death, we avoid feelings that help us discover our legacy. Legacies are more than just really good televised lip syncs; they are the impact you continue to make on other people and the world once you've left this Earth. Legacies can be financial, but can also be social and cultural, and are ultimately acts of service that give our lives meaning and purpose. Over and over again, the top reported regrets of the dying are working too much, not spending enough time with loved ones, and letting fear control too much of their lives. Reflecting on your death can be an antidote to procrastination. It's like a kick in the butt, a reminder to live life full-out, and a way to ensure you've left it all on the table when the bartender yells last call.

Estate planning is separate from the work we do in our 7-word plan and Saving Rate Roadmap, but is incredibly important for both financial preservation and honoring end-of-life wishes. By understanding estate documents like a will, trust, and power of attorney, you can ensure the money you've earned and saved throughout your lifetime goes to the people and causes you care about most. This work also helps inform legacy planning, an umbrella term in which you reflect on who you wanna be when you grow up—and what kind of impact you want to make.

In this chapter, we'll discuss both estate planning and legacy planning in more detail, then give you an ultimate checklist you can use to button everything up and get that final rocket boost of financial confidence.

Why Legacy Planning Matters

1. Nine out of ten queer people don't have a will
2. Legacy planning makes you take a good hard look at your life
3. Once it's set up, estate maintenance is minimal
4. Legacy work helps you connect with your community
5. Charitable contributions have tax breaks

REASON NO. 1: NINE OUT OF TEN QUEER PEOPLE DON'T HAVE A WILL

A survey of two thousand queer Americans in 2023 found that 90 percent didn't have a will or trust.[1] (Non-queer people aren't faring much better: two in three have no estate plan.) We'll explain what a will and trust actually are later in this chapter. First, let's take the *Scared Straight* approach (the show on MTV, not conversion therapy) to better understand what happens when you don't have these documents in place.

When someone dies and they don't have a will, they are considered **intestate**, and the state they lived in ends up determining who gets what assets. The state courts that determine this stuff are called **probate courts**, and all the lawyers and administrators who work on your probate case are paid out of your assets—money that could have gone to your loved ones or causes you care about instead. The administrator compiles assets, pays off debts, and works with a probate judge to determine who your beneficiaries should be, then locates and contacts them.

The probate administrator won't know about the ongoing beef you had with your parents or that you cut them off. They're simply going to follow the rules and regulations of the state, and in most states biological family are first in line as your beneficiaries, unless otherwise specified. If the administrator can't get in touch with any of your beneficiaries, all of your assets are eventually taken by the government (oof). Not all queer people have great relationships with their blood relatives; it's important for us to know how end-of-life succession works so that we can direct resources toward chosen family instead if desired.

Despite all this, people are terrible about estate planning, and it rarely makes the news—until a celebrity dies without a will, that is. Then every estate planning lawyer in America tries to insert themselves into the conversation. ("See? SEE what's happening right now?! WE TOLD YOU SO.") The digital peanut gallery picks up a lot, too: "They were worth so much money, how could they not have sorted this out?"

These artists' legacies are undeniable, but their estates weren't quite buttoned up, and in some cases that led to family members' claws coming out when unresolved assets were up for grabs:

- **Prince** died in 2016 without a will, and because he had a $300 million estate, but no spouse or children, the ensuing legal battle took over six years to settle.
- **Aretha Franklin** died without a formal will, but a handwritten letter functioning as her will was found *stuffed in her couch cushions*. After a legal battle ensued, this piece of paper was recognized as valid, and it determined the destiny of her $18 million estate. (#diva)
- **Pablo Picasso** never wrote a will because he was superstitious that it would portend his death (a popular opinion, unfortunately). When he died in 1973, it took seven years and $30 million in legal fees to divide his estate up among his seven heirs. Think about what that $30 million could have gone to instead.

Celebrity estate conflicts are compelling to us because of the amount of money involved. But even if we don't have millions of dollars to our name, probate court can be expensive. One study of probate court cases in San Francisco from 2014 to 2016 found that disputes amounted to an average of $17,000 in additional attorneys' fees.[2] This is in addition to all the time and energy your loved ones have to spend on legal documents while also navigating grief. The more paperwork you have squared away in your estate planning, the more control you'll have over your end-of-life wishes and assets.

Hiko, 44, California: *The aftermath of my mother's passing has been stressful. I'm trying to find a probate attorney because my mother was unable to officially put together a will before she passed. I'm dealing with her house in Florida, putting it on the market. I was relying on her Social Security income to pay her bills; now that she's gone, the Social Security has stopped, so my expenses have doubled because I'm paying for my apartment and utilities [here in California] in addition to her house and all the maintenance that comes with it. Having now lost both my parents, I'm a lot more future-minded. My financial status is on my mind the most it's ever been.*

REASON NO. 2:
LEGACY PLANNING MAKES YOU TAKE A GOOD HARD LOOK AT YOUR LIFE

And that's why I think you should look into doing it now, no matter how old you are.

Here's why: When you start to set up your will, trust, and other estate documents, you also begin to feel the existential feels. "How do I want to spend the time I have on this Earth?" "What difference do I want to make?" "If it all ended next month, do I feel like I've lived life full-out?" Reflecting on the future can help guide your present, which gives legacy planning serious aura points.

Estate planning and legacy planning are often used interchangeably, but have slightly different meanings. Think of estate planning as all the paperwork and legal stuff. It helps ensure your assets are protected, tax-advantaged, and transferred smoothly after your immediate death. When done well, an estate plan is objective; it's very clear who receives what, who is responsible for doing what, and how the to-dos are to be completed. Organizing your funeral expenses ahead of time is good estate planning. Setting up a trust for your niece or nephew that they'll get access to when they become adults is good estate planning. Telling your bestie to spread your ashes into the street gutters during the Folsom Street Fair, albeit niche, is good estate planning.

Legacy planning is broader and more subjective. It involves thinking about your values, your social impact, and how you want to share your knowledge and experience, then creating action steps for how to fulfill on those, both now and in your estate plan. Legacy planning can refer to generational wealth or charitable giving, but it also can refer to volunteering your time or starting that business or organization to solve a problem you see in the world. These priorities give your life meaning and purpose in ways that day jobs and personal belongings do not.

Josué, 34, California: *I decided to run as Mr. Gay San Francisco because you're part of a nonprofit in which you raise money for the community. I saw it as the best of both worlds: I get to create change in this world, but also go out and have fun. It's been life changing. I've been able to connect with other queer individuals who also want to make a difference through fundraising, and they've become part of my chosen family over time.*

As we've discussed throughout this book, facing the truth head-on and processing your feelings is a cornerstone to healthy personal finance.

REASON NO. 3: ONCE IT'S SET UP, ESTATE MAINTENANCE IS MINIMAL

Similar to investing, the majority of the effort behind estate planning is done up front. The rest is just maintenance and adjustments as you go.

Having your estate paperwork set up gives you peace of mind that everything will be okay, even if you meet your demise suddenly. Nearly 3.3 million people died in the United States in 2022, according to mortality statistics from the Centers for Disease Control and Prevention, and "accidents" were the third leading cause of death that year, only behind heart disease and cancer.[3] Don't wait for a brush with death (or a full-on French kiss) to take care of this stuff.

Outside of documents like a will and trust, a good estate plan also means having life insurance. Yeah, life insurance, that thing you associate with slimy salesmen or true crime motives. Having adequate life insurance ensures your loved ones aren't burdened financially, and queer people are less likely to have it.

LIFE INSURANCE BASICS TO KNOW

It's not just the killer's motive in many a true crime podcast episode: Adequate life insurance coverage takes care of your family. There are also many different types of life insurance. Here's a cheat sheet to give you an initial foundation.

- **Term life insurance.** The most common life insurance, and usually the cheapest. Insures you for a set number of years, then expires.
- **Whole life insurance.** One insurance policy that remains the same throughout your lifetime (permanent). Set it and forget it, but typically more expensive.
- **Universal life insurance.** Also a permanent life insurance policy, but lets you adjust your premiums as you go.
- **Variable life insurance.** Also a permanent life insurance policy, but with a fixed premium and a little more control over how the cash value is invested.
- **Burial insurance.** A small policy designed to cover the cost of your funeral or other end-of-life expenses. Usually a low payout

cap, around $25,000 as of this writing, but doesn't require medical information, making it a good option for people with preexisting medical conditions who may not be approved for other forms of life insurance.

Term life insurance is best for most, because it's inexpensive but still gets the job done. One *Business Insider* story citing data from Policygenius found that the average twenty-year, $500,000 term life insurance policy cost $30 a month for a 30-year-old, whereas the same 30-year-old would pay $451 a month for whole life insurance.[4]

We've done a ton of work throughout this book to get you out of debt and start building wealth. Don't flush it all down the drain just because those late-night life insurance infomercials were a turnoff.

Many employers include life insurance coverage in their compensation packages. If this applies to you, learn your way around these options and make the decision that's right for you. If you're not employed, look for options you can purchase for yourself.

REASON NO. 4: LEGACY WORK HELPS YOU CONNECT WITH YOUR COMMUNITY

Being of service is cool.

Legacy planning can inspire you to educate yourself on the many LGBTQ+ and local organizations that have a positive impact on your community. Being of service helps us advance causes we care about, help others in need, and cultivate an attitude of gratitude, and it can be an antidote to the feelings of isolation and loneliness queer people often experience. How many people over the years have passed away rich, but also lonely and unfulfilled? Millions? *Hundreds* of millions? You deserve to be a part of something meaningful, and you deserve to experience that feeling now.

The first question to ask yourself is what resources you have available to contribute. Let's bucket resources into three categories: time, money, and attention.

Donating your time. If you can swing it, donating your time in the form of volunteerism is perhaps the most fulfilling way to support an organization. When you dedicate your time, you break up your usual routine and are out in the world, making a direct impact and meeting other like-minded people along the way. Time donation encourages human connection and a sense of belonging, and it's another reason we define time freedom as an expression of wealth.

Donating your money. Donating money is another way to contribute to organizations you care about. While it's completely up to you what organizations you give to, larger organizations often already have the attention of wealthy donors and companies. Your monetary donation might make a bigger difference with a smaller organization you care about that does important work at the local level.

Donating your attention. Yes, attention is currency these days, too! Taking the time to highlight and amplify causes you care about can also be an act of service. This is a great option for people who are short on both time and funds (which is pretty common, actually). I want you to think of both your attention and your ability to *direct* attention as resources, too. Like and share a social media post from a cause that interests you. Tell a friend about it IRL. Attend an event or webinar that an organization you care about is putting on. Value lifelong learning. Value yourself.

LGBTQ+ ORGANIZATIONS TO SUPPORT

Time to earn our "I know my LGBTQ+ nonprofits" merit badge.

The only thing better than being queer is helping other queer people live a great life. There are many nonprofits and charitable organizations solely dedicated to advancing the safety, integrity, and prosperity of queer people; the more knowledgeable we are about these entities and their various causes, the more connected to our queer selves and community we become. There are national organizations fighting for systemic change as well as local organizations looking to improve your very neighborhood.

A few national organizations to know about:

- **HRC (Human Rights Campaign).** The HRC is an LGBTQ+ advocacy group and the largest LGBTQ+ lobbying group in the Americas.
- **GLAAD (Gay and Lesbian Alliance Against Defamation).** GLAAD advocates for accurate media representation and was founded in 1985 as a reaction to the *New York Post*'s inflammatory coverage of the AIDS epidemic.
- **PFLAG.** PFLAG advocates for straight allyship to the LGBTQ+ community.
- **GLSEN (Gay, Lesbian and Straight Education Network).** GLSEN works to end discrimination, bullying, and harassment of queer youth in K-12 schools.
- **The Trevor Project.** The Trevor Project is a suicide prevention nonprofit focused on resources and advocacy for queer youth.
- **Lambda Legal.** Lambda Legal advocates for the civil rights of LGBTQ+ people through legal action, representation, and policy activism.
- **SAGE (Services and Advocacy for LGBTQ+ Elders).** SAGE is a nonprofit focused on the well-being of LGBTQ+ elders.
- **Lambda Literary.** Lambda Literary advocates for LGBTQ+ stories and literature.
- **Modern Military Association of America.** Modern Military, a merger of multiple LGBTQ+ veteran-focused nonprofit organi-

zations, advocates for the rights and well-being of LGBTQ+ military servicepeople and their families.

Also take a few minutes to research your local LGBTQ+ organizations. Search for local organizations online, or check your local queer hospitality establishments, like bars and restaurants, to see what organizations they've connected with in the past.

REASON NO. 5: CHARITABLE CONTRIBUTIONS HAVE TAX BREAKS

And for some rich people, that's the only reason they give a shit about charitable giving (along with doing the step-and-repeat at the gala, of course).

In the US, when you donate to a charitable organization, you can deduct this contribution from your adjusted gross income. The organization has to be a registered 501(c)3 or 501(c)4, which is why you see that weird number plastered ALL OVER those websites and donation forms (be sure to check this; unfortunately, charity scams are a thing now, but it's easy to confirm an organization is real on a website like Charity Navigator). When you donate money, you can deduct the donation on your taxes using the aptly named charitable contribution deduction.

Now that you're an investing superstar, here's something neat to know: There's a way to donate money right from your investments—without even selling them first if you don't want to—and still get all the charitable tax breaks. The way to do this is with an account called a **donor-advised fund (DAF)**.

For many of us, contributing to charity directly from a checking account might put strain our cash flow. But investments like stocks, bonds, funds, and cryptocurrencies probably aren't being relied on for your day-to-day expenses. DAFs make it easy to donate a portion of those investments, and are available at most large investment firms that also offer retirement accounts and brokerage accounts. Fidelity Charitable and Vanguard Charitable are two popular options. Fidelity Charitable is popular because there's no minimum required amount to open an account, the fees are low, and you can gift money to charities in increments as low as $50.

Here's what else to know about donor-advised funds.

- **The investments grow tax-free.** Any future earnings on the investments are tax-free once you put them in the DAF. Once you've contributed the money, it's considered donated, so you can't take it back later.
- **Immediate tax deduction when you donate.** You take the deduction when you put the money or investments into the DAF, not when you actually donate to the organization. This lets you space out your charitable giving as you please.
- **Option for privacy.** When you tell the DAF to give to a charity of your choosing, you have the option of being anonymous. You won't get your name printed in the program pamphlet in a tiny-ass font, but maybe you'd prefer it that way.

I personally became more curious about donating money to charity when I learned I could donate investments, money that I've put away for the long game anyway. Donor-advised funds let you sprinkle your newfound investing mojo into areas of philanthropy and social impact, and they're easy to incorporate into an estate plan. If this sounds interesting, read up on DAFs online and consider opening one up today.

ICONIC IN DEATH: YOUR ESTATE PLAN

Legacy planning and estate planning are powerful tools that help you get real about what really matters to you in your life. Planning brings you peace, and it sometimes has a "hurry up and live" effect because you remember your time on this planet is short. A basic understanding of estate planning will also help you navigate end-of-life conversations and challenges that may arise with loved ones, which can quickly spiral into a stress mess otherwise.

When you know everything is good to go in the event an asteroid falls out of the sky and vaporizes you instantly (which would be kind of iconic, honestly), feelings of groundedness and confidence emerge. For our final exercise together, I've created a legacy planning checklist for you to work through in the coming months, with a sweet incentive to keep you moving forward, and we'll explain the various definitions and documents as we go.

BEFORE YOU START: CHOOSE A PUSH PRESENT

Legacy planning takes personal organization, preparation, and a willingness to overcome procrastination. Depending on how much you have to coordinate, completing this checklist could take a few days, weeks, or months. This work goes deep, and will be confronting and perhaps emotional at times. To stay motivated, I want you to decide on how you'll reward yourself—a "push present," if you will.

Think about how you're going to treat yourself once you're done with this checklist. This could be a trip, a nice meal, a massage, or just taking a day or two off work and enjoying some guilt-free leisure time. Choose something that's a big treat and will really excite you! Then, create a sinking fund and start funding this push present so you can pay for it entirely in cash.

Remember that you only have to set up estate planning once. Everything after that is maintenance. Incentivize this process so that you're motivated to finish what you start.

STEP 1: DECIDE HOW YOU WANT YOUR ESTATE PLAN TO GO

Healthy personal finance often begins with a journal, not a spreadsheet.

Take a moment to think about who you want your assets to go to after you pass away. This "who" usually refers to biological or chosen family members, but can also refer to organizations, charities, and other causes. End-of-life paperwork also means giving instructions on how to handle your death, including medical instructions, communications, and final wishes for your cold, lifeless (but still fabulous) corpse, so think about who you might want to entrust with these responsibilities. We'll get to the technical stuff later; for now, really focus on the who.

Bust out a journal or open up a new note on your phone and jot down answers to the following questions:

Who do you want your money, investments, and assets to go to after you pass away? (It's easy to allocate different percentages of an account to different people, if that helps.)

Who do you want to make decisions on your behalf if you become medically incapacitated and are unable to make decisions on your own?

How do you want your online presence to be handled (social media accounts, email addresses, photos on your phone, and any other digital assets)? Who would you trust to handle this?

STEP 2: HAVE THOSE HARD CONVERSATIONS

Next, sit down and have initial conversations with people who will have responsibility in your estate plan. You don't necessarily have to share who is getting what, but you do want to tell people who have a role what their role will be and confirm they actually want this responsibility before you put it in writing.

These roles include:

- **Executor:** The person who will execute your will.
- **Trustee:** The person or organization that will manage your trust, if you have one.
- **Power of attorney:** The person who can oversee your financial affairs and/or health-care wishes in the event you are incapacitated.

Even if your paperwork isn't extensive or perfectly buttoned up, having these roles clearly assigned will be a big help and prevent your assets from being tangled up in all the red tape that comes with the probate process. You have to tell them what their responsibilities are and where your estate planning documents are; otherwise, they'll never know!

STEP 3: SET UP YOUR ESTATE PAPERWORK

Take a deep breath. Let's go through each of the foundational documents to a good estate plan. These include:

- A will
- A trust
- Power of attorney documents
- Beneficiary designations
- A personal financial statement

1. **A will.** This is the single most important document in your estate planning. Your will communicates how you want your assets to be distributed. Writing one means naming an executor, who will

be the person that carries out these wishes and is the point of contact for any legal to-dos. Your will is your final smackdown, your mic drop moment, a legally valid document that communicates what you want in the event of your passing. If you only do one legacy planning document, have it be this one.

You can write a legally valid will by yourself (Aretha did this, then stuffed it in her couch, and it was still valid!), but paying a small fee to an estate attorney or online service might be worth it for the extra peace of mind. You won't be able to clarify later if something is legally ambiguous in what you wrote because, well, you're dead now.

For parents of young kids, also know that your will is where you can name the guardians of your children.

2. **A trust.** If a will is the "what," a trust is the "how." Trusts typically cost a little money to set up, but they're valuable in that they allow your heirs and loved ones to bypass most of the probate process. In some cases, trusts also have tax perks.

   In trusts, there are three roles:

   - **Grantor.** This is the person who creates the trust (*taps shoulder* that's you).
   - **Trustee.** This is the person who manages the trust. It can be you to start; the idea is that after you're gone, the trustee becomes someone else, or an organization.
   - **Beneficiaries.** These are the people or parties who will receive assets from the trust. You can be your own beneficiary, too. Hell, you can give EGOT energy and be all the roles if you want to (fairly common, actually).

Additionally, there are two main categories of trusts: revocable and irrevocable.

A **revocable trust** is like a jumbo plastic container that makes transferring your assets smoother once you drop dead. Since you created the trust, you're the grantor; you're managing it, so you're also the trustee; and since you're still using the assets in the trust, you're its current beneficiary. You don't need to put all your assets in a revocable trust up front. Instead, you just name the trust as the beneficiary on your other accounts, like savings and investment accounts, and those assets will get dumped into the container upon your death.

In contrast, an **irrevocable trust** is a trust in which you irreversibly transfer assets into the trust, which means they're no longer part of your estate. You lose control, but your assets will be protected from villains like debt collectors should you ever become deeply indebted or bankrupt in the future. An irrevocable trust would be like if you took some of your Monopoly money and set it over on the kitchen counter, with instructions to have it pay you 40 bucks every turn, then pay the rest out to your mom once you get knocked out. This money would then be shielded from your goddamn cousin, who's already snatched up all the red and orange properties and is about to run away with the game. Since the money and assets you put into an irrevocable trust become separate from your estate, they're a way to "hide" wealth from tax liability.

Charitable trusts are irrevocable trusts in which one or more charities are beneficiaries. You and your family members can also be beneficiaries. There are two types.

In **charitable remainder trusts**, the non-charity beneficiaries (you, family, friends, the dog) get the annual income distributions, and when you die the rest of the trust goes to charity. A **charitable lead trust** does the opposite: The trust gives some of its money to a charity every year for a set number of years, but the moment you die, that plan is shut down and the remaining assets go to your other beneficiaries. I'm telling you all this for your own good, but also so you can understand what the hell is going on when your friend who works in nonprofit fundraising is going off about their donor drama (again) at happy hour.

Irrevocable trusts can be complex, so consider working with a financial professional if you want to explore this in your estate plan. Revocable trusts, however, are great proactive planning, and many people just open the trust, then write in their will that all of their assets should be moved into the trust, a move that speeds along a lot of the probate process. If your will says to move all your assets into your trust after your death, that's called a **pour-over will**.

TEA

Pour-over will: Pour-overs aren't just for coffee and fancy garnishes anymore! In a pour-over will, most of your remaining assets get dumped into a trust when you die. It still goes through probate, but since all the instructions are clear, your assets won't be governed by intestate laws. This is important for queer people.

3. **Powers of attorney and/or health care proxies.** Power of attorney refers to a set of documents that together allow someone else to make decisions about your estate on your behalf. A will has an executor, but the executor can't do much until you actually die. What happens if you have a period where you become incapacitated while still alive, and are no longer able to make decisions? When these documents are set in place, it is crystal clear who is responsible for and has authority to do what.

   A **health care proxy** is a type of power of attorney. This is a person you designate to make decisions on your behalf in the event you are medically incapacitated. Think about who will honor your wishes in the event you are incapacitated, and have a conversation with this loved one. A related document is the **advance healthcare directive**, also known as the living will, in which you explain how you want health-care decisions to be handled (a "Do Not Resuscitate," or DNR, is one example).

   My memory trick for these is that the health care proxy refers to a *person* (proxy/person) whereas the advance directive is a *document* (directive/document). A health care team would have the information they need from a directive in the event your proxy can't be reached. Most experts advise having both a proxy and a directive so everything is clear.

4. **Beneficiaries, payable on death (POD) designations, and transfer on death (TOD) designations.** You're already designating beneficiaries in documents like a will or a trust. If you also put your beneficiary's name on file for each specific asset or account (like your savings account), the transfer of that asset will go faster.

   For example, if you name in your will that you want the money in your savings account to go to your younger brother, you'd also want to put that beneficiary designation on file with the bank holding the savings account. Having beneficiary, POD, or TOD designations in place can help ease the burden when it comes time to transfer assets, and in most cases they are both easy and free to set up.

5. **A personal financial statement.** This document isn't as important legally as the others, but it will make your loved ones' lives a lot easier. Give us a one-pager that provides an immediate overview of your financial situation. Think of it as your "I'm dead now" cover letter that will help your loved ones get themselves oriented.

   Your personal financial statement should include all of your bank accounts, all the money coming in, and all your liabilities—debts, loans, and so on. This helps your loved ones avoid surprises and ensure your accounts can be wound down without going delinquent when you're already six feet under.

AN ADDITIONAL DOCUMENT QUEER PEOPLE MIGHT WANT TO CONSIDER

Queer people want to be preserved and memorialized in their gender identity, be dressed in appropriate clothing, and have a kickass tagline on their tombstone (and certainly not their deadname). To overrule both government instructions and the wishes of unaccepting family members, consider also having an **agent for disposition of remains**.

Sometimes known as a funeral representative or a final disposition agent, this person will have the authority to oversee how your body is handled and that your wishes are honored. The designation is simple, but setting it up varies a lot from state to state. In some states, you need to appoint this person in your will or advance directive, whereas in others you'll need a separate document. Also, some states require that the document be notarized, whereas others don't.

STEP 4: SET UP YOUR DIGITAL LEGACY PLANNING

Do you want your mom to have to go through your nudes on your phone if you die suddenly? No? Then you need to include instructions on who should tie up your digital life, too.

In recent years, our digital lives have become nearly as complex as our finances. When you pass away, it's very possible that your loved ones will be tasked with shutting down dozens if not hundreds of accounts and logins. From memorializing social media accounts and posting to your networks on your behalf to shutting down paid subscriptions, digital memorialization has become an increasingly important part of legacy planning.

Consider setting up a password manager to help support your legacy plan. Password managers are good for online security because they let you create a separate secure password for every login. We cybersecurity nerds have been begging you to set a password manager up for years now, but some of y'all are just gonna keep ridin' "password123!!" until the wheels fall off, so let me try a different approach.

Many password managers have end-of-life features like emergency kits. These are printable PDF documents that give clear login instructions and access to all your passwords, and you can include this printout in your estate planning documents. Say you're responsible for logging in and paying the rent each month, but suddenly become unable to do so—someone else needs to be able to do that, and you can make those logins easy to access using a password manager's emergency kit. Estate planning isn't just about you taking care of other people; it's also about other people being able to take care of you in the event you become temporarily incapacitated.

STEP 5: CREATE YOUR DOCUMENT STASH

Now we want to put these documents and resources together in a place where people will be able to easily access them. An envelope in a drawer would be sufficient, or if you want some extra adulting points, you could purchase an inexpensive safe that holds other valuables. (Tell someone the code to the safe!)

To make this 100 percent watertight, there are some other documents you'll also want to include. Here's a rundown of what to have in your documents trove:

Estate Documents

- Most recent will
- Most recent trust
- Powers of attorney

Personal Documents

- Password manager access instructions
- Past tax returns—the last seven years' worth, if you have them
- Marriage certificate, prenuptial agreement, marital settlement agreement, or divorce decree, if any of those apply
- Citizenship papers if you're a naturalized citizen
- Discharge papers if you served in the military
- Gender recognition paperwork, if you have it

Life Insurance Information

- Most recent annual policy statement
- Insurance beneficiary information
- Long-term care insurance contract

Personal Financial Statement

- List of your accounts
    - Where they are
    - Type of account
    - Beneficiary, POD, or TOD information

A List of Contacts

- Doctors
- Bank contact, if you have one
- Insurers for your auto, home, liability insurance
- Lawyer, if you have one
- Accountant, if you have one
- Other professionals you work with or points of contact

Medical Information

- Personal medical history and any drugs you're taking
- Authorization to release health-care information to your health care power of attorney
- Anatomical gifts—if you want to donate your organs, say that somewhere in writing

Funeral Information

- A cemetery deed, if being buried in a cemetery
- Any funeral instructions

- An agent for disposition of remains, if needed
- A draft of an obituary—if you don't write it, someone else will

Ownership Documents

- Deed if you have a house
- Title if you have a car or other vehicle
- Recent mortgage statement
- Any physical bonds or stock certificates (rare, but maybe you're vintage like that)
- Any business formation documents and operating agreements, if applicable
- Any details on patents, trademarks, copyrights, or royalties
- Homeowners' insurance or renters' insurance that lists specific valuables

Don't forget to tell the loved ones in your life where your document stash actually is.

∘ ∘ ∘

The good news is that once your estate documents are set up, it's largely coasting from here on out. Revisit your legacy documents as your wealth and relationships evolve.

THE BIG FAT LEGACY PLANNING CHECKLIST

Here's your checklist. Finish this bad boy off and that push present is yours. Some people can tear through this checklist in a few weeks, but for most the timeframe will be in months. Move intentionally, but thoughtfully; these are weighty decisions that deserve plenty of consideration.

- □ First and foremost, I have decided on an awesome way I will reward myself when this checklist is completed—something that will inspire me to really do the work.
- □ I have done the legacy reflection exercise and journaling to clarify my passions and purpose.
- □ I have had conversations with:
    - The executor of my will
    - The trustee of my trust, if I have one
    - Any powers of attorney and/or health care proxies
- □ I have written a legally valid will.
- □ I have created a trust, if deemed necessary.
- □ I have created legally valid powers of attorney documents.
- □ I have provided beneficiary, payable on death, or transfer on death designation information to any financial accounts that require these details.
- □ I have set up a password manager or other password management system.
- □ I have communicated to my loved ones where all my estate documents are.
- □ I have written a personal financial statement.
- □ I could explain my estate plan and who will do what to a fourth grader if I really had to.
- □ I have assembled my legacy planning documents:
    - Password manager access instructions
    - Past tax returns
    - Marriage certificate and/or prenuptial agreement
    - Most recent life insurance policy statement
    - Life insurance beneficiary information
    - Long-term care insurance contract
    - A list of contacts:
        - » Doctors
        - » Bank contact, if you have one
        - » Insurers for your auto, home, liability insurance

    - Lawyer, if you have one
    - Accountant, if you have one
    - Other professionals you work with or points of contact
- Medical information
    - Personal medical history and any drugs you're taking
- Authorization to release health-care information to your health care power of attorney
- Funeral information
    - A cemetery deed, if being buried in one
    - Any funeral instructions
    - A draft of an obituary
- Ownership documents
    - Deed if you have a house
    - Title if you have a car or other vehicle
    - Recent mortgage statement
    - Any physical bonds or stock certificates
    - Any business formation documents and operating agreements, if applicable
    - Any details on patents, trademarks, copyrights, or royalties

IN CLOSING: LIVE A CONFIDENT, QUEER LIFE

When my then-boyfriend and I relocated from Houston to Los Angeles in 2021, we drove. We planned to do the nearly 1,700-mile drive in three legs, with the second leg ending in Arizona, about an hour away from Grand Canyon National Park. Since neither of us had ever seen the Grand Canyon, we figured it'd be worth tacking an extra day onto the trip to see one of the seven wonders of the world. Yes, it was beautiful, and yes, the swag at the merch shop was cute.

Think of managing your money like planning a road trip. We're going somewhere, and it's important we make it to our destination without running out of gas. But we also want to be comfortable along the way. Snacks. Epic playlist. A cushy pillow to put behind your low back if you need one like I do. And, of course, time and space for both planned and spontaneous side quests. Personal finance isn't just about restriction—it's also about cultivating adventure. When we don't define our queer lives for ourselves, politics and capitalism will define them for us. Don't let them win.

You might feel how I felt back when I first arrived at that personal finance editor job: overwhelmed. There's a lot of new information to absorb here, and unless you're Carrie-Anne Moss in *The Matrix,* and can just make a phone call whenever you suddenly need to know how to fly a helicopter, I don't expect you to have it 100 percent memorized on the first pass. Revisit the various chapters of this book as needed and start using the tools we've hard-launched together: your Bedazzled Budget, your Increase My Income action plan, your Saving Rate Roadmap, and your FIRE number. And if you start feeling cluttered or stressed, just go back to the 7-word plan for building wealth: Lower expenses, increase earnings, invest the difference. It works.

Queer people deserve to live long, fulfilling lives. Money is the primary currency of our generation, and it'll likely stay that way for a while. We should start talking about it more, because when we master how to make, save, and spend our money, it becomes a tool we can use to shape the life we want for ourselves. Cultivating financial independence and security are some of the most activist things we can do: They not only help us take better care of ourselves and one another, but also model for young queer people what responsible adulthood looks like—and how to have fun along the way.

This book gives you the roadmap you need to reach financial independence, regardless of your current money situation. Like all road trips, it will take a while to get to your destination, and that's okay. Use this book to both secure your future and realize a more expressive, fulfilling queer life in the present. You deserve it. And *reading is fundamental!*

ACKNOWLEDGMENTS

Pro tip: If you're visiting someone's city, send them a DM to meet up in person for coffee or a drink. It might turn into a book.

That's what happened to me when I caught up with Peter Kispert at a cocktail bar at 146th and Broadway in Manhattan in the spring of 2024. I talked about my finance column in *Out,* the many underreported data sets we have about queer people, and why self-help guidance around money will never become obsolete. (I also probably bitched about #FinTok multiple times.)

"Why isn't this a book yet?" he asked. Peter, you saw the potential of this book before I did, it exists because of you, and it was the cherry on top to end up working on it together months later with you as my editor. ☺

The team at William Morrow helped me raise my game in so many ways, and it took a village to create the sassy money manual you hold in your hands. Thank you to Liate Stehlik, Benjamin Steinberg, Mauro DiPreta, Kyle O'Brien, Andrew DiCecco, Yeon Kim, Hope Ellis, Cliff Haley, my publicist Lindsey Kennedy, and my marketing partner in crime Rachel Berquist. Hope Breeman and Leda Scheintaub gave this book the thoughtful copy edits writers dream about.

My literary agent Dan Milaschewski has infinite patience for beginner questions, of which I have had many. Thanks to United Talent Agency for throwing their weight behind a starry-eyed queer kid who grew up in rural Illinois; the best is still ahead.

Thank you to everyone I interviewed for this book. For many, it meant getting on a Zoom call with a complete stranger and spilling their guts about their money stressors and failures. Interviewees donated their time because they were inspired by this book and how it might help our community. I'm grateful for their generosity, and their kindness.

Ron Czar is the physical therapist who healed the back pain I talked about in this book. He owns FulHaus club in West Hollywood, is at that gym seven days a week (on top of midday visits to various hospitals and senior centers), and is one of the hardest-working people I know. Thank you for the magic hands, Ronnie, and I'm still terrible at bird dogs.

When I pivoted from self-employment to media-editor life in 2022, I was pretty much the village idiot in the newsroom. Adam Auriemma and John Puterbaugh helped me learn the ropes of personal finance journalism on the fly, while still being myself. Later, when I moved from NextAdvisor to CNET, I reported to Sharon Profis, an ideal mentor for how to get things done in corporate media and sustainably build a portfolio career.

Daniel Reynolds at *Out* magazine took a chance on me. We met at a random party, I mentioned I wanted to write more money stuff for LGBTQ+ people, and we decided to take a swing at doing a personal finance column in an iconic entertainment magazine. Those first few stories revealed to me and others why a book like *Money Proud* is needed in the world. Go to the parties!

I'm not a credentialed financial professional, but fortunately for all of us, Ben Galloway at Greenspring Advisors is. Thank you, Ben, for the pro bono review and fact checks. Any lingering mistakes in this book are mine.

In those first years of self-employment, I noticed how much snake oil there is in online entrepreneurship. I escaped most of it (but not all of it). Part of that was because I had good mentors early on who helped me stay focused on what matters. This quality foundation is why I have a sunny outlook on entrepreneurship and how it can change queer people's lives for the better.

A big shoutout to the Williams Institute and other organizations that do independent data collection and analysis on LGBTQ+ people.

These groups step in and do the community measurements our government isn't willing to do, and their data sets are often the origin point of policy change. They're also a jumping-off point for talking heads like me to advocate for queer equality in mainstream media.

Thank you to our queer ancestors, the many activists, organizers, artists, and community builders who laid the groundwork for our culture to thrive. Your impact lives through us and teaches us how to navigate tumultuous times with power and grace.

RESOURCES

Saving Rate Roadmap: check. Four-hour playlist of pop divas: check. Now get the real-time weather forecast for the journey ahead.

For additional resources and my most up-to-date recommendations, exclusively for *Money Proud* readers, visit https://nickwolny.com/book-resources or scan the QR code below.

NOTES

INTRODUCTION

1. "Money Income in the United States: 1995 (With Separate Data on Valuation of Noncash Benefits)," U.S. Census Bureau, September 1996, https://www.census.gov/library/publications/1996/demo/p60-193.html.

2. Charles P. Hoy-Ellis, "Minority Stress and Mental Health: A Review of the Literature," *Journal of Homosexuality* 70, no. 5 (2021): 806–30, https://www.tandfonline.com/doi/full/10.1080/00918369.2021.2004794.

3. "2023 U.S. National Survey on the Mental Health of LGBTQ+ Young People," The Trevor Project, https://www.thetrevorproject.org/survey-2023/.

4. "Mental health," *Merriam-Webster*, https://www.merriam-webster.com/dictionary/mental%20health.

5. "The Wage Gap Among LGBTQ+ Workers in the United States," Human Rights Campaign, https://www.hrc.org/resources/the-wage-gap-among-lgbtq-workers-in-the-united-states.

6. "Homelessness Among the LGBTQ Community," National Coalition for the Homeless, https://nationalhomeless.org/lgbtq-homelessness/.

7. "2025 Anti-Trans Bills Tracker," Trans Legislation Tracker, https://translegislation.com/.

8. PRRI Staff, "Views on LGBTQ Rights in All 50 States: Findings from PRRI's 2023 American Values Atlas," Public Religion Research Institute, March 12, 2024, https://www.prri.org/research/views-on-lgbtq-rights-in-all-50-states/.

9. Jeffrey M. Jones, "LGBTQ+ Identification in U.S. Now at 7.6%," *Gallup*, March 13, 2024, https://news.gallup.com/poll/611864/lgbtq-identification.aspx.

10. "The Economic Well-Being of LGBT Adults in the U.S. in 2019," Center for LGBTQ Economic Advancement & Research, https://lgbtq-economics.org/research/lgbt-adults-2019/.

11. "The LGBTQI+ Economic and Financial Survey," Center for LGBTQ Economic Advancement & Research, https://lgbtq-economics.org/research/leaf-report-2023/.

1 | THOUGHT PATTERNS

1. Melanie Hanson, "Average Cost of College by Year," Education Data Initiative, September 9, 2024, https://educationdata.org/average-cost-of-college-by-year.
2. "As Nationwide Fraud Losses Top $10 Billion in 2023, FTC Steps Up Efforts to Protect the Public," Federal Trade Commission, February 9, 2024, https://www.ftc.gov/news-events/news/press-releases/2024/02/nationwide-fraud-losses-top-10-billion-2023-ftc-steps-efforts-protect-public.
3. Kevin Schaul and Rachel Lerman, "Are Home Prices Still Rising? See How Prices Have Changed in Your Area," *Washington Post*, May 14, 2024, https://www.washingtonpost.com/business/interactive/2024/housing-market-price-trends-zip-code-map/.
4. Stacy Jo Dixon, "Average Daily Time Spent on Social Media Worldwide 2012–2024," Statista.com, April 10, 2024, https://www.statista.com/statistics/433871/daily-social-media-usage-worldwide/.
5. Matthew N. Berger, Melody Taba, Jennifer L. Marino, Megan S. C. Lim, and S. Rachel Skinner, "Social Media Use and Health and Well-being of Lesbian, Gay, Bisexual, Transgender, and Queer Youth: Systematic Review," *Journal of Medical Internet Research* 24, no. 9 (September 21, 2022), https://www.ncbi.nlm.nih.gov/pmc/articles/PMC9536523/.

2 | DEBT

1. "Federal Student Loans: Preliminary Observations on Borrower Repayment Practices after the Payment Pause," U.S. Government Accountability Office, August 14, 2024, https://www.gao.gov/products/gao-24-107150.
2. Christopher S. Carpenter, Kabir Dasgupta, Zofsha Merchant, and Alexander Plum, "Sexual Orientation and Financial Well-Being in the United States," Federal Reserve Board: Finance and Economics Discussion Series, June 2024, https://www.federalreserve.gov/econres/feds/files/2024048pap.pdf.
3. Shameek Rakshit, Matthew Rae Twitter, Gary Claxton, Krutika Amin, and Cynthia Cox, "The Burden of Medical Debt in the United States," Peterson-KFF Health System Tracker, February 12, 2024, https://www.healthsystemtracker.org/brief/the-burden-of-medical-debt-in-the-united-states/.
4. Statista Research Department, "U.S. Wage and Salary Workers Median Hourly Earnings 1979–2023," Statista.com, January 14, 2025, https://www.statista.com/statistics/185335/median-hourly-earnings-of-wage-and-salary-workers/.

5. CFPB Office of Markets, "The High Cost of Retail Credit Cards," Consumer Financial Protection Bureau, December 18, 2024, https://www.consumerfinance.gov/data-research/research-reports/issue-spotlight-the-high-cost-of-retail-credit-cards/.

6. "Credit Reports & Scores," Center for LGBTQ Economic Advancement & Research, https://lgbtq-economics.org/issues/credit-reports-and-scores.

7. "The LGBTQI+ Economic and Financial Survey," Center for LGBTQ Economic Advancement & Research, https://lgbtq-economics.org/research/leaf-report-2023/.

8. Jessica Beck and Sarah Holder, "Billions in Phantom Debt Is Lurking In 'Buy Now, Pay Later' Services," *Bloomberg*, June 14, 2024, https://www.bloomberg.com/news/articles/2024-05-07/americans-are-spending-billions-with-buy-now-pay-later.

9. Lane Gillespie, "Bankrate's 2025 Emergency Savings Report," Bankrate, January 23, 2025, https://www.bankrate.com/banking/savings/emergency-savings-report/.

10. Elizabeth Sweet, Arijit Nandi, Emma Adam, and Thomas McDade, "The High Price of Debt: Household Financial Debt and Its Impact on Mental and Physical Health," *Social Science & Medicine* 91 (August 2013): 94–100, https://pmc.ncbi.nlm.nih.gov/articles/PMC3718010/pdf/nihms482461.pdf.

3 | SAVING RATE

1. James Grubman, "There Is No 70% Rule—Improving Outcome Research in Family Wealth Advising," Globe Law and Business, June 2022, https://jamesgrubman.com/wp-content/uploads/2022/06/2022-06-There-is-no-70-rule-JGrubman-IFOJ.pdf.

2. Chris Stokel-Walker, "How a Squid Game Crypto Scam Got Away with Millions," *Wired*, November 2, 2021, https://www.wired.com/story/squid-game-coin-crypto-scam/.

3. Danielle Commisso, "More Americans Are Living Paycheck to Paycheck—Here's Who They Are," *Civic Science*, September 11, 2024, https://civicscience.com/more-americans-are-living-paycheck-to-paycheck-heres-who-they-are/.

4 | BUDGETING

1. "Paycheck-to-Paycheck Economy Moves to Higher-Income Brackets," PYMNTS, April 5, 2024, https://www.pymnts.com/consumer-finance/2024/a-third-of-those-earning-200k-live-paycheck-to-paycheck/.

2. Bryn Healy, "One-Quarter of Americans Didn't Call an Ambulance During a Medical Emergency for Fear of Costs," YouGov, June 13, 2024, https://today.yougov.com/health/articles/49738-one-quarter-americans-didnt-call-ambulance-medical-emergency-costs-poll.

5 | INCOME

1. "Number of Jobs, Labor Market Experience, Marital Status, and Health for Those Born 1957–1964," Bureau of Labor Statistics, August 22, 2023, https://www.bls.gov/news.release/pdf/nlsoy.pdf. "Labor Market Experience, Education, Partner Status, and Health for Those Born 1980–1984," Bureau of Labor Statistics, April 2, 2024, https://www.bls.gov/news.release/pdf/nlsyth.pdf.
2. Lane Gillespie, "Survey: More Than 1 in 3 Americans Earn Money Through Side Hustles, 32% Think They'll Always Need Them," Bankrate, July 10, 2024, https://www.bankrate.com/credit-cards/news/side-hustles-survey.
3. Daniel Kahneman and Angus Deaton, "High Income Improves Evaluation of Life but Not Emotional Well-being," *PNAS* 107, no. 38 (September 7, 2010): 16489–93, https://www.pnas.org/doi/10.1073/pnas.1011492107.
4. Matthew A. Killingsworth, "Experienced Well-Being Rises with Income, Even Above $75,000 per Year," *Proceedings of the National Academy of Science* 118, no. 4 (January 26, 2021), https://pubmed.ncbi.nlm.nih.gov/33468644/.
5. Michele W. Berger, "Does More Money Correlate with Greater Happiness?" *Penn Today*, March 6, 2023, https://penntoday.upenn.edu/news/does-more-money-correlate-greater-happiness-Penn-Princeton-research.
6. Sharita Gruberg, Lindsay Mahowald, and John Halpin, "The State of the LGBTQ Community in 2020," Center for American Progress, October 6, 2020, https://www.americanprogress.org/article/state-lgbtq-community-2020/.
7. "The Wage Gap Among LGBTQ+ Workers in the United States," Human Rights Campaign, https://www.hrc.org/resources/the-wage-gap-among-lgbtq-workers-in-the-united-states.
8. "Remote Workers Were 24% Less Likely to Be Promoted in 2023," Resume Builder, December 4, 2023, https://www.resumebuilder.com/remote-workers-were-24-less-likely-to-be-promoted-in-2023/.
9. "Freelance, Side Hustles, and Gigs: Many More Americans Have Become Independent Workers," McKinsey & Company, August 23, 2022, https://www.mckinsey.com/featured-insights/sustainable-inclusive-growth/future-of-america/freelance-side-hustles-and-gigs-many-more-americans-have-become-independent-workers.
10. "73% of Employers Would Negotiate Salary, 55% of Workers Don't Ask," CareerBuilder, https://resources.careerbuilder.com/news-research/73-of-employers-would-negotiate-salary-55-of-workers-don-t-ask.
11. "How to Negotiate a Job Offer," Fidelity Smart Money, https://www.fidelity.com/learning-center/smart-money/how-to-negotiate-salary.
12. Rakesh Kochhar, Kim Parker, and Ruth Igielnik, "Majority of U.S. Workers Chang-

ing Jobs Are Seeing Real Wage Gains," Pew Research Center, July 28, 2022, https://www.pewresearch.org/social-trends/2022/07/28/majority-of-u-s-workers-changing-jobs-are-seeing-real-wage-gains/.

13. Alison Doyle, "What Is the Hidden Job Market?" The Balance, January 21, 2022, https://www.thebalancemoney.com/what-is-the-hidden-job-market-2062004.

14. "What Is the STAR Method?" Development Dimensions International, https://www.ddiworld.com/solutions/behavioral-interviewing/star-method.

6 | INVESTING

1. Jack Caporal, "The State of LGBTQ Finance: A Survey of 2,000 Americans," *The Motley Fool*, April 17, 2024, https://www.fool.com/research/lgbtq-money-study/.

7 | TAXES

1. "The Equal Credit Opportunity Act," U.S. Department of Justice Civil Rights Division, https://www.justice.gov/crt/equal-credit-opportunity-act-3.

2. Erica York, "Summary of the Latest Federal Income Tax Data, 2025 Update," Tax Foundation, November 18, 2024, https://taxfoundation.org/data/all/federal/latest-federal-income-tax-data-2025/.

3. "Policy Basics: Where Do Our Federal Tax Dollars Go?" Center on Budget and Policy Priorities, January 28, 2025, https://www.cbpp.org/research/federal-budget/where-do-our-federal-tax-dollars-go.

4. William C. Boning, Nathaniel Hendren, Ben Sprung-Keyser, and Ellen Stuart, "A Welfare Analysis of Tax Audits Across the Income Distribution," *Quarterly Journal of Economics* 140, no. 1 (February 2025): 63–112, https://academic.oup.com/qje/advance-article/doi/10.1093/qje/qjae037/7888907?login=false.

5. "SOI Tax Stats—Tax Stats at a Glance," Internal Revenue Service, https://www.irs.gov/statistics/soi-tax-stats-tax-stats-at-a-glance.

6. "More than 2.5 Million LGBTQ Adults Are Parenting Children Under the Age of 18," Williams Institute, UCLA School of Law, July 17, 2024, https://williamsinstitute.law.ucla.edu/press/lgbtq-parenting-2024-press-release/.

7. "The Extra Costs of Living with a Disability in the U.S.—Resetting the Policy Table," National Disability Institute, https://nationaldisabilityinstitute.org/reports/extra-costs-living-with-disability/.

8 | ENTREPRENEURSHIP

1. Statista Research Department, "U.S. Number of New Business Q4 2012–Q4 2023," Statista.com, August 26, 2024, https://www.statista.com/statistics/771207/quarterly-business-starts-us/.
2. "Survival of Private Sector Establishments by Opening Year," Bureau of Labor Statistics, https://www.bls.gov/bdm/us_age_naics_00_table7.txt.

9 | FINANCIAL INDEPENDENCE

1. German Lopez, "The Reagan Administration's Unbelievable Response to the HIV/AIDS Epidemic," *Vox*, December 1, 2016, https://www.vox.com/2015/12/1/9828348/ronald-reagan-hiv-aids.
2. "Savings Goal Calculator," U.S. Securities and Exchange Commission, https://www.investor.gov/financial-tools-calculators/calculators/savings-goal-calculator.

10 | LEGACY PLANNING

1. Jack Caporal, "The State of LGBTQ Finance: A Survey of 2,000 Americans," *The Motley Fool*, April 17, 2024, https://www.fool.com/research/lgbtq-money-study/.
2. Reid Kress Weisbord and David Horton, "Why a Handwritten Will Found in Aretha Franklin's Couch Got R-E-S-P-E-C-T from a Jury," *The Conversation*, July 13, 2023, https://theconversation.com/why-a-handwritten-will-found-in-aretha-franklins-couch-got-r-e-s-p-e-c-t-from-a-jury-209657.
3. "About Underlying Cause of Death, 2018–2023, Single Race," CDC Wonder, https://wonder.cdc.gov/ucd-icd10-expanded.html, https://wonder.cdc.gov/controller/datarequest/D158;jsessionid=151F8AD9764AD62BCF431EC43000#Options.
4. Liz Knueven and Alani Asis, "How Much Does Life Insurance Cost? Average Life Insurance Cost and Factors," *Business Insider*, September 17, 2024, https://www.businessinsider.com/personal-finance/life-insurance/average-life-insurance-rates.

ABOUT THE AUTHOR

Nick Wolny is the personal finance columnist for *Out* magazine and a frequent television correspondent. He has previously written about LGBTQ+ topics for *Fast Company, Business Insider, Fortune, Entrepreneur* magazine, and *The Advocate,* and currently publishes *Financialicious,* a weekly newsletter on queer money matters. A classically trained French hornist by upbringing and rural Illinois boy at heart, he now lives in Los Angeles.